1988

University of St. Francis
GEN   801.95 G648p
Goodheart. Eugene.

W9-AED-631

3

Pieces of resistance

Pieces of resistance

EUGENE GOODHEART

The right of the
University of Cambridge
to print and sell
all manner of books
was granted by
Henry VIII in 1534.
The University has printed
and published continuously
since 1584.

CAMBRIDGE UNIVERSITY PRESS

Cambridge
New York   New Rochelle   Melbourne   Sydney

LIBRARY
College of St. Francis
JOLIET, ILLINOIS

Published by the Press Syndicate of the University of
    Cambridge
The Pitt Building, Trumpington Street, Cambridge CB2 1RP
32 East 57th Street, New York, NY 10022, USA
10 Stamford Road, Oakleigh, Melbourne 3166, Australia

© Cambridge University Press 1987

First published 1987

Printed in the United States of America

Library of Congress Cataloging-in-Publication Data
Goodheart, Eugene.
Pieces of resistance.
1. Criticism – United States – History – 20th century.
2. American periodicals – History – 20th century
3. American fiction – 20th century – History and criticism.
I. Title.
PN99.U5G66   1988   801'.95'0973   87–11801

British Library Cataloguing in Publication Data
Goodheart, Eugene
Pieces of resistance.
1. Literature, Modern – 19th century –
History and criticism   2. Literature,
Modern – 20th century – History and
criticism
I. Title
809'.034   PN671

ISBN 0 521 34036 5

Contents

Preface

Pieces of Resistance is a collection of essays and essay-reviews written over a period of twenty-five years, 1960–85. It responds to the political, cultural, and literary changes that occurred during that period as these changes expressed themselves in the writings of novelists and critics and in the "personalities" of certain influential magazines. The exemplary figures are Lionel Trilling, Philip Rahv, and V. S. Naipaul, among others, that is, writers with a particular sensitivity to ideological tendencies in the literary imagination and the cultural life that distort and diminish our understanding of the world. My own critical stance shares their resistance to these tendencies, hence the title of my collection. The journals that I discuss are *The New York Review, Commentary,* and *The Evergreen Review,* which over the years and particularly in the late sixties and early seventies provided illuminating intersections of political, cultural, and literary themes. Eros, radical politics, pornography, avant-gardism, racism, and Stalinism are among the themes that crop up in various forms in these essays, themes of continuing interest.

Not all the essays in this collection are polemical. A number of essays – for instance, those on Bashevis Singer, Daniel Fuchs, and Meyer Liben – are interpretations of works of imagination that speak to personal experience and have moved me. Fuchs and Liben are not writers central to American literary life, but they have a power and charm that deserve serious consideration. Some of the themes in the more polemical pieces are, to be sure, present in these essays. In the short pieces on Donald Barthelme and Raymond Carver I have tried to capture the ways in which they represent the quality of our lives: their "realism," so to speak.

The book, for all its diversity, is of a piece. It is criticism of a kind that not only looks at a work or event closely but tries to see in the work or event a larger cultural and political significance. Nor does it pretend to an impersonal objectivity. The historical moment, present

vii

as well as past, and personal experience condition the critical act. Criticism, as I understand and practice it, is evaluative as well as interpretative. My commitment to evaluation is not a naive holdover of an obsolete mode of criticism but a deliberate response to current ways of thinking about literature that put in doubt the evaluative function of criticism.

I have made only small stylistic changes and revisions, preserving the substance of the essays, even where I am no longer in precise agreement. The long essay on Naipaul, which concludes the book, represents a conflation of two separate essays on this remarkable writer, originally printed in *Salmagundi* and *Partisan Review*.

Acknowledgments

The essays in this collection appeared in the following journals: *ADE Bulletin*, "The Creativity of Criticism," Spring 1981. *Bennington Review*, "The New York Review Loves an Englishman," June 1982. *The Boston Review*, Review of Donald Barthelme's *The Dead Father*, Spring 1976, and Review of Raymond Carver, *Cathedral*, February 1984. *Chronicle of Higher Education*, "Lionel Trilling 1905–1975," November 17, 1975. *Commentary*, "Tenderminded Fiction: *The New Country: Stories from the Yiddish about Life in America*," November 1961. *Dissent*, "The New York Review: A Close Look," March–April 1970. *Midstream*, "Leslie Fiedler and the Mythic Life," a review of *No! In Thunder*, Spring 1961; "Eros, Politics and Pornography: A Decade with *The Evergreen Review*," April 1969; "The 'Radicalism' of Susan Sontag," December 1969; Review of Ralph Ellison's *Shadow and Act*, March 1965; Review of William Styron's *The Confessions of Nat Turner*, January 1968; Review of three novels of Daniel Fuchs, Winter 1962; "The Demonic Charm of Bashevis Singer," Summer 1960; Review of Bernard Malamud's *New Life*, Autumn 1961; and Review of Meyer Liben's *Justice Hunger and Other Stories*, June–July 1967. *The Nation*, "The New Apocalypse," Sept. 20, 1965, © 1965; "The Deradicalized Intellectuals," Feb. 8, 1971, © 1970; and "The New Reformation of Paul Goodman," Aug. 3, 1970, © 1980. *New Boston Review*, Review of Joseph Frank's *Dostoevsky: The Seeds of Revolt 1821–1849*, 1977. *Partisan Review*, Review of William Chace's *Lionel Trilling: Criticism and Politics*, 1981; "V. S. Naipaul's Mandarin Sensibility," 1983; and Review of Saul Bellow's *Him with His Food in His Mouth and Other Stories*, 1985. *Salmagundi*, "Naipaul and The Voices of Negation," Fall 1981, and "The Claustral World of Nadine Gordimer," Winter 1984. *Sewanee Review*, "Philip Rahv and *Image and Idea*," Winter 1984. I am grateful to the editors for permission to reprint the articles.

I would also like to thank Morris Dickstein and Mark Schechner for their extremely useful suggestions about what to include and what to exclude. Both of them helped me discover the abiding concerns in these occasional pieces.

Autobiographical

Growing up in Brooklyn, in a small world of Yiddishist "progressivism" in the forties and fifties, I did not choose my political or cultural views. They chose me. A child of immigrant parents, who had left Russia during the upheaval of 1917, I had identified the progressivist conviction with the sentiment of being Jewish. The vanguard of progress was of course the Soviet Union, which had not only created a worker's state, but had emancipated the Jews from the Pale of Settlement. I remember May Day parades, summer camps, and theatrical spectacles in which we declaimed our twin beliefs in a socialist future and Yiddishkeit. Among my childhood heroes were Paul Robeson, Howard Fast, Theodore Dreiser, Pete Seeger, and Itzhik Pfeffer, the Soviet Yiddish poet who wrote a poem in which each of fifteen or twenty lines celebrated one of Stalin's virtues. Pfeffer was killed by Stalin during a flare-up of anti-Semitic paranoia after the establishment of the State of Israel.

I remember quarreling with Zionists about Israel as a solution to the Jewish problem, *before* the establishment of the State of Israel. My anti-Zionism did not imply contentment with American life. On the contrary, I believed with my radical friends that American society should be transformed, and that we should be agents of transformation. We did not think of ourselves in *golus* (or exile), but as different from the mainstream, and we were prepared to cultivate our difference within the society. If we were unassimilated Jews, we were nonetheless New Yorkers whose difference from the rest of America we would discover later in our travels through the country. "The Final Solution of the Jewish Problem" made my quarrels with Zionism irrelevant, but I cannot say that I was ever converted to Zionism. When I visited Israel for the first time, I was almost fifty. On a visit to the writer Amos Oz, I was asked by General Israel Tal, the former deputy defense minister, who was also visiting Oz, why it had taken me so long to make my first visit to Israel. He did not wait

1

for an answer and guessed with absolute accuracy that I was a New Yorker from a radical Yiddishist anti-Zionist background and that my resistance to visiting Israel took longer to overcome than my commitment to radical ideology.

I had a lot to live down when I entered Columbia College in 1949. The trial of Rudolph Slansky, the Jewish General Secretary of the Czech Communist party, for treason against socialism, made a deep impression on me. As with my elders who had witnessed the earlier travesties of justice in the purge trials of the thirties, scales fell from my eyes. My political conversion would have doubtless occurred if I had not been at Columbia, but it did occur there and in the presence of professors of the political experience and sophistication of Lionel Trilling, Fred Dupee, and Richard Hofstadter among others. I came to see not only the deceit and horror of Stalinism, but the cultural philistinism associated with it. This was particularly hard on me as a student of literature. I had much to unlearn as well as to learn. I recall being wounded by a remark made by a professor at Columbia, that my admiration of Dreiser might prevent me from experiencing the higher triumphs of imagination. (The remark in retrospect seems harsh and unjust to Dreiser, an expression of the cult of James at the time.)

It was Lionel Trilling who had the most decisive influence on my intellectual and political development at Columbia. Before I encountered him, I was already unhappy with my ideological habits and increasingly aware of the grim realities of Stalinism but unable to find any real alternative in the vacuous conventional politics of the fifties. I was drawn to Trilling through what I thought was a quite independent interest in and love of literature. What I found to my surprise was the possibility of a dialectic between literature and politics that was to reform my whole way of thinking. I still remember the enormous impact on me of *The Liberal Imagination* when I first read it. What Trilling offered was not an escape into Art, but art or literature as a paradoxical political activity, subversive of ideological rigidity, responsive in its imaginative capacities to the adversary. One of the book's deep attractions was that it did not foreclose the possibility of a radical position, though Trilling himself was not a radical.

My first visit to Europe came at a propitious moment. I spent most of 1956 in Paris on a Fulbright. It was the year of the Hungarian Revolution and the Khrushchev Report. I seemed to have learned to speak French with a certain fluency, if not accuracy, if only to be able to argue with Communist students, who were not easily disillusioned by Soviet actions or admissions. I thought I had exorcised Marxism, only to find myself performing the ritual of exorcism in my daily encounters with militant spokesmen for oppressed colonials (black students from Africa) and articulate members of a self-conscious working class.

I was shocked by a brutal "realism" in their talk, which I had never experienced among American fellow-traveling radicals whose politics tended to be more sentimental and abstract. I recall in particular a man with a lame arm and brutal theories. Despite Hungary and Khrushchev he remained a *dur* – a Stalin and Rakosi man. Orwell once characterized the euphemism as the naming of things "without calling up mental pictures of them. Consider for instance some comfortable English professor defending Russian totalitarianism. He cannot say outright, 'I believe in killing off your opponents when you get good results by doing so.' " Here was a man incapable of euphemism. He had rid himself of all moral or sentimental encumbrances, he had a vision of political reality as revelation. His harshness proved to be tonic. He strengthened my opposition to the ideology of my youth.

Writers like Wordsworth, Stendhal, Dostoevsky, and Conrad confirmed my growing suspicion of all revolutionary ideologies, though I felt uncomfortable with the reactionary conclusions that some of the writers whom I admired seemed to have arrived at. I did not want to be defined by a hostility to a past to which I was still attached through old friendships. In my early years as teacher and critic, political concerns yielded to ideas of personal development and fulfillment. Lawrence's reactionary politics were irrelevant to my fascination with his exploration of personal relationships and states of consciousness.

The radicalism of the sixties caught me, like everyone else, by surprise, and it reawakened my anti-Stalinism. Though the ideologies of the sixties were decidedly un-Stalinist, even anti-Stalinist, I kept recognizing the Stalinist type in the arrogance and deceit of the new ideologues; I found the philistinism of the counterculture worse than anything I had experienced in my youth. What made the radical sixties possible was that it was a movement of the young, who had not experienced the ideological embitterments of those who were ten, fifteen, or twenty years older. I recall an argument in the sixties with a well-known young radical about ten years younger than I, who thought it absurd that he be made to suffer the guilt of Stalinism, since he had never had anything to do with it. He was unwilling to entertain the thought that there might be Stalinist tendencies in his own thinking and activity. (He has recently declared himself a neoconservative.) I reacted strongly to the radicalism of the sixties, but I tried, as I had tried in my quarrel with my Stalinist upbringing, to keep my balance. I didn't want to be a case of the inverted ideologue, who is nourished by the passion of constant hostility to radical ideology.

This is the case of the neoconservatives, who emerged as an immediate reaction to the illusions of the sixties, but who represent a deeper tendency that began with the disillusionment with Stalinism and went underground in the sixties. As a conservatism without roots, it has a curious resemblance to the object of its revulsion. One has to listen or read for voice as well as sense, and I hear in the accents of neoconservatism some of the old ideological patterns from the past. While traditional conservatives have the equanimity of those who have nothing to exorcize, neoconservatives, or at least those of whom are embittered ex-leftists, recoil from their past with particular intensity. I find them stridently confident, predictable, and even fanatical in their opposition to every liberal or radical tendency (e.g., homosexual culture, feminism), in their habit of dividing the world too neatly between good and evil. They tend to be intolerant of softness, hesitation, equivocation, the contemptible faults of liberals. I recall the same scornful guilt inducing dismissal of liberals by Stalinists and sixties radicals. I think it a mark of strength in the liberal to scorn the scorners. The cultural corollary of the neoconservative position is, curiously enough, philistine in its cherishing of popular feeling and its mistrust of what it regards as avant-garde pretension. (In sketching a portrait of the neoconservative type I risk falling into the trap of ideological reduction. As with people on the Left, I know admirable people of neoconservative persuasion who do not fit the type. The first humanizing wisdom about ideology is that type and reality do not coincide. It is a wisdom that makes possible friendship across political lines, though these friendships are difficult to sustain in proportion to the intensity of ideological conflict.)

In comparison with the thirties and the sixties, the present time is, relatively speaking, devoid of ideological passion. The dominant conviction in most areas of thought is skepticism. I had been drawn to Matthew Arnold's idea of literature as a criticism of life and in particular of the political life. For all of his skepticism about the ideologies of his own time, he remained confident to a fault about the values of the literary imagination. But now for many of us whose business is the study of literature, the confidence seems to be misplaced. A radically skeptic disposition has recently overtaken the discipline of literary study and has brought with it a loss of authority in the literary intellectual to reflect on matters that are not strictly linguistic. Not only is the critic uncertain about the objective meaning of the text, he is uncertain whether meaning inheres in the text. Deconstruction, the most radical of literary skepticisms, holds the view that written discourse is unreliable, that no matter how hard a text may try to sustain the illusion of unity, coherence, meaning, truth, it is incorrigibly prone to disunity, incoherence, meaninglessness, and error. For such skeptics, "reading" becomes a process of discovering the illusoriness of our knowledge of texts and of the world. Who can complain against a healthy skepticism, but skeptics should be modest and uncertain. The current breed strikes me, as it strikes others, as often dogmatic and arrogant, engaged in a power trip at the expense of literature. T. S. Eliot's caveat about radical skepticism still seems persuasive. "Scepticism is a highly civilized trait, though, when it declines into pyrrhonism, it is one of which civilisation can die. Where scepticism is strength, pyrrhonism is weakness: for we need not only the strength to defer a decision, but the strength to make one."

It may be that what appears to be an internal development in literary study represents another recoil from the illusions of the sixties, though its anti-authoritarianism may suggest an affinity with the radical gestures of that decade. The skeptical sensibility prides itself on its unblinking view of human reality. There is much that is wrong-headed, pretentious, and even dogmatic in current skeptical formulations, but it is not a challenge to be ignored. For someone like myself who has spent much of life in a defensive position, reacting against ideological thinking, the new skeptical spirit is a challenge of another kind.

A sympathetic and astute reader of my essays has remarked what others may sense: a "disturbing . . . overall skewness of vision" in the essays. He notes that despite my concern to maintain a liberal distance from the neoconservatives, most of my criticism is directed against the Left in the sixties. Odd as it may seem, my severity with the Left may be read as an expression of my closeness to it. (The bitterest struggles, we know, are often familial struggles.) I had grown up believing that radicalism and justice were synonymous terms, only to find constant betrayals of the cause of justice on the

Left. In reading thinkers like Burke, a conservative, and Tocqueville, a complex figure who transcends conservative and liberal categories, I learned something about the impulsions and tendencies within the Left that lead to these betrayals. But I have never been tempted to embrace the conservative position, because of what I have always felt to be a deficiency in social compassion and social justice. I cherish John Stuart Mill's model of the political life as expressed in his justly celebrated essays on Bentham and Coleridge, because they envisage political and moral truth as distributed on a spectrum from "left" to "right" (terms that I often find used in unilluminating ways).

It is also true, as my astute critic pointed out to me, that there is a "persistent admonitory tone," which overbalances the affirmative pieces. The word "resistance" in my title is not fortuitous. I have no excuses to make, except to say that in these essays (though not necessarily in my other work), I felt that my contribution to political and cultural discourse would be most salutary in the posture of resistance rather than of embrace and affirmation.

I   Critics and criticism

1   William Chace's *Lionel Trilling: Criticism and Politics*

William Chace's study of Lionel Trilling is the work of a young man who is not Jewish and not from New York and who "was born exactly one year before the German invasion of Poland." For Mr. Chace Stalin "is . . . a name, not an experience," and he scrupulously warns us that he does "not know at first hand many aspects of the modern experience of ideological conflict." My own perspective is precisely the opposite. I am Jewish and from New York. Both World War II and Stalin were more than names for me, they were experiences. Despite the difference in perspective, I find Chace's portrait of Trilling's mind both recognizable and congenial. Chace has none of the sixties' rage against the weakness of the liberal imagination, nor is there that passionate revulsion from the experience of Stalinism that can create another kind of distortion. His view has the disadvantages as well as the advantages of distance, but his study succeeds in touching upon most of the important issues in Trilling's work in a way that enables the reader to advance and complicate the discussion.

The first three chapters of the book attempt to place Trilling in his historical context, particularly in his relation to politics and his Jewish identity. I will return to them later, but I want to begin by addressing myself to Chace's first consideration of a major work by Trilling, the novel *The Middle of the Journey* (1947), published eight years after the book on Matthew Arnold.

The political center of the novel is the liberals' experience of Stalinism in the thirties and forties. Trilling was not alone among his contemporaries in his repudiation of Stalinism, but he had perhaps a deeper understanding of the problematic character of alternatives to the Stalinist temptation (it was not called Stalinism by fellow traveling liberals until the Khrushchev Report of 1956) than his contemporaries. Against the two absolutisms in *The Middle of the Journey*, one incarnated by the passionate commitment to communism (i.e.,

9

Stalinism) of Nancy Crooms and the other by the fanatical, though deeply meditated Christianized anticommunism of Gifford Maxim, Trilling posed the liberal sensibility of John Laskell. Trilling demystified the anger of the two fanatics in a way which clearly suggests the superiority of the liberal idea. "It was the anger of the masked will at the appearance of an idea in modulation." But the burden of the novel strongly qualifies the sense of superiority, for if the liberal resists ideologizing his anticommunism (not wanting to become a distorted mirror image of his adversary) he remains insufficient in character and doctrine. Chace acutely, if not with entire accuracy, notes Trilling's modulated response to "the idea in modulation":

The "liberalism" of this novel, then, is at best a piety. Precariously maintained, and made uneasy in the presence of another force that mixes intelligence, aggressiveness, and a strange honor in shrewd proportions, it exists only to be threatened. It finds its solace in reflection upon death, and with death in mind it judges the effusions of political passion stridently surrounding it. Trilling's loyalty to such liberalism is odd and diffident. Perhaps the nature of that loyalty is one sign of the malaise and discomforts of political engagement in the 1940's in the United States. That so important a university intellectual in that "haunted" postwar time could put forward as a protagonist such a figure as John Laskell, and yet offer him such frail support in his contests of mind and will, reveals that even the more skeptical forms of liberalism had been placed under great stress. Liberalism in that time was provisional and wary.

The liberalism is not a piety, but an anxiety, a necessarily inadequate response to the twin temptations of Stalinism and ideological anticommunism. To see why the response is necessarily inadequate (and the source of anxiety) one would have to understand the choices felt to be available at the time. What Chace omits in his account (a consequence of his distance from the time) is the spectre of Nazism. The very force of Nazism had made liberalism, even in the eyes of the liberals, seem insufficient. Communism (or at least fellow-traveling) was the alternative forced upon liberals, because it had – or seemed to have – the capacity to meet force with force. Such an alternative, of course, entailed the suppression or repression of knowledge of the Soviet labor camps and of the Nazi-Soviet nonaggression pact. But the bad faith of liberals who were utterly without the idea in modulation does not evaporate the overwhelming fact of the threat of Nazism. Nor is bad faith the whole story of fellow-traveling liberal antifascism in the thirties. George Orwell's unillusioned witnessing of the Spanish Civil War (as recorded in *Homage to Catalonia*) did not destroy his conviction that he was on the right side and that he was in the company of many gifted and courageous men who were willing to sacrifice and indeed sacrificed their lives for a worthy cause.

It is an odd but significant fact of Chace's study (which covers a period of fifty years from the mid-twenties to the mid-seventies), itself perhaps a symptom of the American intellectual history that he is recording, that there is scarcely a reference to the experience of Nazism. It almost seems as if American intellectuals had been deflected by Stalinism from contemplating the enormities of Nazism. One cannot imagine a comparable study of a European intellectual with such a conspicuous absence. One must turn to a European intellectual, Hannah Arendt (a refugee from Nazism), in order to see Stalinism in a perspective which includes the phenomenon of Nazism. One of Hannah Arendt's achievements (particularly in *The Origins of Totalitarianism*) is in her powerful demonstration that rather than alternative phenomena, Stalinism and Nazism were part of a single historical and ideological continuum. (Outside the community of New York intellectuals, this view was promulgated by conservative thinkers with a libertarian bias like Peter Viereck and Frederich von Hayek.)

American intellectuals, at a distance from the war, did not have the either/or experience of European intellectuals. They could afford the luxury of "an idea in modulation." In *The Middle of the Journey*, the liberal Laskell is seen by the impressive Maxim as the last of a dying breed, even complicit in its own extinction. ("The supreme act of the humanistic critical intelligence – it perceives the cogency of the argument and acquiesces in the fact of its own extinction.") But the death sentence has turned out to be premature. "The idea in modulation" helped spare American intellectuals as a class from the insidiousness of Stalinism. It took the sophisticated left-wing Europeans much longer to learn the lesson, and it is a question whether they have fully learned it yet.

What is the source of "the idea in modulation" in *The Middle of the Journey*? Chace accurately notes that "the novel turns, in its complexity, upon death. Death imitates, conditions and gives character to all of its main events. The people in the novel approach death in many different ways, and in their encounter with it invite understanding of their selves. Death delineates and judges them. Thus it stands central to everything, subsuming politics as it subsumes all other phenomena, but doing so with suppleness and never with the morbidity one might imagine it possessing."

Trilling saw a certain kind of political aspiration, having its provenance in the Enlightenment and finding its contemporary apotheosis in Stalinist "radicalism" as an attempt to deny the conditioned character of existence (our finitude, our mortality) in a dream, or worse, a doctrine of utopian fulfillment. It is not hard to choose the side of wisdom if the polarities are finitude and infinity, mortality and immortality. In a century wracked and disgraced by political absolutisms that have arrogated the religious dream of infinite possibility and immortality, the view of man as conditioned is a noble view. The trouble arises when the polarities exclude alternatives. Death may be a premature perspective. The young grow old and die, but they are not only entitled to the illusion that they will live forever, such an illusion may inspire the will to produce, to achieve, even to transcend. Indeed it is precisely the encounter, the conflict between the will to achieve (and even transcend) on the one side, and the limiting, thwarting conditions of existence on the other, that makes for the sense of tragedy. If one must surrender to conditions (as one inevitably must), the test of heroism, of courage is in the capacity one has to persist against those conditions and the grace with which one finally submits to them.

This youthful radical dream of transcendence should not be conflated with Stalinism – though youthful radicalism, persisting unmodified in old age, may systematize and bureaucratize itself into Stalinism. Trilling never conflated Stalinism with radicalism. His commitment to "the idea in modulation" left open the possibility of other kinds of radicalism for people with temperaments different from his own to follow. Nevertheless, I sometimes find wanting in his work a sharper discrimination between a possible radicalism and an absolute radicalism, which denies conditions. Death tends to cast a premature shadow.

All of the changes in Trilling's intellectual career can be viewed, I think, as the tracings of "an idea in modulation." Trilling had his heroes and even his causes, but I think it a mistake simply to see Freud or Arnold in the background of the mutations of his thinking about political and cultural situations. It was an aspect of Trilling's genius that he could turn on ideas and commitments that he had long cherished, when he found them a threat to what he felt to be the health of self and society. Mind, art, and the idea of culture itself are not exempt from an often penetrating skeptical scrutiny. It has scarcely been remarked how far Trilling traveled from an Arnoldian view of culture in his later career, however much he continued to admire Arnold's spirit and sensibility. No one knew better than Trilling that Culture could no longer be counted on to supply a fresh stream of thought to our stock habits of thought and feeling.

In the concluding essay in *Beyond Culture*, "The Two Environments: Reflections on the Study of English," Trilling asks "whether in our culture the study of literature is any longer a suitable means for developing and refining the intelligence." It should be noted that Trilling asks the question (in a manner characteristic of a mind in modulation), leaving open the possibility of dialogue and debate. Chace engages the question by challenging the attempt to go beyond culture and liberature "as hazardous and dubious as was his earlier one to find a politics appropriate to the antinomian, adversarial, and deathly aspects of the culture he fears," but he does not say why, apart from challenging Trilling's effort to find support in Keats's apparent preference for philosophy over poetry ("for the same reason that an eagle is not so fine a thing as truth"). "Hazardous and dubious" aborts our understanding of Trilling's brave attempt to think through our cultural situation. By literature Trilling means something quite different from Arnold's secular scripture; he means "the antinomian, adversarial literature," that richest expression of the modern creative mind, which diffuses itself, for instance, in our recent counterculture. Literature as secular scripture never lost its value for Trilling, but he was acutely sensitive to its weakness as an antidote to mass culture. In *Beyond Culture* Trilling turns to biological instinct, which as Freud has taught him "proposes to us that culture is not all powerful. It suggests that there is a residue of human quality beyond the reach of cultural control." As Chace and others point out, biology (or instinct) cannot provide the kind of resistance Trilling wished to attribute to it. What is of interest, however, is Trilling's keen sensitivity to the hegemonic tendencies of modern culture.

Like any political absolutism, culture itself can become an expression of the aggressive will. Trilling characteristically recoils from every imperializing manifestation of the will, whether it takes the form of politics or intellect or creative imagination. What attracts him to "biological instinct" (be it myth or actuality) is its resistance to the will to dominate. It is important to keep this aspect of Trilling's thought in mind, because it provides a qualification, if not a corrective to the persuasive view (first put forward by Joseph Frank in his brilliant review of *The Opposing Self*) that his long-standing antipathy to the will leads Trilling "to endow social passivity and quietism *as such* with the halo of aesthetic transcendence." There are moments in Trilling's work which invite this kind of judgment, but I believe with Chace that they betray his best intention. Chace aptly cites a passage from Trilling's essay on Edith Wharton. "The morality of inertia, of the dull, unthinking round of duties, may, and often does, yield the immorality of inertia. . . . No: the morality of inertia is not to be praised, but it must be recognized."

The distinction needs development. The morality of inertia is not in its acquiescence in things, but in its resistance to system, coercion, all the life-destructive violent assertions of the will. It is precisely the work of the mind in modulation to discover at any given moment the strongest source of resistance to the destructive exercises of the will. Such a mind can never come to rest in a system or a position, it must even question its own assurances from time to time. It may be mistaken in its particular judgments, it may take myth for fact, but it is protected from scandal by its conservative conscientiousness about the hubris of the will. Trilling's criticism never shares the righteous indignation of the oppressed not because he is out of sympathy with those who are oppressed, but because he has a special sensitivity to the resentful will that is often masked by righteous indignation. It is the "conservative" or "aristocratic" bias of his criticism. We may understand the "sentiment of being" (a phrase Trilling derived from Wordsworth) in this context. Trilling does not advocate a mindless acquiescence in the brute force of life, but rather the wise passivity of relaxed will as a resistance to its more brutal expressions.

The phases of Trilling's career (represented by *The Middle of the Journey, Matthew Arnold, The Liberal Imagination, Beyond Culture,* and *Sincerity and Authenticity*) are carefully distinguished and discussed by Chace, who wants to show the consistency of this effort to defend self and society against the various guises of the imperial will.

In *The Middle of the Journey*, as we have seen, the encounter with death inspires a more powerful resistance to the political absolutisms which beleaguer the liberal "hero" than any political argument he may offer against them. In *Matthew Arnold,* Trilling found a commitment to mind and literature that provided him with another center of resistance to the ideological will. But his own innate gift for modulation enabled him to see the inherent weaknesses and histor-

ical limitations of Arnold's thought. Writing in the aftermath of the
Enlightenment belief in progress, Arnold envisaged the possibility of
a perfect state (the expression of the best self), "standing," in
Chace's words, "above all classes and resolving all contradictions."
Trilling demurred from this view (calling it "banter") *partly because it was unrealistic;* it ignored the conditioned (i.e., class) character of social existence. But Trilling also saw in the middle classes a
source of valuable resistance to an increasingly powerful modernism, which he was to call in *Beyond Culture* "the adversary
culture." (At times he seems almost willing to forgive, if not forget,
its philistinism.) If in *The Liberal Imagination* Trilling is very much
the Arnoldian or Millian critic, discriminating for example between
the higher triumphs of the imagination (e.g., James) and the crudities
of a simpleminded realism (e.g., Dreiser), he is capable of finding in
the values of art and intellect threats to social life. "The middle
class . . . has been losing its love of society," Trilling writes with
a note of complaint. There is much to love in community, not at all
clear what there is to love in actual society. Trilling himself, I
suspect, does not value society as much as he mistrusts the reactive
alternatives to it, or rather withdrawals from it: anarchism, even
authoritarianism. "Often our anarchism takes the form of disgust
with the very idea of society. On the upper levels of our taste this
disgust is expressed for us by Baudelaire, Rimbaud, Céline, and
Kafka." The adversary can be found in the most privileged reaches
of art. In *Sincerity and Authenticity,* written against the background
of the sixties, Trilling deepens his critique of modernism for its
"antinomian reversal of all accepted values, of all received realities." His adversaries are Herbert Marcuse, Norman O. Brown,
David Cooper, and R. D. Laing. The effect of their attempt to
transvalue values (through erotic revolution and the validation or
authenticating of insanity) is to destroy the authority of *character.*
But the reduction of *Sincerity and Authenticity* to a polemic against
the counterculture fails to acknowledge the extraordinary modulations of the argument. Trilling's last book reads as if he wanted to
resist his own will to annihilate the adversary, for the effect of
Trilling's historical perspective (including among others Rousseau,
Diderot, Goethe, and Jane Austen) is to allow the adversarial view
its full claim upon us. Unlike Stalinism, modernism remained an
object of deep ambivalence for Trilling.
     Chace concludes his study of Trilling with an oblique disparage-
ment of a tendency in contemporary criticism, that has in effect put

into question the achievement of "old-fashioned" critics like Trilling and Edmund Wilson. Trilling "reminds us all, and has reminded me for many months in writing this book about him, of something we can never wholly forget: literature is important by virtue not of its textuality but of its entry into our moral lives." It is true that Trilling rarely applied himself to a text in an exhaustive exegetical manner as if all that mattered was the fullest possible understanding of what a text meant or did. Trilling perceives an old adversary in "the masked will" of text: its attempt to dominate the reader through its implicit demand for a suspension of disbelief, a full immersion in the text as it understands itself. In his essay "On the Teaching of Modern Literature," Trilling speaks of the intimidation by the text. Modern criticism "has taught us how to read certain books; it has not taught us how to engage them. Modern literature (it need scarcely be said again) is directed toward moral and spiritual renovation: its doctrine is damnation and salvation. It is a literature of doctrine, which although often concealed is very aggressive. The occasions are few when criticism has met this doctrine on its own fierce terms. Of modern criticism it can be said that it has instructed us in an intelligent passivity before the beneficent aggression of literature. Attributing to literature virtually angelic powers, it has passed the word to readers of literature that the one thing you do not do when you meet an angel is wrestle with him." Trilling's style with its practiced hesitations, its self-regarding convolutions, its capacity to create distance as well as engage is an expression of resistance to textual domination. Works of literature became occasions for speculative understanding about the nature of literature and life, though it should be said that Trilling's literary tact matched and surpassed the capacities of most professional close readers.

But there is another tendency in contemporary criticism to which Trilling's achievement implicitly speaks: the tendency to deconstruct and disassemble works of literature in order to discover the linguistic elements of which they are composed. This view of literature rests upon a radical skepticism, if not nihilism, about meaning and reality that Trilling would undoubtedly have experienced as adversarial. Trilling himself, as we have seen, had an abundant capacity for skepticism. It is simply that skepticism never completely defined his intelligence, which remained rooted in convictions about virtue, character, and truth that it had no interest in deconstructing. Trilling's skeptical intelligence served a critical humanism that he questioned only to test and strengthen.

The early chapters of Chace's book deal with Trilling's uneasy, ambivalent relation to his being a Jew. Chace reminds us that Trilling was always sensitive to the "conditioned" nature of existence and that Jewishness was one of the conditions of existence, which he apparently sought to escape or transcend, though he confessed that he owed to his Jewishness his imagination of society. Chace subordinates the theme of Jewishness to what he considers to be a paradox of Trilling's work. Though Trilling always insisted upon the inescapability of conditions, his own manner is usually transcendental and abstract. Trilling was a *clerc* in Julien Benda's sense of the word, a man "who speak[s] to the world in a transcendent manner," even if his message is opposed to abstraction, system, and the unconditioned view of things. Trilling's ambivalence towards Jewishness, however, remains a troubling and interesting question, which Chace does not adequately address, again because he is distant from the experience.

Trilling was only one of a number of New York Jewish intellectuals who needed to liberate themselves from the parochialism of the world in which they grew up. That world is given to us uncritically in stories by sentimental Yiddish writers. It is given to us critically, though with affection, by Alfred Kazin in *Walker in the City*. I don't know much about the particular circumstances of Trilling's early life, so I may be wrong to extrapolate from what I know of the lives of other writers of Trilling's generation and of my own experience. The world of our fathers may have valued intellectual ambition, but it did not provide adequate conditions to foster either the intellect or the creative imagination. (I am not referring simply to the obstacle of anti-Semitism that lay in the path of the Jewish intellectuals of Trilling's generation.) It is, of course, true that a writer may later find in the circumstances of his early life the subject of his art, as Joyce did in the claustral and paralytic circumstances of Dublin life. But it is sheer sentimentality (to which Joyce never succumbed) to pretend that the life was very nourishing to the intellect. Trilling represented for many Jewish students at Columbia in the forties and fifties (I was one of them) the possibility of entering into a world of letters and cultivation not to be found in the boroughs of New York where we grew up. It is easy retrospectively to take the view that we were all suffering from Jewish self-hatred, but the phrase doesn't accurately encompass the range of experiences of young Jewish intellectuals whose minds were being formed in the thirties, forties, and fifties. I myself don't recall ever feeling ashamed of being Jewish, I even confess to its having been on occasion a source of pride. But I sensed in the books I read, in the teachers I encountered at Columbia another air in which it was possible to breathe another kind of life, richer and more ample. Aspirations of this kind risk snobbery and, worse, self-falsification, but the risk does not discredit the aspiration. A number of Jewish intellectuals, who freed themselves of the parochialism of their origins, rediscovered in later life pleasure and value in their early lives. That Trilling was not one of them has to do with the particularities of temperament and experience.

With incisiveness and elegance (he has learned from Trilling's manner), Chace traces the consistencies and the modulations of Trilling's work. Chace has the distance from Trilling which enables him to see his man with clear-eyed sympathy. Without a trace of hagiolatry, Chace never loses respect for his subject. Whatever agreements and disagreements one may have with Chace's arguments, one must admire the scrupulous spirit of the book.

2 Philip Rahv and *Image and Idea*

Philip Rahv wrote essays and reviews. Though he intended to complete a book on Dostoevsky, it is doubtful that the book would have been more than a collection of essays. In saying this, I disparage neither Rahv's achievement nor the essay. Literary success in our culture is defined in terms of the book, whether it be a novel or a book of criticism. The writer of stories or essays can never feel content with his achievement because the shorter works, according to the cultural view, are either a preparation for the larger effort or chips off the workbench. Because the real book is always a rarity, this is unfortunate. Most "books" are made from ambition, not genuine conception; and the fine short-story writer or essayist may betray his true gift by working in an uncongenial form. Moreover the emphasis on the book is achieved at the expense of an appreciation of shorter forms.

Rahv had all the powers of the essayist. He had something important to say about the subjects or occasions of his essays. Unlike most books Rahv's essays had genuine occasions, reasons for being written. What he had to say involved bold and challenging statements about large areas of experience: literature, history, culture, society, politics. In books such statements tend to become so hedged and qualified that they lose their shape. The provocation of the essay gives way to the density of exposition. A true essayist, Rahv was impatient to make his statement with maximum force and incisiveness. This impatience was served by an appropriate gift for the resonant and suggestive phrase.

Rahv, one of the two founding editors of *Partisan Review,* was an editor of great distinction. We speak of the native endowment necessary for poets and novelists. We do not tend to think of the editor as a creature of talent or genius. Yet a true editor (there are of course countless facsimiles) cannot be made of whole cloth. He must have both the talent and the disposition, if he is to be any good at all. He

19

must know his own mind and have the courage of his convictions. Without a genuine instinct for the significant issue and the incisive formulation, he (or she) is no more than a collector of articles, a mediator of the eclectic.

The editor of conviction risks encroaching upon the autonomy of the writer. Rahv's editorial character was sometimes overwhelming. During the last years of his life, after he had severed his connection with *Partisan Review* and launched the abortive *Modern Occasions,* Rahv in a rage against the trendiness (his favorite word of disparagement) of what proposed itself as the avant-garde sought writers who would perform like troops in a battle in which he was the master strategist and tactician. One enemy was pornography and its exemplary villain Norman Mailer. Rahv sought recruits, me among others, to attack both the personality and the work. When I wondered why Mailer and not Philip Roth as well, he reprimanded me for my naïveté. Roth was a friend, an ally on other matters. Editorial character and strength do not always depend on fairness. I never wrote the article.

I mention Rahv's editorial character early in this essay because it was not just another role that he performed. It entered deeply into his work as a critic. One hears the voice of the editor in the very first essay of his first volume of essays, *Image and Idea* (1949). "Paleskin and Redskin" is perhaps the best known of his essays. In no more than five pages Rahv divides American literature between writers confined to the "drawing room" (James serves as his principal example) and writers who breathe "the open air" (Whitman is the chief exemplar). American literature suffers from the "ills of a split personality" – excessive insularity from experience and refinement on the one hand, the crudity and vulgarity of raw experience on the other. Characteristically Rahv contrasts the American situation with that of Europe in which "the aristocrat Tolstoy and the tramp Gorky found that they held certain values and ideas in common." And he concludes with the hope that Whitman and James will be reconciled, that there are "available the resources of effort and understanding" which will create the conditions of the kind of mature literature that exists in Europe.

This most influential of Rahv's essays is in retrospect unconvincing and flat. The oppositions are crude. Melville is associated with the "drawing-room fictions" of Henry James. Even James's confinement to the drawing room is something of a travesty. The presence of the "ambassador" Strether in Paris, observing the scene of

Chad and Mme. de Vionnet in love, is hardly to be reduced to the comportments of genteel fiction. On the other side Whitman's songs in "the open air" are not illuminated by phrases such as "gross, riotous naturalism" to which the redskin is supposed to incline. Rahv speaks of the nineteenth century as the period of paleface dominance and of the twentieth as the rule of the redskin. But Faulkner, who is not even mentioned in the essay, can hardly be reduced to either type. The essay reads more like an editorial challenge to the fraternity of writers, a challenge necessarily issued in bold, broad, even crude strokes to think about the condition of American writing and to consider that condition in a perspective larger than the one in which American academics specializing in fields normally think.

The essays that follow "Paleface and Redskin" take us far beyond its stereotypic contrasts. In "The Cult of Experience in American Writing" Rahv erodes the contrast he makes between James and Whitman:

James's attitude toward experience is sometimes overlooked by readers excessively impressed (or depressed) by his oblique methods and effects of remoteness and ambiguity. Actually, from the standpoint of the history of the national letters, the lesson he taught in *The Ambassadors,* as in many of his other works, must be understood as no less than a revolutionary appeal. It is a veritable declaration of the rights of man – not, to be sure, of the rights of the public, of the social man, but of the rights of the private man, of the rights of personality, whose openness to experience provides the sole effective guaranty of its development.

Rahv, of course, has in mind Strether's "pronouncements in favor of sheer life"; and though he acknowledges that life in Strether's (and James's) imagination tends to be an abstraction, "something distilled . . . from the total process of living," he wishes now to emphasize that "it represents a momentous break with the then dominant American morality of abstention." This view has become a staple of our understanding of and feeling for James. But what is now familiar is the consequence of the pioneering efforts of Rahv and Trilling among a very few others. (As Rahv notes, the essays on James in the collection "were written before the James boom so-called was touched off, in the fall of 1944, by the publication of two anthologies of his shorter fiction.")

"The Cult of Experience" explores the positives and negatives of "the primacy of experience in late American literature." One of the benefits is the "relative immunity [of American literature] from abstraction and otherworldliness." Rahv translates abstraction into "the rocks and sands of ideology" that impede "the stream of life." *Ideology* is a powerful negative in Rahv's vocabulary, usually an expression of the Stalinist mentality that *Partisan Review* combated from its inception in the thirties when Rahv and William Phillips rescued the journal from the John Reed Club and established its independent life. Though the context in "The Cult of Experience" does not refer at all to Stalinism (here the villain is Puritanism), the Marxist analogy is present in the imagery of Rahv's understanding of the relation of experience to ideas:

> The part experience plays in the aesthetic sphere might well be compared to the part that the materialist conception of history assigns to economy. Experience, in the sense of this analogy, is the substructure of literature above which there rises a superstructure of values, ideas and judgments – in a word, of the multiple forms of consciousness. But this base and summit are not stationary: they continually act and react upon each other.

This is the language of analogy, not theoretical dogma, and it enables Rahv to pursue the argument that he makes throughout the book – that American literature, even in its most notable expressions, is deficient in "values, ideas and judgments." Thus even writers who would seem not to exemplify the cult of experience become illustrations of it: "poetic technique became the special experience of Ezra Pound, language that of Gertrude Stein, . . . Kenneth Burke experienced ideas (which is by no means the same as thinking them)." Experience, in Rahv's view, is another kind of specialization, even abstraction, which ultimately can be redeemed only by its integration with ideas. Yet in another essay Hawthorne is faulted not for a deficiency of ideas but for the poverty of his imagination of experience. Hawthorne "was haunted not only by the guilt of his desires but also by the guilt of his denial of them." In denying his desires, he is denied "free access to experience . . . the necessary condition of the novel's growth." Hawthorne is a "romancer," as he described himself, rather than a true novelist. "The conflict in him is clearly between a newborn secular imagination, as yet untried and therefore permeated with the feeling of shock and guilt, and the moribund religious tradition of old New England." Thus the "unregenerate temptress" of *The Scarlet Letter,* Hester Prynne, becomes a symbol of novelistic possibility, ultimately undermined by Dimmesdale's confession, which reduces the experience of passion between the lovers to an allegory of sin.

It is not entirely clear from the essay on Hawthorne why the desire for experience doesn't itself count as a kind of experience (early in the essay Rahv characterizes Hawthorne's work as one of "submerged intensity and passion – a tangled imagery of unrest and longing for experience and regret at its loss") or why the conflict of feeling and idea is not an instance of the creative contradictions that Rahv asserted to be the mark of the greatest literature. (The idea of creative contradiction is probably derived from Marx and functions in Rahv's criticism the way ambiguity and paradox functioned in his New Critical contemporaries Ransom, Brooks, and Tate.) In any case what is characteristically Rahvian is the way in which questions of genre and subject are linked and seen in the perspective of national history. And that national history in turn becomes part of a larger perspective. The essay concludes with a contrast between Dostoevsky and Hawthorne, who was considered by the critics of what Rahv calls "the school of 'original sin'" as "a kind of puritan Dostoevsky." In Dostoevsky's work the preoccupation with sin occurs in "a society suffering from a surfeit of experience"; whereas Hawthorne's (and James's) America suffers from a poverty of experience, the paradoxical result of an excess of practical life. Cultural, aesthetic, and subjective experience "had gradually been lost to the migrant European man in the process of subjugating and settling the new world." It is an odd conclusion of Rahv's view of American literature that its classic writers should be devoid of experience. Implicit is the view that idea and experience must nourish each other. Experience loses its character if ideas have not penetrated it. Ideas become abstractions if they are not tested in the crucible of experience. The cult of experience differs from a true mastery of experience.

Critical views of American literature are too often characterized by excessive praise or excessive disparagement. And perhaps no writer has been more the object of oscillating views than James. As Rahv notes in "Attitudes toward Henry James," he is "at once the most and least appreciated figure in American writing." He is for some readers the supreme novelist, the very exemplification of the genre (at once its Sophocles and its Aristotle), and for others the novelist of an experientially impoverished imagination who wrote stories about ghosts (Chesterton's characterization) instead of about people.

Nowhere is Rahv's Johnsonian balance and wisdom more evident than in his writing about James. First comes nothing but scorn for the disparagers of James who banish him from American literature for the twin sins of being a critic of America and an admirer of Europe. In Rahv's view critics like Ludwig Lewisohn, Vernon Parrington, and Van Wyck Brooks are little more than cultural chauvinists who simply misread and misunderstand what they read. The disparagers of James fail to see what Rahv sees so clearly: that "he is the only really fine American writer of the nineteenth century who can truly be said to have mastered [the] 'principle of growth.' " And it is a principle of growth, as Rahv makes clear, that has an exemplary American character: "What is to be admired in a late narrative like *The Wings of the Dove* is James' capacity to lift the nuclear theme of his first period – the theme of the American innocent's penetration into the 'rich and deep and dark' hive of Europe – to a level of conscious experience and aesthetic possession not previously attained." Indeed even James's onesidedness in his appeal to a "high refinement" and his artificial stylization can be seen as an American phenomenon – an attempt, although a possibly self-defeating one, to enrich an American consciousness impoverished by an excess of practical life.

Rahv's sensitivity to James's onesidedness is no mere concession to the disparagers of James. It stands at the very heart of his view, so that he is as severe with academic adulators like Leon Edel (see the corrosive review of Edel's biography, collected in the posthumous collection entitled *Essays on Literature and Politics, 1932–1972*) as he is with the disparagers.[1] Rahv also demolished Maxwell Geismar's know-nothing leftist position on James (in "Pulling Down the Shrine," *The Myth and the Powerhouse*, 1965). To compare Geismar's attack on the cult of James with that of Rahv is instructive. The difference is between sheer animus and genuine criticism.

In Rahv's view James is not a supreme classic in world literature like Balzac, Proust, Dostoevsky, and Tolstoy. Rahv notes the indisputable fact that James's reputation as a novelist is limited to the English-speaking world, and the reason for it in Rahv's view is his

---

[1]   Throughout his discussion of James (though not confined to that discussion) we are reminded that the reading of literature is the subject of a custody battle between the critics and the academics, between those with capacity for genuine and independent thought and perception and those who timidly and without judgment distort, inflate, and deflate the opinions of others. Though Rahv held an academic position (he was a professor at Brandeis), he was, like R. P. Blackmur, an autodidact without academic degrees. Whereas Blackmur's writing was often marked by a creative eccentricity, unchastened by academic decorum, Rahv's writing had a Johnsonian directness and acerbity, uncluttered by academic pedantry.

Americanness. "European readers, lacking a deep background in American or at least Anglo-Saxon culture of the Victorian age, make very little of him" ("Henry James and His Cult"). Rahv's specific criticisms of James's achievement amount to a considerable correction of the academic cult of James. James knew "the heights, and those of a very selected kind," but one doesn't find the concern for fundamental and universal experience that one finds in Tolstoy and Dostoevsky. His "exquisite economy" is something of an illusion, for his late work in particular is marked by either "undue loquacity" or "undue reserve." The passion for nuance and discrimination is pushed to "an unworkable extreme." He "took the social order of his time too much for granted, a position that is wholly contrary to the spirit of modern literature." The contrast between New World innocence and Old World corruption tends to become stereotypic. For all its air of refined intellectuality, James's work shows an American paucity of ideas. And Rahv voices other objections.

What is of particular interest, however, is the way Henry James is restored to his proper place in American literature, and the way Rahv's affinity for and difference from him reveal Rahv's own character as a critic. The critic in Rahv's view must never allow himself to be the thrall of local or national prejudices. He must have a knowledge of the national traditions and prejudices, but he must be able to stand and be judged on the ground of world literature. In James's effort to enrich American consciousness through an experience of Europe Rahv doubtless found a reflection of his own effort as a critic to bring to the understanding of American literature an international consciousness. Rahv finds James wanting precisely in a failure of realization. In a sense James never transcended his own American provinciality.

In "The Native Bias" (collected in *The Myth and the Powerhouse*) Rahv directly challenges James's influential explanation for the "poverty of materials" in America. The poverty does not consist in the absence of "high civilization," as Cooper and Hawthorne as well as James concluded. "If that were strictly the case, we would be utterly at a loss to explain the appearance in backward Russia, and early in the nineteenth century at that, of so great a poet as Pushkin and a master of narrative prose like Gogol." Rahv then cites the vulgar ingredients in the art of Balzac, Flaubert, and Zola and attributes the imaginative limitations of American writers to a puritan "lack of inner freedom to break with tradition so as to be able to say the seemingly unsayable." As one reads his essays

128,189

College of St. Francis Library
Joliet, Illinois

there is an increasing sense that, as much as Stalinism, American Puritanism (in its obsession with original sin) is a bête noire for Rahv. As a modern incarnation of the Enlightenment, he regarded American Puritanism as an offense to the spirit of Reason and Art. *Image and Idea* contains essays on Tolstoy, Dostoevsky, and Kafka, the most considerable of which is the essay on *The Possessed*. Rahv later published four more powerful essays on Dostoevsky. There are essays on *Notes from Underground, Crime and Punishment*, and *The Brothers Karamazov*. The essays on the European writers have a twofold importance. They are writers of great, indeed the greatest, interest; they demand the full exercise of Rahv's critical powers; they are also the touchstones which contribute significantly to his perspective on American literature. A Russian immigrant, Rahv had linguistic and cultural advantages in his discussion of Russian writers.

The essay on *The Possessed* begins with a series of beautiful aphorisms on the nature of a classic:

The tendency of every age is to bury as many classics as it revives. If unable to discover our own urgent meanings in a creation of the past, we hope to find ample redress in its competitive neighbors. A masterpiece cannot be produced once and for all; it must be constantly reproduced. Its first author is a man. Its later ones – time, social time, history.

Rahv's choice of *The Possessed* is not fortuitous: "Of all the novels of Dostoevsky" it "now seems closest to us." It at once embodies the religious fervor of *The Brothers Karamazov* and a profound concern with the political and revolutionary ideas that preoccupy our own age. The political timeliness of *The Possessed* involves the emergence of Stalinism, a phenomenon that compels a revision of the judgment that the novel is "a vicious caricature of the socialist movement." Dostoevsky's invention of the terrorist Peter Verhovensky is a prophetic stroke, for in his histrionic performance we have an anticipation of the duplicities of contemporary communism. Rahv shows with enviable deftness how Dostoevsky's possessed characters are imaginative renderings of the various events in Russian history contemporary with Dostoevsky (see, for instance, the linking of the activity of Verhovensky's circle to Nechayev, the revolutionary terrorist who invented the slogan: "Everything for the revolution – the end justifies the means"). But the real power of *The Possessed* derives from how Dostoevsky imagines the dialectic between religious fervor and political passion.

Rahv cuts through the knotty question of Dostoevsky's reactionary politics to what is the essential rarely expressed truth of the politics of the novelist's imagination:

The truth is that Dostoevsky, despite the commitment of his will to reactionary principles, was at bottom so deeply involved in the spiritual and social radicalism of the Russian intelligentsia that he could not help attempting to break through the inner rigidity of the orthodox tradition toward a dynamic idea of salvation; and in a certain sense what this idea came to is little more than an anarcho-Christian version of that "religion of humanity" which continued to inspire the intelligentsia throughout the nineteenth century and by which Dostoevsky himself was inspired in his youth, when together with Belinsky, Petrashevsky, and other social enthusiasts of the 1840s, he took for his guides and mentors such heretical lovers of mankind as Rousseau, Fourier, Saint-Simon, and George Sand.

The very energy of commitment to religion becomes a species of revolutionism, which makes the secular radicalism of the time seem conservative. "There is no stasis in Dostoevsky's religiosity but rather a dynamism destructive of dogma and seeking fulfilment in the triumph of Christian love and truth in the human world." By connecting Dostoevsky with "the religion of humanity," Rahv can develop his view that Dostoevsky was a spokesman not of the *narod*, the peasantry, but of the oppressed intelligentsia. It may be more accurate to say that Dostoevsky was the most searching and penetrating critic of the intelligentsia, and he was able to penetrate so deeply because he was on intimate terms with every type and idea he scrutinized. Stavrogin, Kirillov, Shatov – each one is a significant perversion of the spiritual life, the ground of both the politics and the religion of Dostoevsky's time. Shatov's God is the providential termination of the national destiny. Kirillov's atheism ("of a desperate intensity without parallel in world literature") becomes the conviction of the most unmitigated nihilism. "His absence is so agonizing a negation of meaning that he cannot help reacting to it by attempting to blow up the world, and since the world is not his to destroy he can only destroy himself." And Stavrogin is the demon himself, the experimenter with ideas beyond good and evil that become incarnated in Shatov and Kirillov. "Such people," Rahv reminds us, "are unknown in countries like America, where social tension is at a relatively low point and where, in consequence, the idea counts for very little and is usually dismissed as 'theory.'" Dostoevsky's greatness does not spring simply from his capacity for ideas but from his ability to create characters who live by ideas. The polarities of experience and theory, image and idea (which Rahv finds everywhere in American literature), collapse in the art of Dostoevsky and in the art of other great European novelists.

One of the most difficult things to evaluate is the Marxist theme in Rahv's work. In *Image and Idea* it makes appearances only when it serves arguments that do not have Marxism itself as the focus. The focus is usually Stalinism, and Marxism is the stick with which to beat it. Rahv's scorn for Stalinism is most severe when he discovers it in its seemingly benign fellow-traveling form, because there he finds it in association with naïveté and stupidity, qualities as detestable in his eyes as knavery. Unlike recent Russian dissidents, however, Rahv did not discover the sins of Stalinism in Marxism itself. With his acute sense of history (the sixth sense he called it, using the phrase for the title of his last collection) he could not accept the view that ideology unfolds in a vacuum. "No ideology, whether secular or religious, exists in some ghost-like fashion apart from the men who believe in it or merely use it for their own ends," he said in reviewing Chambers's *Witness*. Since these men live in a particular time and place, they must be understood as historical creatures and not ideological machines. Rahv saw the Stalinist outcome as a Russian phenomenon rather than an inevitability of the Marxian idea. The difficulty in understanding Rahv's politics, however, is in knowing what is left of his commitment to Marxism after he had criticized every perversion of it. The Stalinists betrayed Marx, liberal fellow-travelers were suckers for Stalinism, and the sixties' radicals lacked the true revolutionist's understanding of history, strategy, and tactics. What is left is the negativism of the critic, who remains intransigently opposed to bourgeois society, but without any genuine positive alternative.

Rahv was a vigilant advocate of the autonomy of the literary process, and he had nothing but scorn for ideologues of whatever persuasion (e.g., Geismar, Hicks, De Voto) who judged works of art by ideological standards. At the same time, unlike critics of an exclusively "aesthetic" disposition, he was fully alive to the political implications of art. A literature of ideas in the modern period often means a literature of politics. Practical politics aside, Marxism (as opposed to Stalinism) may have given Rahv a body of ideas – or, better, an intellectual character – in which American literary criticism is often deficient. Though severe in his judgment of the Stalinism of the European left, Rahv had an implicit affinity for the

Europeans in their commitment to a literature and a criticism of ideas. Perhaps this is all that his Marxism amounts to.

There is an analogy between Rahv's view of modernism and his view of Marxism. True conservative that he was, he was a model of orthodoxy in his attachment to the inaugural figures: Joyce, Yeats, Eliot in the case of literary modernism, Marx and Lenin in the case of Marxism. The subsequent history of both movements was for Rahv a history of betrayal and degeneration. One thinks of Coleridge (in J. S. Mill's appreciation of him) recalling institutions and movements to their original idea. In the case of Stalinism Rahv was almost always right, but one feels in his view of the course of modern literature at times an almost willful refusal to find much good in anything after the classical period. Rahv was at best ambivalent toward modernism. He had little, if any, feeling for contemporary experimental writing. When he values a contemporary work like Bellow's *Herzog* it is "above all" because the novel "positively radiates intelligence." Writers like Mailer and Genet who provoke his contempt are seen in moral and intellectual terms: *An American Dream* is violent, empty of real ideas, and "eccentric"; Genet's *A Thief's Journal,* a piece of "moral idiocy." It is not that Rahv is wrong in his judgments – only that one feels a strong disposition in him as he grew older to suspect and mistrust the new. I can imagine his response to the recent rage for literary theory: a snorting and absolute contempt for those lovers of abstraction at the expense of literature. There was something of the Grand Inquisitor in Rahv's critical personality. If the inaugural figures had returned, Rahv might have used his considerable powers of persuasion to send them away.

In her moving eulogy Mary McCarthy mentions the fact that he never learned to swim, which she then turns into an emblem of his strength: his resistance to the tide. But there is more than a little fear, or distaste, for the current, which makes his weakness as a critic, a weakness that masked itself as strength. I can still hear his brusque "bullshit!" as the final term of an argument he made against the shallow, the spurious, or what he simply and uncritically found disagreeable.

Rahv's sixth sense was at its best reflective and retrospective. In full and disinterested possession of his critical gifts he was a superb discriminator of the various powers of classic European and American writers. At his best Rahv managed to maintain sufficient distance from a writer, so that he could see both the limitations and the strengths. (Lionel Trilling, a contributor to *Partisan Review*, was of course a master of the art of distance.) Rahv's New Critical contemporaries too often lost the necessary perspective for evaluation because of their ideological insistence on being close to the text.[2] To read a work closely may enable one to see it in its detail and perhaps its complexity, but it may also involve a loss of perspective, which comes from comparison with other works and traditions and with the possession by the reader of a set of interests and values that are not purely literary. The critic who reads only lyric poems or American literature will not have the larger perspective to make the necessary judgments. And he will not have the larger perspective if he does not inhabit a world larger than the one defined by literature – for example the worlds of history and politics. Together with these conditions the critic must possess the qualities of intelligence, taste, and judgment. In Rahv we have an exemplary convergence of conditions and gifts. Though not nearly so productive as Edmund Wilson and Lionel Trilling, Rahv in his criticism in comparable to them in kind and quality.

---

[2] Evaluation of imaginative literature has virtually disappeared from the contemporary practice of serious criticism, and its disappearance can be attributed in part to the elevation of interpretation as the supreme activity of criticism. New Critics never denied the evaluative function, but New Critical practice, especially in its more pedestrian expressions, became routines of explication of virtually any text. The evaluative function tended to atrophy. Most devastating to the practice of evaluation has been the case made against it by Northrop Frye, structuralists, and deconstructive skeptics. Whatever the differences among them, they seem to agree that evaluation belongs not to the professional study of literature but to the history of taste. For Rahv, of course, evaluation was the essence of criticism.

3 Joseph Frank's *Dostoevsky: The Seeds of Revolt 1821– 1849*

Dostoevsky: The Seeds of Revolt 1821–1849 (the first of four vol- umes of the life and works) is a salutary event in a time when the Newest Criticism is declaring the bankruptcy of the unified text. Not that a great text like *Notes from Underground* or even a lesser one like *The Double* is susceptible to easy solutions. If Joseph Frank believes Dostoevsky's work can be convincingly interpreted in the terms of the novelist's intentions, he knows how formidable the critic must be. He must have judgment, a gift for literary interpreta- tion, a deep knowledge of Russian political and social history, a sensitivity to individual psychology, and a general culture that make it possible for him to place Dostoevsky in currents that flow beyond Russia. As important as these powers is the capacity to integrate them.

Joseph Frank has the requisite combination of powers, and his book is an exemplary interweaving of history, psychology, and liter- ary criticism. Unlike most critical biographers, Frank is never gra- tuitous in his use of information. Nothing is ever given simply for the sake of creating the density of a life. Frank's patient detailing of the class affiliations of the Dostoevsky family life, for example, is not meant simply to satisfy the reader's curiosity. He wants to establish a true perspective on values in works that might appear ambiguous or obscure without the family history. Thus Dostoevsky satirizes the old aristocracy at the same time that he values ''aristocratic'' status (in *A Raw Youth* and *The Idiot*, to cite two instances), because like his declassed father he felt the injustice of being denied ''the consid- eration to which they felt entitled by right of descent from noble forbears.'' It would be easy, too easy, to view Dostoevsky's attitude as an exercise in *ressentiment*. With his keen literary sense of how the imagination transforms experience, Frank sees in the thwarted vanity of the Dostoevskys the seeds of Feodor's extraordinary sen- sitivity to injustice: the incommensurability between merit and reward that so profoundly characterized Russian society of the nineteenth century. The sensitivity extends beyond a sense of grievance at the injustice done to the declassed gentry to the most passionate indignation ever expressed by any writer (modern here seems to be an unnecessary qualification) at the sufferings of all the insulted and injured, whether they be master or serf.

Frank has set for himself an interesting and difficult problem. Without domesticating Dostoevsky he wants to correct what he regards as a false view of him as a sick artist. This view is expressed in Freud's famous and influential essay, "Dostoevsky and Parricide." Frank convincingly demolishes the "factual" basis of Freud's reading, which connects the onset of Dostoevsky's epilepsy with his knowledge of his father's murder. (Dostoevsky, in Freud's account, is a Hamlet-like figure who vicariously identifies himself with his father's murderer and therefore must be judged.) In a letter written before he composed the essay on Dostoevsky, Freud connected the epilepsy with a putative "castrating" punishment by a tyrannical father. Frank effectively demonstrates the absence of evidence both for the castrating event and for the connection between Dostoevsky's knowledge of the murder and the beginning of his epileptic seizures. Moreover, he establishes the probability that the epileptic seizures began during Dostoevsky's Siberian exile. Freud's interpretation would have been confirmed (so Freud believed) if Dostoevsky had experienced a remission from the seizures in Siberia, since the Siberian exile would have provided Dostoevsky with the punishment that he was supposed to have craved after his father's death. Frank's own guess (he is admirably scrupulous about distinguishing informed speculation from scholarly knowledge) is that Dostoevsky's epilepsy had an organic basis.

The important point about his elaborate (almost legalistic) refutation of the Freudian view is to resist any and all efforts to cloud our perception of Dostoevsky as the normative artist that he was. To say with Freud that Dostoevsky's epilepsy represents an unresolved conflict within him between submission and rebellion against authority is to circumvent the essential question about the existence of the conflict and the forms it took in his life and work, if that conflict indeed existed. Dostoevsky's powerful imagination of murderers (Raskolnikov, the Ivan-inspired Smerdyakov) can be converted to a view of a masochistic parricidal Dostoevsky only if one has the most primitive conception of the imaginative possibilities of art. In defense of Freud, it should be said – as Frank does indeed say – that he did not set as much store by these admitted speculations as did some of his literary followers. Though not intended as such, Frank's work is a valuable warning to psycho-historians against the ignorant misuse of psychoanalytic categories in treating literary and historical figures. To know the categories of psychoanalysis is not necessarily to know the life of a historical character, since no life can simply be deduced from the categories.

Family history is, of course, an insufficient means by which to establish an understanding of Dostoevsky's achievement. Much of Frank's book is given over to an account of the literary and political life of the time, which nourished Dostoevsky's formation as a writer. In the nineteenth century the literary and the political are indissolubly linked, for as Trotsky once remarked, literature was often the only dissident politics. The chapters on Dostoevsky's association with various literary and political coteries (particularly the Belinsky Pleiade and Petrashevsky Circle) gives us the milieu that was to be imaginatively transformed into the world of *The Possessed*. Of particular fascination is the personality of Speshnev, the man of fire and ice, who was to become Stavrogin, the destructive messiah of Dostoevsky's great novel. What emerges from these chapters is the reality which is shown to be susceptible to the *melodramatization* of the novel. The injustice of Russian life and the sense of frustration about the possibility of social reform encourage an extravagance of behavior and fantasy, which Dostoevsky was to transmute into a masterly art. In all these debates Dostoevsky was both observer and participant, whose vanity and resentment were constantly being exacerbated by other members of the various circles. We are given a glimpse of the underground man and his friends in Dostoevsky's various dealings with the other members of the radical intelligentsia.

Dostoevsky always stood at a distance from the political debates (which Frank characteristically presents in careful detail), because of a deep feeling that any political solution was inadequate to what Russia needed.

Socialism offers a thousand methods of social organization, and since all these books are written intelligently, fervently, and often with genuine love for mankind, I read them with curiosity. But precisely because I do not adhere to any of the social systems, I studied Socialism in general, all of its systems, and this is why (though my knowledge is far from complete) I see the faults in every social system. I am convinced that the application of any of them would bring with it inescapable ruin, and I am not talking about us but even in France.

This statement by Dostoevsky was made under police interrogation, but Frank believes it to be not only expressive of Dostoevsky's real sentiment, but of a representative sentiment of many of his contemporaries and friends as well. It is certainly consistent with what was to become Dostoevsky's "solution": a profound belief in the saving passion of Christ.

The religious solution, however, was no simple leap of faith, expressive of a facile aversion to the political life. On the contrary, as Frank has argued in earlier essays, Dostoevsky is an ideological artist, if that means that he invented obsessed characters who live out their ideas to their absurd logical conclusions and thereby disclose their destructive power. This tendency toward the extreme enactment of ideas is no mere intellectualist exercise on Dostoevsky's part, but is an imaginative rendering of the reality of the Russian intelligentsia in its impotent rage for justice and fulfillment.

What makes this volume something of a tour de force is Frank's capacity to make the early life and work so interesting, despite the relatively minor importance of the early fiction. The two most notable works of that period are *Poor Folk* (which Belinsky hailed as the work of a new genius, establishing Dostoevsky's reputation overnight) and *The Double*. The discussions of these novels are models of literary and social analysis. Frank is concerned to show the accomplishment and the limitation of the work, always with a sense of anticipation of the great work to follow.

The stress laid on [honor] shows Dostoevsky's acute awareness that the spiritual is of equal importance with the material in alleviating the lot of the unfortunate – even, perhaps, of greater importance, since poverty only heightens the need for self-esteem and self-respect to the point of morbidity. Indeed, the prominence of this motif in *Poor Folk* already reveals a tension in Dostoevsky's work that will have extremely important consequences later. In *Poor Folk,* this tension between the spiritual and the material is still latent and in a state of equilibrium; the emphasis accorded the spiritual (or, if one prefers, the moral-psychological) dimension of human experience only heightens the pathos of the material injustices that Dostoevsky's characters have to suffer. But when, beginning in the early 1860's, an aggressive and blinkered materialism became the ideology of Russian radicalism, Dostoevsky broke definitely with the radicals in defense of the "spiritual" in a broad sense. This opposition between the material and the spiritual – between the satisfaction of man's material needs, and his equal inner need for dignity and self-respect – will one day, of course, culminate in the Legend of the Grand Inquisitor.

One of Frank's most interesting "discoveries" is the voice of the underground man in the feuilletons that Dostoevsky wrote in the

1840s. Frank promises fuller treatment of the connection between the feuilleton and *Notes from Underground* in a later volume, but in his rich account of the feuilleton style, he enables us to hear what has always been experienced as singular and unprecedented, the voice of the underground man: fantastic, parodistic, satirical, high-flown, profane. It is a voice with an unparalleled freedom for making the most subversive, the most corrosive criticisms of Russian reality and indeed of human reality generally.

Though one can speak only provisionally about Frank's ultimate achievement, there is already substantial evidence that he is on his way to producing a classic, a monumental study of Dostoevsky beyond what anyone else has yet achieved. The paradox of the achievement promises to be what I would call the *de-monumentalizing* of Dostoevsky. The prevailing view of Dostoevsky has been that of the proto-existentialist, the world-literary figure who discovered not only *ressentiment*, but absurdity, angst, and abysmal existence as well. The Dostoevsky of existentialism is without local roots, he exists in an abstract space of burning metaphysical issues. Even his Russian character is *de-localized* and is seen as a species of soul. The existentialist Dostoevsky has been immensely seminal for modern European literature, but also he has not been entirely credible as a human being. By returning Dostoevsky to his local habitation, Frank in effect humanizes him without depriving him of his demonic qualities.

As an admiring reader of Frank's earlier essays on Dostoevsky's major novels, especially those on *Notes from Underground, Crime and Punishment,* and *The Possessed,* I have always had reservations about his open hostility to the existentialist reading of Dostoevsky's work. If that reading has been productive of creative literature as well as interesting philosophic criticism, why not honor it as valuable? Or at least one might account for the value, despite the mistaken interpretation. In the light of Frank's book, the reservations have all but disappeared, so convincing is his presentation. I am still impressed with the existentialist appropriation of Dostoevsky, but I share with Frank the view that a true reading remains an ideal for the critic, especially when the ideal is as beautifully realized as it is in Frank's book.

Frank's interest in Dostoevsky is at once intense and self-justifying. But one feels in this book as well as in the other essays that the interest may be partly motivated by a more general concern with the relations between literature and society in Europe since the French Revolution. As a liberal and a democrat, Frank shares Dostoevsky's aversion to mindless radicalism and revolutionism. What Frank discovers in Dostoevsky is the sanity and penetration of the normative ideological artist, despite the obvious aberrations and extravagances in his life and work. The completed study of Dostoevsky should be an inspiration for all students of Stendhal, Flaubert, Conrad, Malraux, indeed of all the major writers of the nineteenth and twentieth centuries who tried to grasp imaginatively the revolutionary reality of their times.

4 Leslie Fiedler and the mythic life

No! In Thunder (1960), the second collection of Leslie Fiedler's essays, is bound to add to the fame and notoriety that have attended Fiedler ever since he began to publish. In particular, the Foreword and the introductory essay, from which the book takes its title, will confirm Fiedler's reputation for being toughminded, arrogant and iconoclastic. Appropriately, he begins his Foreword with an expression of hope that his essays will have the intended effect of "offending all those with cemeteries to defend," whether they be the pieties of "the avant-garde revolt in the twenties, Marxism of the thirties, the enlightened middlebrowism of the forties or the hip pieties of the fifties." Fiedler has already established a reputation for himself as toughminded and unsentimental in *An End to Innocence*, and more recently in *Love and Death in the American Novel*. He obviously wants to make it clear that, if anything, he has hardened in the interim between *An End to Innocence* and the current collection of essays. The Foreword is a piece of unabashed self-revelation. Fiedler speaks of himself as a legend from which he hopes to disentangle his real self, and though he repudiates as part of the legend reports of friend being separated from friend, lover from lover by arguments over one or another of his essays, one can nonetheless detect an unmistakable note of pride. "At least, my essays have brought certain dull parties to a long overdue end."

The "No! in Thunder" refers both to what Fiedler regards as the essential function of the artist and to what he conceives his own essays to be saying. The phrase is from a letter Melville wrote to Hawthorne in which, attempting to characterize Hawthorne's art, he in effect characterized his own. "He says No! in thunder; but the Devil himself cannot make him say *yes*. For all men who say *yes*, lie; and all men who say *no* – why, they are in a happy condition of judicious, unencumbered travellers in Europe; they cross the frontiers into Eternity with nothing but a carpetbag – that is to say, the

Ego.'' Fiedler's commentary on Melville's text is meant to explain his book and vindicate himself.

The "No! in thunder" is never partisan; it infuriates Our Side as well as Theirs, reveals that all Sides are one, insofar as they are all yea-sayers and hence all liars. There is some evidence that the Hard No is being spoken when the writer seems a traitor to those whom he loves and who have conditioned his very way of responding to the world. When the writer says of precisely the cause that is dearest to him what is always and everywhere the truth about all causes – that it has been imperfectly conceived and inadequately represented, and that it is bound to be betrayed, consciously or unconsciously, by its leading spokesmen – we know that he is approaching an art of real seriousness if not actual greatness.

The Hard No! then is the *radical* refusal to be taken in by piety; it is the willingness and the courage to stand alone, if necessary, and abide by one's personal convictions about the truth – in a word, the willingness and courage to be *egoistic*.

There could be no ultimate quarrel with Fiedler's manner, if the essays were all that Fiedler made them out to be. What offends is not the arrogance of the Foreword and the Introduction, but the failure of the essays to make good on the promise that the arrogance implies. For even Fiedler's superb polemical manner, the original "insights" that he delivers with such *éclat,* the wit and colloquial grace of his language cannot make the book what it is not: a radical action against the Modern Age. The result is that the book comes off as somewhat pretentious.

Having had his expectations raised so high at the outset, the reader is more impressed with his disappointment than with the genuine accomplishments of the essays. And the disappointment is immediate. Part I, entitled The Artist, begins with two able, though quite academic, performances on Dante and Shakespeare, an interesting though somewhat misleading essay on Whitman,[1] a rescue operation on Robert Louis Stevenson, followed by pieces on Peretz, Malamud, Faulkner and Warren among others. The impression of discontinuity between the introductory essays and Part I is so striking as to seem significant. What the essays have in common is not the Hard No!,

---

[1]   It is Wordsworth, not Whitman, who is the first truly modern poet with epic ambitions, the first to derive a mythology "from his own experience, lived or dreamed" and make himself the hero of his poetry.

but a preoccupation with the mythical content of life and literature: the recurrent patterns that manifest themselves in the actions of men in the world and in books that express the eternal rituals of the soul. In an essay, "In the Beginning Was the Word," placed misleadingly towards the end of the book, Fiedler states with admirable succinctness the real subject matter of his essays: "Myths, those ancient Greek stories that are our Archetypes par excellence, preserving for us the assurance which belongs to ritual alone: that what is done below is done above, what is done here and now is done forever, what is repeated in time subsists unbroken in eternity."

Fiedler, of course, means to connect the mythical content of life and literature with the Hard No!; myth, which is for him almost identical with Life (or Truth), is the Supreme Court of Appeal against the ideologies and pieties that impoverish and destroy Life. The deeper the connection between the individual imagination of the artist (or the social critic) and the myth, the greater the art, the more thunderous the No! But it is precisely Fiedler's failure to apply to this assumed connection the same toughmindedness that he applies to certain middlebrow pieties, for instance, that makes for the discontinuity and the disappointment. The connection between myth and the Hard No! is an unexamined assumption, a problem that Fiedler is able to avoid through his rhetorical gift. Dialectical exploration of difficulty and ambiguity (one of Fiedler's favorite words) yields to the cleverly turned sentence – or the sentence so cleverly turned that the writer outsmarts himself. ("In the end the negativist is not a nihilist, for he affirms the void.")

The preoccupation with the mythical content of life and literature – as these essays unwittingly testify – leads not to the Hard No!, but to a kind of stoicism. Every cultural situation that Fiedler writes about is conceived as a manifestation of an archetypal pattern in human consciousness which emerges from the timeless world of myth with the inevitability of, say, history as the Marxists conceive it. The archetype of myth, which is prior to person or society, is the fate from which there is neither escape nor finally even understanding. How is it possible then to make the leap – as Fiedler apparently does – between myth and Nay-Saying? For Nay-Saying presupposes the freedom to say No even to myth – for instance to the Myth of Innocence. Not once does Fiedler show how the will can free itself from the thousand rituals that determine it and make the gesture of freedom that the No! implies. The essays are a testimony to the

Devil's power to coerce our imaginings and utterances; even the No!
– Melville to the contrary notwithstanding – is the Devil's
inspiration.

The moral of every essay of social criticism, whether it be on the
Leopold and Loeb trial or the Negro and Jew in America or the Un-
Angry Young Men, is that every event is a symbolic event "in which
a whole society objectifies and acts out its inner conflicts, its most
pressing archetypal errors." We are all caught in the grip of a deter-
minism against which even courage, wit, intelligence and talent are
impotent. Thus Fiedler writes:

> How hard it is for those who did not *live* the mythic life of their own
> generation to realize that so far as our imagination is concerned, they had
> never existed at all! It is not a matter of talent or intelligence or wit (the
> dullards Ethel and Julius Rosenberg are relevant and hence real, the brighter
> Harold and Bernard Rosenberg irrelevant and unreal) . . .

This! (to borrow an exclamation mark from Fiedler) from a man who
begins his book by celebrating the Nay-Sayer's power to refuse, in
effect, to live the mythic life of his generation.

In the very interesting essay on the Negro and the Jew, Fiedler,
living the mythic life of his generation, remembers the experience of
reading *Uncle Tom's Cabin* as a boy and of making a vow to take a
heroic stand in a fight to wipe out racial inequality ("Needless to
say, no heroic exploits followed."); and again, bravely confessing
that "none of [his] best friends is black," he resigns himself to the
knowledge of "the distrust we would have to overcome, the masks
we would have to penetrate, to discover our real selves, much less
become real friends." These moments in Fiedler call to mind George
Orwell, who also in a sense lived the mythic life of *his* generation.
The kind of paralysis of the will that seems to go with Fiedler's
recognitions, Orwell never shared. Who can read *Homage to Catalonia* without perceiving the limitations of the mythical view of
history? The Orwell who remained a socialist, despite every disillusionment, because he could not forget the brief and glorious time
when Barcelona was a working-class city is a superb counterinstance
to Fiedler's portraits of men and self as incarnations of the mythic
life fulfilling a destiny not of their own making.

No! in Thunder belongs, paradoxically, to the ethos of what I
should like to call the new Stoicism – the kind of response to life that
was so clearly reflected by the symposium conducted in *The New*

Leader several years ago in which the members of the generation presently in their thirties sought to define its character. The consensus of the symposium was that this generation, having been denied the mature experience of the depression and having inherited the previous generation's disenchantment with Marxism, had grown up prematurely oriented to notions of conformity and success. All that remains to the sensitive highbrow element, as the articles bear witness, is an uneasy and inactive dissatisfaction with it all and a capacity to endure the dissatisfaction. To place Fiedler in such company might at first glance appear perverse. Or it might seem to those who have read *An End to Innocence,* that, if this judgement of his latest book is accurate, Fiedler has changed from his earlier rebelliousness. The truth is that the two collections of essays are of a piece. To be sure, there is nothing in the latest collection that compares with the essays on the Rosenbergs or the Hiss trial or *Huck Finn* for sheer provocation. *No! in Thunder* is a tamer book. But it must be insisted that the two books are *ideologically* similar in spirit, as a rereading of *An End to Innocence* makes clear. Fiedler's No!, like his toughmindedness in *An End to Innocence,* is little more than an incapacity to act with the paralyzing knowledge of the dubious motives which every idea, attitude, gesture and action conceal.

But why the insistence on the No? Before we can decide whether Fiedler himself is not a victim of the sentimentalism that he so deplores by refusing to face the bitter consequences of what he has seen and become, it would be useful to consider the inconsistent role that *myth* plays in the essays. In a brief review of Malamud's *The Natural,* Fiedler, after demonstrating the presence of the Grail legend in the novel – the manager of the team called the Knights is Pop Fisher, etc. – speaks of the special achievement of Malamud: ''in this book the modern instance and the remembered myth are equally felt . . . he has not felt obliged to choose between the richness of imagined detail and that of symbolic relevance.'' What Mary McCarthy has called the Novel's ''deep love of fact and of the empiric element in experience'' is found to serve in Malamud's case the mythic ambition of literature. In the essay on ''The Un-Angry Young Men'' we find this account of the mythical dimension of ''the New York academics'':

. . . the New York academics, who represent the latest form of status-striving among descendants of East European immigrants. In the first gener-

ation, there was a simplehearted drive to found fortunes in woolens, ladies'
underwear, junk – no matter; in the second, an impulse to enter the (still
financially rewarding) respectability of the public professions, law and med-
icine; in the third, an urge to find a place in publishing and the universities,
to become writers and intellectuals. In my own generation, there are notorious cases of men with no taste (much less any love) for literature becoming
critics out of sheer bafflement. Never have so many natural operators and
minor Machiavellians pushed so eagerly and with less reason into the academy. The old tragedy of the poet forced into manufacturing paper bags
becomes the new comedy of the proto-tycoon lecturing on the imagery of
Wallace Stevens.

It is clear that the "I" of Fiedler – that part of him that can disengage
from myth – wants no part of the archetypal pattern that he is
describing above. And there are many instances of Fiedler's hostility
towards comparable social "myths." The whole animus of the essay
on the Rosenbergs in *An End to Innocence* is the resentment that
"the Rosenbergs were not able to think of themselves as real people," that they saw themselves "only as cases, . . . [like] Scotts-
boro and Harry Bridges and the Trenton Six, replaceable puppets in a
manifestation that never ends" and that finally they permitted the
Stalinist press to "share in the ritualistic exploitation of themselves."

There is a split in Fiedler's attitude towards myth which divides
the literary critic and the social critic. Wherever Fiedler discovers
myth in a work of literature, there is a chance that he has discovered
seriousness, or even greatness. On the other hand, though one must
live the mythic life in order to be "real and relevant," Fiedler says
No!, or at least would like to, to the social myth – that is, if he were
not rendered neutral by the myth.

This, of course, is oversimplification; for instance, as the essay
"Archetype and Signature" makes clear, the mythical dimension
does not itself decide the seriousness or greatness of a work of
literature. Every work of literature is the product of a dialectic between the mythic pattern (the archetype) and the personal idiosyn-
cratic imagination of the artist (the signature). Yet despite this recognition, Fiedler on another occasion will speak of myth as a category
of value and still on other occasions make comparisons among works
of literature with similar mythical preoccupations in which no basis
is proposed for distinguishing among the merits of the different
works. ("From Uncle Tom, in particular, there descend such important characters of our literature as Mark Twain's Nigger Jim and
Faulkner's Lucas Beauchamp, who symbolically grant the white

man forgiveness in the name of their whole race, redeem him by their enduring the worst he can inflict.'') As a practical critic, Fiedler is apparently not interested in the *signature* of the artist. He has the taste and the intuition to recognize value when he encounters it, but literary criticism in the sense of the demonstration of the discrimination of value in literature seems alien to Fiedler's purposes. Indeed, one of the interesting paradoxes in Fiedler is that he exploits his literary training as a social critic and his sociological and anthropological talents as a literary critic. Thus, in the Preface of *An End to Innocence,* he speaks of '' 'a close reading' of recent events that I should like to think I have achieved, a reading that does not scant ambiguity or paradox, but tries to give to the testimony of a witness before a Senate committee or the letters of the Rosenbergs the same careful scrutiny we have learned to practice on the shorter poems of Donne.''

I have spent so much time pointing out the inconsistencies in Fiedler not out of pique. I do not know him, nor do I have proprietary interest in any of the cemeteries that he chooses to desecrate. On the contrary, I go along with most of the praise that has been accorded him. He is one of the most incisive of our critics. His perception of the ritual content of our life and literature is probably quicker and keener than that of any critic writing today. But he has seriously misconceived his role, and that misconception is, in Fiedler's terms, an enactment of an aspect of the mythic life of our time.

The decline of the radical imagination in America has left a residuum of recalcitrant rebellious energy. Failing to discover the appropriate forms through which this energy can express itself, the would-be rebel becomes fantastical and willful. Mailer's *Advertisements for Myself on the Way Out* may be in certain ways a preposterous book (Fiedler in a review for *Midstream* characterized Mailer as The Fool), but folly, as we know, can be serious and significant, and it is hard to read Mailer's book without being moved by the plight of the radical imagination in America. Even a reader completely out of sympathy with the vision of the radical as psychopathic personality cannot fail, if he has the sensitivity and intelligence, *to see* that Mailer's book – indeed, his recent public career – is what happens when a society deprives the radical imagination of occasions for expression or when the occasions which it does provide have the effect of emasculating it. Fiedler is certainly sensitive to this situation, and the No! that he delivers early in the book belongs to that rebellious energy that survives even his fulfilled wish "for maturity and an end to innocence – in short, middle-age itself." There is simply too much energy and youthful imagination in Fiedler for him to be content with that. But he is also too knowledgeable, too much burdened with the past, the guilty past, to go out on the radical limb. Indeed, all his effort to portray himself as a Nay-Sayer, a rebellious spirit, is betrayed by what is the deepest truth about Fiedler – that his is a conservative mind. Perhaps nowhere else is this made so clear as at the conclusion of his essay "The Profanation of the Child" in the group entitled "The Eye of Innocence" in which Fiedler describes with approval a new kind of "revolutionary" literature.

. . . The work of recent writers for whom tales of childhood are inevitably tales of terror, represents a literature blasphemous and revolutionary. Such writers have come to believe that the self can be betrayed to impulse as well as to rigor; that an Age of Innocence can be a tyranny no less terrible than an Age of Reason; and that the Gods of such an age if not yet dead must be killed, however snub-nosed, freckled-faced or golden-haired they may be.

Revolutionary indeed! Concealed in this passage is the cult of maturity and social responsibility that has plagued the radical enterprise in recent years. To be sure, "the self can be betrayed to impulse as well as to rigor," but to characterize this statement as revolutionary is sheer disingenuousness, an attempt to have one's cake and eat it. Lionel Trilling's *Liberal Imagination,* which is in a sense the "archetype" for both of Fiedler's collections of essays, was at the time a fresh and much profounder response to the neglected values of the Conservative Mind. Consequently, Fiedler's potshots at the young New York Intellectuals, "the little Trillings and Riesmans," seem like pure gratuitousness.

Finally, my deepest irritation with the book has to do with something not only in Fiedler, but in myself as well – indeed, in the times in which we live. I have just been rereading *Homage to Catalonia* and *Down and Out in Paris and London* and coming to Fiedler from Orwell, I have been struck by what I surely would not have seen so clearly in Fiedler if Orwell's books were not there to serve as contrast. Fiedler's world is *literary* through and through, whether the subject matter be Robert Penn Warren's latest book or the Leopold and Loeb case. There is hardly an event in social or cultural history that is not immediately perceived in terms of middlebrow and highbrow responses and the corresponding literary documents. How narrow the mythic life of our time has become! It is not simply that the political imagination has become enervated or that the will to act in behalf of a cause has all but died, it is that the wider world in which Orwell lived and suffered gave one the sense of possibilities and that our world, shrunken in the age of conformity, aviation and the universal fear of war, has become something of a claustrophobe's nightmare. In Fiedler's essays the shrinking of the world is documented, and his own response to this shrinking is, if I may once more render it in his own terms, an enactment of the mythic life of our times.

Author's note: *No! In Thunder,* as well as my review, predated the political turbulence of the sixties. My response to Fiedler's book reveals an impatience with the "cult of maturity and social responsibility." The explosiveness of the sixties was a response to this cult, among other things. As will be clear from subsequent pieces, I did not find myself in sympathy with the new radical mood. But Fiedler did. He did not rock the boat by continually reminding his reader, as he did in the late fifties, that self-betrayal is the law of radical causes – indeed, of all causes. In the late sixties, Fiedler would write the following:

The kind of criticism the age demands is death-of-art criticism, which is most naturally practised by those who came of age since the death of the new poetry and the new criticism. It seems evident that writers not blessed to be under 30 (or 35, or whatever the critical age is these days) must be reborn in order to seem relevant to the moment and to those who inhabit it most comfortably: the young. But one hasn't even the hope of being reborn unless he knows first that he is dead.

Now the apocalypse is "in" – and that, after all, is *all* that matters: Perhaps the deep consistency in Fiedler's work is his fidelity to the mythic life of his times, whatever that mythic life may be at the moment.

5 The "radicalism" of Susan Sontag

With the publication of "Notes on Camp" in 1964 Susan Sontag became for a while the most talked about critic in America. She had been publishing essays since 1961 in which she was making a reputation for herself as the critic furtherest "in" or "way out," depending on one's linguistic preferences. She has always been responsive to the new, as much an exponent as a critic of the avant-garde, a term she uses with a certain reluctance, because she is intelligent enough to know that the avant-garde has its problems now. She has created the impression – without posturing or immodesty – of being dead center, of knowing where the action is. Her essays have the considerable virtues of seriousness, forcefulness and clarity of exposition, genuine intelligence and often humility. They are virtues rarely, if at all, found together in exponents or critics of the avant-garde. She writes a vigorous, reasoned and thoughtful criticism that makes her manner seem almost traditional. And this is very much to her advantage, because even those readers who are hostile to her views are disarmed by her lucid and informing way of speaking of the strange world of post-modern art.

But the attractiveness of her essays has diverted her readers from a serious consideration of what she is in fact saying. Most discussions of her work focus on her as performer rather than critic. Her critical doctrine of style in great part provokes this view of her. Indeed, she might well object that what is important is not what she says, but the way she says it. But the *way* and the *what* are inextricably connected, and not in a manner which would make the *what* "very tiny – very tiny" (to paraphrase De Kooning's characterization of content, a statement which provides the motto for her essay "Against Interpretation"). The recent publication of *Styles of Radical Will,* her second volume of essays, provides an opportunity for seriously examining and evaluating what she has been saying in her essays. In

46

the process we may learn something about modern art and contemporary politics. Sontag's characteristic subject is art and her viewpoint and doctrine are aesthetical. One gets the feeling of *déjà vu* from her theoretical aesthetics. In the essay "On Style" (printed in her first book, *Against Interpretation*) she reasserts the (by now) traditional view that style and content are indissoluble, because she claims that though everyone is quick to affirm the view, in the *"practice of criticism . . .* the old antithesis lives on, virtually unassailed." She departs from the formalist view by refusing to accept the antithesis that formalism usually makes between art and morality.[1] She argues that what makes the art "morally" valuable is that it responds to and awakens qualities not normally cherished by a culture: attentiveness, grace, intelligence, expressiveness, energy, sensuousness. "The ambivalence toward style is not rooted in simple error but in the passion of an entire culture to protect and defend values traditionally conceived of as lying 'outside' art, namely truth and morality, but which remain in perpetual danger of being compromised by art." For Sontag serious art must try to show up the failures of a culture and in itself satisfy spiritual, moral and sensuous needs not satisfied by the culture.

What need or needs should a seriously radical art respond to? For Sontag much of the spiritual failure of America is in its sensual poverty. Her admiration for the Dionysian "message" of Norman O. Brown provides the conscious rationale for much of her work:

> We are nothing but body; all values are bodily values, says Brown. He invites us to accept the androgynous mode of being and the narcissistic mode of self-expression that lie hidden in the body. According to Brown, mankind is unalterably, in the unconscious, in revolt against sexual differentiation and genital organization. The core of human neurosis is man's incapacity to live in the body – to live (that is, to be sexual) and to die.

Thus in an interesting essay she values pornography because she sees the "deepest spiritual resonance of the career of pornography in its 'modern' Western phase (as) this vast frustration of human passion and seriousness since the old religious imagination, with its

---

[1] Sontag derives her formalist position from French phenomenological criticism rather than from New Criticism, but this makes little practical difference in her critical writings.

secure monopoly on the total imagination, began in the late eighteenth century to crumble.'' And she lays the blame upon modern capitalist society, which has failed ''to provide authentic outlets for the perennial human flair for high-temperature visionary obsessions, to satisfy the appetite for exalted self-transcending modes of concentration and seriousness.'' It is revealing that she does not respond to ''the spiritual resonance'' of Lawrence's effort, a writer for whom sexuality became an absolute and yet who rejected pornography as degrading. Indeed she adds her voice to a growing chorus of disapproval of D. H. Lawrence's ''puritanism,'' though in sheer sensuality, sheer bodily imagination none of the writers, cinéastes or artists whom she values can hold a candle to Lawrence. The reason is that she is less interested in sexual vitality than in what William James called ''morbidmindedness.'' The value of morbidmindedness is that it ranges over '' 'a wider scale of experience' than healthy-mindedness.'' In the concluding section of the essay she concedes that ''most people don't need 'a wider scale of experience.' It may be that, without subtle and extensive psychic preparation any widening of experience and consciousness is destructive for most people.'' But she sees the hostility to pornography as misplaced in the light of society's tolerance of items in the culture which are much more pernicious – murder, genocide, exploitation. Moreover in her view, pornography need not be for most people, but for the happy or unhappy few for whom the goal of consciousness is ''a wider scale of experience.''

The essay is not without effect as an argument against censorship or at a higher level against the protests of certain intellectuals (e.g., George Steiner) that pornography is a noxious form of imagination. But the *achievement* of pornography remains dubious. As a revelation of psychic capacity (e.g., ''Justine of [Sade] lives in a perpetual state of astonishment, never learning anything from the strikingly repetitive violations on her innocence''), pornography strikes one as an exhaustible genre. The extreme exercise of lust complicated by sadism and masochism, which is rendered unpsychologically and behavioristically, will tend to be repetitive within a work and from work to work. The element of novelty is in the working out of all the permutations and combinations. It is pretentious to view pornography as Sontag views it, as a spiritual operation in the following terms:

But O is an adept; whatever the cost in pain and fear, she is grateful for the opportunity to be initiated into a mystery. That mystery is the loss of the self. O learns, she suffers, she changes. Step by step she becomes more what she is, a process identical with the emptying out of herself. In the vision of the world presented by *Story of O,* the highest good is the transcendence of personality. The plot's movement is not horizontal, but a kind of ascent through degradation. O does not simply become identical with her sexual availability, but wants to reach the perfection of becoming an object.

The wisdom in pornographic self-transcendence, in Sontag's view, is that " 'the obscene' is a primal notion of human consciousness, something much more profound than the backwash of a sick society's aversion to the body." This may well be the case, though the mere assertion of such a view can hardly do the work of persuasion. But even if this were the case, it is hard to see why pornography deserves a religious vocabulary (except perhaps as sheer parody). *Gulliver's Travels* provides an instructive analogy. Gulliver's discovery of the ineluctable corruption of the human body and soul (beyond the shaping force of society) can be viewed as a commanding and terrible truth but it does not merit the language of self-transcendence. On the contrary, the discovery reveals the terrible fixity of human nature, man's essential incapacity for transcendence. To quote Sontag against herself:

An idea becomes false and impotent when it seeks reconciliation, at cut-rate prices, with other ideas. Modern seriousness, in numerous traditions, exists. Only a bad intellectual end is served when we blur all boundaries and call it religious, too.

The instances of "the perennial human flair for high temperature visionary obsessions" and of "self-transcending modes of concentration and seriousness" that come to mind are the Dionysian spirits like Blake, Keats, Nietzsche and Lawrence, whose death-seeking is not the emptying of oneself that characterizes *The Story of O* or the work of Beckett, but a courting of the sensual richness before death. ("Oh now it would be rich to die" [Keats] "Only those who have unlived lives in their bodies are afraid of death" [Rilke].) Sontag's romantic vocabulary conceals the harsh reality of the pornographic imagination. The sensuousness that she responds to tends to be anemic in the manner of a Robbe-Grillet novel or cruel and death-dealing in the manner of *The Story of O* or disgusting in the manner of Michel Leiris's autobiography:

Manhood begins not with "I was born in . . ." but with a matter-of-fact description of the author's body. We learn in the first pages of Leiris' incipient baldness, of a chronic inflammation of the eyelids, of his meager sexual capacities, of his tendency to hunch his shoulders when sitting and to scratch his anal region when he is alone, of a traumatic tonsillectomy undergone as a child, of an equally traumatic infection in his penis; and, subsequently, of his hypochondria, of his cowardice in all situations of the slightest danger, of his inability to speak any foreign language fluently, of his pitiful incompetence in physical sports. His character, too, is described under the aspect of limitation: Leiris presents it as "corroded" with morbid and aggressive fantasies concerning the flesh in general and women in particular.

She is an exponent of the sensuousness of spiritual impoverishment rather than the full-blooded Dionysianism of a Blake or a Keats or a Lawrence. She allows her sensibility to betray her theory; which, given her view that sensibility has priority, is a fine thing. But it makes for an intellectual incoherence in her criticism, for she has not yet found an adequate theoretical expression for her "aesthetic case studies." Despite his ready availability, Norman O. Brown (on the evidence of these essays) is not for her.

It is a real question whether her aesthetic theorizing or her practical criticism is radical on her own terms. She operates on a tacit and dubious assumption shared by a great many people that one can speak of the radical and the modern interchangeably. The *modern* is too protean an idea to be summarily defined, but one of its essential characteristics is the value of changefulness. The modern artist is never content with an old form or an old idea and seeks forever to displace what is traditional with what is new. I doubt that the real motive for the pursuit of the new is the desire for a "definitive art form," as Sontag states. Everything in the ethos of modern and postmodern art suggests that changefulness has become an end in itself, a symbol of vitality. As McLuhan has argued, the industrial and technological revolutions in their perpetual innovativeness constitute the appropriate breeding ground for such an aesthetic. And indeed Sontag's interest in technique (e.g., the ingenuities of Robbe-Grillet or Godard) and technology (e.g., the world of pop art and of happenings, Marshall McLuhan's romance of technology) seems her deepest interest. She will speak at length about cinematic technique. This interest generates a paradox to which no attention is given in the essays. The feeling for technique and technology, especially when the works which incarnate technique and technology are spiritually and sensuously impoverished (often programatically so), would hardly suggest the subversive relation that she feels should exist between art and conventional social values. In a society that exalts the lunar module as its highest imaginative and intellectual achievement the valuing of the technique and technology of art is hardly the "stylistic" move one would expect from a radical aesthetics.

One could argue that given the pervasiveness of technique and technology in our society the necessary task of aesthetics is to concern itself with the artistic *use* of technology. But this implies a will to dominate the "materials" of art, which seems to be proscribed in the current art scene. It is the happening rather than the organizing artistic will that determines the contemporary work of art. In a society of urban sprawl, in which the valuable past is often destroyed, there is nothing particularly radical or subversive in endorsing pop art or the happening. Sontag says at one point that "a radical position isn't necessarily a forward-looking position." Yet this awareness of the problem rarely communicates to her aesthetic sensibility. Her feeling for a comparatively old-fashioned writer like Cioran is genuine, but in the context of her essays her praise of him reads like a diplomatic concession to the other view. Her heart belongs to Cage. "Styles of Modern Will" would come close to defining the intention of the essays. For political reasons she wants the term radical but I am not sure she deserves it.

When she values the anti-McCarthy film *Point of Order,* because it "aestheticized a weighty public event," she is hardly exercising radical judgment. Or when she defines the new sensibility (again in *Against Interpretation*) as one involving "anguish, followed by anaesthesia and then by wit and the elevating of intelligence over sentiment . . . as a response to the social disorder and mass atrocities of our time," we can well understand her confession of failure in *Styles of Radical Will* to incorporate her political convictions into her essays. She would have to change her sensibility for Ho Chi Minh to settle comfortably in her consciousness alongside Pauline Réage's *The Story of O.* l don't see that her sensibility changed significantly between 1965 (*Against Interpretation*) and 1968 (*Styles of Radical Will*).

She understandably shies away from defining "radical," hoping that its meaning will emerge contextually. But it is sometimes hard to resist the suspicion that the word is there more for its prestige than its reality: "The question each artist must ask is: What is *my* radicalism, the one dictated by *my* gifts and temperament?'' Why must the artist ask this question? Why shouldn't he ask himself (if self-questioning is indeed the creative process), what are my gifts and temperament and what will genuinely express them?

The difficulty with the terms radical and modern extends to "avant-garde.'' The essays are not remarkably sensitive to the problems of being avant-garde these days. For instance, how much in the contemporary art scene is really new (let alone interesting) and how much of it is simply a reenactment of "the modern'' – that is, the persistence of the surrealist and dadaist strains in modernism? In her essay on Cioran she shows an ambivalent attitude toward the historicizing consciousness which may help account for her unwillingness to examine the status of the avant-garde today. She offers as an alternative mode to the historicizing consciousness of Cioran whose "thought is halfway between anguished reprise of the gestures [of the past] and a genuine transvaluation of them'' the work of John Cage: "All that is necessary . . . is an empty space of time and letting it act in its magnetic way.'' The emptying of the space of time demands the cultivation of innocence – the dissolving of the constraining sense of necessity and difficulty that goes with historical consciousness. Sontag is in the tough spot of trying to cultivate and understand this innocence at the same time, which at best is a precarious enterprise.

It may yet turn out that the really new element in the post-modern "avant-garde'' is its populism. The surrealist and dadaist strains in modernism have emerged as the characteristic art of the post-modern. The contingent, the arbitrary, the accidental, the spontaneous: these are the features of the new sensibility. Whereas the older surrealists presupposed the artistic grace of the individual artist, the new surrealism has gone populist. The dadaist gesture, as exemplified by the happening for instance, has become possible for everyone. And this creates another difficulty for the exponent of the avant-garde. Resistance to the new gave an edge and savor to the work of the avant-garde. The avant-garde artist had to sharpen his weapons against the formidable indifference or hostility of the philistine. But this is no longer the case. As soon as Sontag published her "Notes on Camp,'' she became a celebrity of *Time* magazine. This is not necessarily the fault of Sontag or the avant-garde. We all know that America has a way of gobbling up its dissenters by offering them money, status, prestige, even against their will, though the aesthetics of Sontag and McLuhan offer little resistance to the temptation –

indeed seem to encourage it. Nothing seems too radical for assimilation.

One could hardly expect a critic, no matter how talented, to resolve the predicament of the avant-garde in a culture which offers it so little resistance, in which the avant-garde loses its reason for being. But the surprise in the essays is that so little attention is paid to the problem. Perhaps an artist can deliberately cultivate innocence: I am not sure that it is the prerogative of the critical essayist.

Not that she is without the gift for self-criticism or for putting her convictions and commitments into question. Much of the interest of the essay on her trip to Hanoi is that she allows her experience of the North Vietnamese (their sobriety, their singular moral and political passion, their simple though ceremonious relation to life) to put in jeopardy the validity of her own complex sensibility. She values the simplicity of the Vietnamese, who are not split between their public and private spheres. (Minimal art and the silences of John Cage are quite different from the *genuine* simplicities of North Vietnamese life, which Sontag describes, for minimal art and the silence of Cage depend on a sophisticated – and, I believe, meretricious – innocence.) One symptom of the split in the West, as Sontag sees, is the immense amount of "talk" here, "talk" as an end in itself:

But Vietnam is a culture in which people have not got the final devastating point about talking, have not gauged the subtle, ambivalent resources of language – because they don't experience as we do the isolation of a "private self." Talk is still a rather plain instrumentality for them, a less important means of being connected with their environment than direct feeling, love.

And yet after leaving Vietnam she confesses to one of her companions that she "can't deny the immense richness of [the intellectual and aesthetic pleasures of Western culture]. . . . What came to mind . . . was the sentence of Talleyrand that Bertolucci used as the motto of his sad, beautiful film: 'He who has not lived before the revolution has never known the sweetness of life.' " This despite the strong feeling gained from her experience that the "same culture" coarsens the sensibilities and thwarts the capacities for goodness of most people.

Her essay on her trip to Hanoi begins with the statement that she has not been able to incorporate her evolving radical political convictions into either her essays or her novels. The collection in which the essay appears is titled *Styles of Radical Will*. One assumes that she intended her essays on the pornographic imagination or on the aesthetics of silence to be expressions of radical will. Could it be that there is an ineluctable opposition between "aesthetic radicalism" and "radical political convictions," which Sontag is slipping over when she attributes her divided sensibility to a personal inability? The Puritan discipline involved in political struggle, especially in a place as reduced and crisis-ridden as Vietnam, could hardly be expected to be the breeding ground for an aesthetic sensibility in the mode of John Cage or Allen Kaprow or even Godard. Not that Sontag expects this, but it is hard to envision what "incorporation" would mean for Sontag, short of an abandonment of her aesthetic predilections. She can of course maintain her aesthetic stance and continue to evolve politically in a radical direction, but then her sensibility would become schizophrenic.

There is already some evidence of schizophrenia in her own political rhetoric. She not only believes that the war in Vietnam is an abomination, that our treatment of the Blacks is a moral atrocity, but she has yielded to the venomous Manichean rhetoric of radicalism at its worst. "The white race is the cancer of history."[2] (PR symposium.) When she encountered rhetoric of this sort in Vietnam, she excused "the disease of rhetoric" (Pham Van Dong's phrase) by attributing it to the effect of war or by noting the mechanical way the North Vietnamese utter Marxian shibboleths as indicative of a lack of serious belief in them. ("Even when they use the melodramatic Communist language of denunciation, it comes out sounding dutiful and a little flat.") There is something appealing in this complex, guilt-ridden member of the cancerous white race in her final incapacity for being reduced to the moral simplicities of political rhetoric. She would not put it this way: but her aesthetics act as a sort of cooling agent on her evolving political and moral passions.

There is a sense in which the essay "Against Interpretation" is a good rationale for her own performance. Sontag is essentially an exponent of the arts – of the arts in which she believes. She performs for them through the essay. She is deliberately short on interpretation and theoretical understanding. Intelligent and bright as she obviously is, she is on her own admission primarily concerned with sensibility rather than with "ideas" or "intellect." Even her essays on intellec-

---

2   To Sontag's credit, she has long since abandoned this kind of rhetoric. Her own bout with cancer made her realize the irresponsibility of the metaphorical use of the language of illness. See her *Illness as Metaphor*.

tual performers like Claude Lévi-Strauss or Norman O. Brown treat the sensibility that emanates from their books rather than the logic or cogency of their ideas. And yet there is in her intelligence and interests the promise of a kind of understanding of what she stands for that is never kept. The historicizing consciousness, logical analysis, interpretation, evaluation are the unavoidable activities of the critic. It is very hard to see how the intelligent critic engaged in these activities can be the adversary of art or anything humanly valuable in these barbarous times.

6 Paul Goodman's neolithic conservatism

One must be grateful for Paul Goodman's long-standing independent radicalism. It has the virtues of high intelligence, programmatic resourcefulness, and an ample supply of generosity to adversaries of all camps. Unlike many radicals, Goodman argues with the opposition. In the current scene he emerges as a necessary double critic – of the Establishment (which he has always been) and of recent "radical" idiocies (idiocy is Goodman's word, not mine), which he can talk about with the assurance of a man whose credits with the radical young are many. His evident exasperation with the know-nothing character of recent militancy has not dissolved either his affection for the young or his faith that the promise of a better future is in them.

So he can speak of shrill fanaticism and self-righteous violence, and wonder whether those whose minds are daily blown really have minds at all, without raising his voice to the pitch of indignation. In criticizing the current scene, tone is as important as the substance of the criticism; and tone is a complex matter of temperament, intelligence, good faith and experience.

What I do see is that dozens of Underground newspapers have the same noisy style and stereotyped content: "A brother throws a canister at a pig." Though each one is doing his thing, there is not much idiosyncrasy in so much spontaneous variety. As if mesmerized, the political radicals repeat the power plays, factionalism, random abuse, and tactical lies that aborted the movement in the thirties. And I have learned, to my disgust, that the reason why young people don't trust people over thirty is that they don't understand them and are afraid to try. Having grown up in a world too meaningless to them for them to learn anything, they know very little and are quick to resent it. Their resentment is understandable; what is disgusting is their lack of moral courage.

This is severe criticism, but instructively severe – and without rancor.

56

Goodman does not permit himself the easy self-congratulation of the adult who has found that the young may be no better than the old.

As a citizen and father, I have a right to try to prevent a shambles and to diminish the number of wrecked lives. But it is improper for older people to keep saying, as we do, that activity of the young is "counter-productive." It's our business to do something more productive that they can join if they want to.

The argument in *New Reformation* is that the crisis of the young goes deeper than politics or even moral disaffection. It is a religious crisis generated by the technological dehumanization of American life. Goodman's attitude toward this reformation (he returns several times to the analogy of Luther's revulsion from the corruptions of Rome in 1510) is ambivalent.

It is hard to describe this, or any, religiosity without lapsing into condescending humor. Yet it is genuine and it will, I am convinced, survive and develop, I don't know into what. In the end, it is religion that constitutes the strength of the new generation. It is not, as I used to think, their morality, political will, or frank common sense. Except for a few, I am not impressed by their moral courage or even honesty. For all their eccentricity, they are quite lacking in personality. They do not have enough world to have strong character. They are not especially attractive (to me) as animals. But they keep pouring out a kind of metaphysical vitality.

Goodman's own career explains his ambivalence. For all his sympathy for the need for a radical transformation of conscience and of social institutions, he has always had a strong pragmatic bent. For Goodman, social change means particular remedies for particular diseases, and if he himself doesn't have the know-how for achieving the remedy, his thinking creates an atmosphere in which one is provoked to develop the know-how. "To have no program rules out the politics of rational persuasion, for there is nothing to offer other citizens, who do not have one's gut complaints, to get them to come along." And on another occasion: "unlike most other 'social critics,' I am rather scrupulous about not attacking unless I can think up an alternative or two, to avoid arousing metaphysical anxiety." The current militant attack is directed toward stirring metaphysical anxiety. Without programs the anxiety can only issue in apocalyptic despair. Goodman is not despairing and apocalyptic because his mind continually attaches itself to concrete problems and concrete solutions, though he has in reserve the imagination of despair, which all imaginative men have.

So he not only speaks of the need to make technology an ethical science; he addresses himself to particular situations. He is interested, for instance, in distributing the tasks between "Big Science" and "shoe-string science" in a way that will benefit society.

Perhaps the most efficient use of Big Science technology for the general health would be to have compulsory biennial checkups, as we inspect cars, for early diagnosis and to forestall chronic conditions and their accumulating costs. But up to now, Dr. Michael Halberstam cautions me, mass diagnosis has not paid off as much as he hoped. For this an excellent machine would be a total diagnostic bus that would visit the neighborhoods – as we do chest X-rays. It could be designed by Bell Lab, for instance. On the other hand, for actual treatment and especially for convalescence, the evidence seems to be that small personalized hospitals are best. And to revive family practice, maybe the right idea is to offer a doctor a splendid suite in a public housing project. Here, big corporations might best keep out of it.

One is never sure that Goodman is really addressing himself to the "fundamental" problem; but then he has always insisted that one must go about it in a piecemeal way, changing what has to be changed and can be changed – with maximum rationality and consideration for the general welfare.

On the education of the young, Goodman characteristically makes specific proposals – for instance, "mini-schools" of about twenty children and four teachers. The four teachers are:

1. A teacher licensed and salaried as in the present system. Since the present average class size is twenty-eight, these are available.
2. A graduating college senior from one of the local colleges, perhaps embarking on graduate study. Salary $2,000. There is no lack of candidates, young people who want to do something useful and interesting in a free setting.
3. A literate housewife and mother, who can prepare lunch [*pace* Women's Lib.]. Again there is no lack of candidates.
4. A literate, willing, and intelligent high school graduate or dropout. Salary $2,000. No lack of candidates.

Goodman is for less organized education and more incidental education, gained naturally in life. What this means is not entirely clear, but perhaps the vagueness is in the nature of the suggestion for more incidental education. Yet Goodman's progressivism in primary education does not lead to soft-headed "Third World" curricula in higher education. Somewhere else he distinguishes between teaching kids and teaching a subject – which is the proper business of the university. He is right when he says that much of what passes for college education is worthless, and he is also right that many who are designated students are, properly speaking, not students at all.

What to do? It seems to me that two kinds of change are necessary at the university level. There is, first, the need to create a truly universal higher education (for those 18 and above) that will help the economically and socially disenfranchised to the possibility of professional success in the general society. It is only the elitist radicalism of the offspring of the white upper classes that can afford to dismiss this kind of suggestion with the disdainful word "cooptation." Such an education need not be condescending or conservative. It would be addressed to young people who are not essentially students (and this is not a matter of social class), whose interest in study would be governed by the contemporary. The curriculum need not exclude Shakespeare or Kant or Isaac Newton, as some of the "Third World" curricula have it, but it would have a narrower conception of relevance than what I would call the more disinterested study of the professional student.

Both *disinterested* and *professional* are disreputable, though I don't believe discredited, words nowadays. The professional curriculum would create and sustain intellectually lively disciplines which must in some sense be elitist. Or if not elitist, significantly different from the "universal" curriculum, simply because of the necessary erudition, difficulty and complexity of the disciplines. One should not rule out the possibility of commerce between the two curricula. But what should be emphasized now against the growing confusion and fogginess of academic and intellectual life is the folly of collapsing the two curricula into one curriculum.

Then there is the problem of authority – and legitimacy (the title of the third section of the book). This is a tough one for Goodman, who has a healthy anarchistic mistrust of power and authority. He wants authority diffused ("the young do have an authentic demand for young people's power, the right to take part in initiating and deciding the functions of society that concern them, as well as governing their own lives which are nobody else's business''), but he regards student power as ''springing from a phony situation . . . symbolic and often merely spiteful.''

I began writing this during the nationwide student strike against the American bombing of Cambodia in 1970 – always with the awareness that if things really change, it will be the young who deserve most of the credit. Perhaps the fogginess and self-righteousness of their militancy is a necessary price. It nevertheless seems to me a service to the cause of social change and to the humane values that should survive all change *not* to blink at the serious failures in thought and sympathy of current militancy. Too often the prestige of radicalism is used to discredit truths that are not particularly radical in character but are truths nonetheless, and to provide a cover for herdlike behavior.

Goodman's ambivalent view of the youth revolt strikes me as absolutely right. He sympathizes with the attempt to loosen authoritarian and rigid educational structures, but he is revolted by the mindless hostility to the tradition of humane letters, which has its own instructive radicalism if the young would only care to listen and learn. The implicit McLuhanism in all versions of youth protest has created an ideological impatience with anything that requires long periods of reflection. Goodman is critical of the commercialism of the counter-culture, which is closer to the mainstream culture of television and advertising than it is to any genuine radicalism. To be sure, the communal ethic of the counter-culture is in contrast to the programmatic egotism and rapacity of American middle-class life, but when youth attacks rationality and high culture, it is acting very much in the spirit of mainstream culture.

It is part of the current forgetting of our cultural past that we are no longer aware that high culture has been the counter-culture in America. Egotism and competitiveness are not products of high culture or elitism but rather of the American capitalist spirit, which in its passion for production and its appetite for consumption is the most unbridled of all capitalism. Despite the histrionic poverty of hippie culture, its luxurious appetite for drugs and leisure and movement makes it part of the consumer culture it so vehemently attacks. One value of Goodman as humanist is that he refuses to accept the absurd caricature of high culture that the counter-culture has drawn.

The difficulty facing the independent liberal or radical in separating himself from the prevailing pieties is that there seems no place to go. Those who argue for ''rational'' alternatives cannot satisfy the radical or even liberal conscience, because their idea of rationality too often involves a polarization against the legitimate *passion* for justice. (This is the obvious trouble with a writer like Sidney Hook.) The tone of a magazine like *Public Interest* is wrong, because it is programmatically unresponsive to what is actually occurring in the country. When I think of real alternatives, certain individual performances come to mind – like that of Paul Goodman, who by instinct, experience and imagination has mastered the complex political sentence. Goodman knows where and how to put the criticism and the praise. But there is no party feeling which would connect people of independent sentiment (liberal and radical) into effective political action. This may be the incurable malaise of the independent position and one explanation of the militant contempt for it.

The terms one uses to describe oneself are always significant, now more significant than usual. Goodman's characterization of himself as a neolithic conservative makes sense when one considers what he is dissociating himself from. His maxims are, among others, "The right purpose of elementary schooling is to delay socialization" and "Innovate in order to simplify, otherwise as sparingly as possible." He dissociates himself from the mindless liberal belief in technological "progress" (necessary change, yes).

The social critics he invokes are Coleridge mainly and Arnold "when the vulgarity of liberalism gets me by the throat." His "conservatism" of course has nothing to do with the McKinley variety. But it is salutary that he chose such an opposite word to describe his radicalism. When everyone in one's circle speaks the same political dialect, it becomes increasingly difficult to have one's own individual ideas and perceptions expressed. This in turn discourages individual ideas and perceptions. Goodman's use of the phrase "neolithic conservative" is part of an old habit of being himself, of understanding the present situation in his own way. Unlike many others, he is not intimidated by the reputation of words and ideas.

In any society worth preserving the conditions for fostering this kind of individuality must be preserved. I know the standard rejoinder – that this seems like an irrelevant criticism of the radical militancy of the young at a moment when political repression has become more than mere possibility, and when the fact of Cambodia and Vietnam looms so large. But the rejoinder itself has the habitual prematurity of those who decide in an authoritarian way when it is right to speak, how one should speak. It is not at all clear that the encouragement of diversity within a political group is not healthier for the movement than an insistence on the correct line. The "correct line" is not part of the ideological vocabulary of the new militancy, but it is more and more part of its emotional temper.

The young are leading the peace movement and the movement for social change by default. There was virtually no effective adult Left in America before the advent of the New Left. This accounts for some of the failures of substance and style on the American Left. Whatever the going piety about the young may be, there are real political disabilities in being young – and strengths as well. As Goodman says, "the hostile inexperience of the young, with a chip on the shoulder and fortified by ideology, calls out to the latent lunacy of the reactionaries," who, for instance, gassed the campus of the University of California, "because the hippies were developing a vacant lot of the university, intended to be a soccer field, as a garden." On the other hand, the young do have spontaneity and a continuous access to political energy – which is no small thing.

The disabilities of the youth movement notwithstanding, it is natural and inevitable that those over and under 30 who want change will in some sense be led by the young. To complain about this fact is like complaining about a natural phenomenon. The question remains: what should the quality of the following be? I think the uncritical and mindless adulation of the young by over-30 adults (many of them "guilty" liberals) is repellent and self-destructive. It often involves an unmaking of personality – an affectation in style, vocabulary and ideas, which betray the best in the person.

The power of the adult "follower" is ideally what Barrington Moore calls critical rationality. Whether one is squarely inside the movement or at the periphery of it, it is always a service to it to exercise critical rationality – to tell it like it is – without prematurely worrying about the consequences. Of course, the animus of the counter-culture is against critical rationality because rationality is repressive. For a man like Paul Goodman, however, this is no argument against exercising it.

7 Geoffrey Hartman's *Criticism in the Wilderness: The Study of Literature Today*

"The critic today," Geoffrey Hartman remarks in *The Fate of Reading*, "is as necessary and as ineffectual as ever" – necessary because the poem or novel demands an answer equal to its imaginative claim and ineffectual because the usual answers are either "a hygienic response, deflating every speculation," what Hartman calls plain-style criticism, or system building, which tries to legislate rules for criticism (e.g., the work of Northrop Frye). Of the two types of critics, Hartman prefers the system builders, because they are makers, "the unacknowledged poets of our time"; but he would go beyond them to discover or invent a mode of interpretation that has the freedom of poetic imagination. "To interpret is a creative, and at times willful, act, as everyone knows who has considered the history of a discipline far wider and deeper than 'criticism.'" Unlike Frye, for instance, Hartman believes that the imaginative experience of the creative writer necessarily "contaminates" the study of literature, resulting in a critical style characterized by metaphor, paradox, ambiguity, and ellipsis. Jacques Derrida's *Glas*, which turns "criticism" into an outrageous exercise of Joycean wordplay, becomes for Hartman an extreme provocation, if not a model, for critical style. Hartman fully understands the risk of "contagion," which, he says in *Criticism in the Wilderness*, may "evoke in us a sense of leprous insubstantiality, however witty and explosive, however energetic," the play of language may be.

Though *Criticism in the Wilderness* is not exactly in the plain style, it represents a spirited and successful effort to accommodate those readers who may have found Hartman's style too luxurious, too elusive – in a word, too representative of the kind of criticism he is affirming. This is not to say that Hartman betrays his "program" by paraphrasing the critical ideas of others. Rather he uses his own superb gift for metaphor and wordplay (as well as a certain amount of explication) to elicit the imaginative and intellectual energies in a whole array of critics. The title somewhat misleadingly suggests melancholy or strident voices howling or speaking in a wilderness. The fact is that Hartman is an exuberant and genial critic at polar temperamental odds with some of his deconstructionist friends. Since world and text are a plenum of possibility for Hartman, he can assert with only minimal self-doubt (enough to ratify his sophistication, according to contemporary standards) that criticism is or should be a creative activity.

A short review cannot do justice to the richness of Hartman's creative exposition of critics and criticism and to the occasional illustrative virtuoso readings of poems. The meditations on Carlyle, Arnold, Eliot, Leavis, Benjamin, Frye, Derrida, and others are filled with luminous figured statements, characterizing critical style and voice as well as doctrine. They often beautifully exemplify Hartman's ambition to erode the boundaries between criticism and creative literature.

If this ambition has a model, it is Georg Lukács' "The Nature and Form of the Essay." (I hesitate to say a model for Hartman's own performance because of the temperamental and doctrinal differences between Lukács and Hartman. I think Hartman's irrepressible playfulness puts him closer to Derrida, with this difference: Hartman remains faithful to the pathos of the romantic inspiration; the world is full for him, not empty as it is for Derrida.) In his close readings of Lukács' essay (the call for the close reading of criticism belongs to Hartman's central theme), he remarks Lukács' view that the "inner tendency of all reflective, self-critical discourse" is one of tentativeness: "everything . . . including the ending is always arbitrary or ironic: the one question dissolves into the many, and even the external as distinguished from internal interruptions serve to keep things open." The occasional character of the essay (a book, an event) "prevents closure." The irony of the essay form is the disparity between the critic's "desire for ultimate issues" and the particular works or events he must discuss. The essay is a "fragment" aspiring to a totality it can never achieve. (Hartman might have noted the affinity of this romantic "fragment" with the novel, the fragmentary epic of "transcendental homelessness," as Lukács treats it in *The Theory of the Novel*.)

What draws Hartman to Lukács' essay on the essay is its autotelic ambition: its desire to be its own justification. At the same time, "the essayist critic . . . cannot himself embody the idea. He heralds it, he wakes our sense for it, but he remains its precursor." "Precursor," Hartman suggests, has the resonance of "provisional." The precursor (i.e., the essayist) is "the one who foresees but is a threshold figure; like Moses or John the Baptist, he can bring us no further than the penultimate stage." This is the grandiloquent language of romanticism, for which Hartman has an unembarrassed affection. As Hartman suggests, Lukács draws on Hegel mediated by Pater and on Schlegel for his concept of irony. Lukács alludes as well to Matthew Arnold's "criticism of life."

Hartman's argument for creative criticism can best be understood against the background of what he calls the Arnoldian Concordat: the "agreement" that Arnold effected between creativity and criticism. The metaphor of the Concordat nicely suggests Arnold's authority as well as his ecumenical and hierarchical impulses. What is ambiguous in Lukács' essay (criticism as both a precursor and an activity "in itself") was prematurely, in Hartman's view, resolved by Arnold in favor of a secondary, dependent, and uncreative role for criticism. The title of Hartman's book is appropriately and ironically drawn from a passage in Arnold's "The Function of Criticism at the Present Time":

There is the promised land toward which criticism can only beckon. That promised land will not be ours to enter, and we shall die in the wilderness; but to have desired to enter it, to have saluted it from afar, is already the best distinction among contemporaries.

Hartman's view of Arnold is ambivalent, with the negative side ascendant. I think he significantly misreads Arnold, though it is only fair to say that Arnold himself invites the misreading.

Though Arnold does indeed speak of the inferiority of criticism to creativity, the program that he actually establishes for criticism in a sense belies the distinction that he makes and that is the basis of Hartman's discontent with him. Criticism Arnold understands to be a speculative function that generates an atmosphere of ideas in which imaginative literature can prosper. Though not abstract and systematic like philosophy, criticism is in practice a creative activity. Arnold chooses not to call it creative, because he wants to privilege poetic imagination with that term. Arnold's poetical bias misleads him and readers about the creative character of criticism – of his own criticism. The fact is that for Arnold criticism as a speculative function is not a dependent activity. On the contrary, it is imaginative literature that depends on the prior activity of criticism for its full success. Here is the crucial passage from "The Function of Criticism":

It is the business of the critical power . . . "in all branches of knowledge, theology, philosophy, history, art, science, to see the object as in itself it really is!" Thus it tends, at last, to make an intellectual situation of which the creative power can profitably avail itself. It tends to establish an order of ideas, if not absolutely true, yet true by comparison with that which it displaces; to make the best ideas prevail. Presently these new ideas reach society, the touch of truth is the touch of life, and there is a stir and growth everywhere; out of this stir and growth come the creative epochs of literature.

The failure of romantic poetry, according to Arnold, is in the "fact" that it has been insufficiently nourished by the work of "the critical power." Hartman, of course, acknowledges this passage, but he denies the *creative* function of criticism when he speaks deflatingly of its role as "circulating" or even "stimulating" ideas. Arnold, of course, does not help matters by being obscure about how much invention is involved in making the order of ideas prevail.

What is at issue between Hartman and the Arnoldian Concordat is the question not of whether criticism is creative or autotelic but of what "creative" means and how the creative functions in both theory and practice. Arnold's criticism exhibits its creative power as it applies itself to society rather than to literature. There is a wealth of invention, wit, and irony in *Culture and Anarchy* and "The Function of Criticism." Hellenism and Hebraism, barbarians and philistines are key metaphors in a series of elaborate conceits that body forth a whole society in *Culture and Anarchy*. Consider, as another example, the superb and poignant irony directed against the newspaper squib "Wragg in Custody" or the splendid speculation about Burke's "return upon himself" in "The Function of Criticism."

However vulnerable Arnold's touchstones may be for a contemporary "criticism of life," they enable a literary-inspired criticism to engage the kind of question Hartman raises toward the end of his book. What is the role of criticism in a society where ambition is the higher education of the masses? Arnold ("the greatest of all school inspectors," in Harold Bloom's unfairly witty phrase) produced a body of criticism fully alive to this alarming reality. Hartman wants criticism to respond to our media-saturated culture, but he does not tell us how we can advance beyond Arnold and his epigones in mediating between mature imaginative activity (like poetry) and the business of mass society. Hartman's call for an effort at mediation is commendable, but what is to be done remains unclear.

Though one would want to encourage students with a poetic gift to write creative criticism (as well as poems and novels), it would be foolhardy, as Hartman knows, to offer the poetic model for educating the mass of English majors. The prosaic virtues of lucidity and cogency are the necessary foundation for teaching literature in a society in which the contamination of language by technological jargon and political deceit is as common as the pollution of the air we breathe. It would be philistine (again Arnold offers us the resource of a metaphor) to oppose plain speech to genuine poetry, and Hartman deserves praise for courageously resisting this tendency in the academy. Both are necessary for the health and vitality of language. But creative criticism, in Hartman's sense, must remain a minority activity with indeterminate social consequences. In a mass society pedagogy is motivated by a less exalted ideal, if only because the creative ideal encourages the ungifted in the kind of pretension that helps contaminate the language. The basic goal must be to develop the power of lucid explanation and argument, the power that makes possible self-knowledge and judgment. Hartman acknowledges the distinction between criticism and pedagogy when he argues against the usurpation of criticism by the pedagogical ideal. But he seems less concerned about the possibility of usurpation in the opposite direction. One suspects that he wants it both ways: a criticism with limited responsibility to the pedagogical function, free to fly as high as it can, and at the same time a critical faculty in the minds and sensibilities of the greatest number of students. Arnold understood the price to be paid by "diffusion" of the cultural heritage (the word suggests the price). Hartman's ideal prohibits the paying of such a price. I am suggesting that Hartman and Arnold may be on different terrains and that the issue between them may never be fully joined.

Hartman is arguing for an autotelic criticism that already exists: Burke, Benjamin, Barthes, and Derrida come immediately to mind. The scandal that Hartman has created in some minds is the result of their limited understanding of the critical tradition. In "A Note on Critical 'Autotelism'" Allen Tate has this to say about Kenneth Burke:

Mr. Burke's *A Grammar of Motives* is an independent work, possibly of the imagination, and if we know how to read it, it can be both entertaining and useful; it is edifying, it enlarges one's mind. But if we think of it as criticism we must see it as an example of the atomization of experience which Blackmur feels has all but undone us. Burke seems not to be concerned with literary works as wholes, he picks off the work illustrative fractions to be devoured by his Five Master Terms.

Notwithstanding his bias, Tate in 1949 understood the power and claim of autotelic criticism. One might qualify Tate's comment and note that autotelic criticism in some sense depends on other texts (even if they are fractions of other texts). Roland Barthes (who could have substituted for Burke in the quotation above) disintegrates *Sarasine* in *S/Z*, but he attempts to account for every fraction of it. The autotelic critic does not defer to the *whole* of the text. With his master terms or codes (or, in Hartman's case, the poet's gift for metaphor), the creative critic closely sensitive to the text releases hitherto concealed energies. As Hartman would say, the transaction between text and reader is symbiotic rather than parasitic.

One does not need the gifts of a Burke or a Barthes or a Hartman to see a misdirected humility in insisting on the secondary role of criticism. In his introduction to *The Sense of an Ending*, Frank Kermode says, "it is not expected of critics as it is of poets that they should help us make sense of our lives; they are bound only to attempt the lesser feat of making sense of the ways we try to make sense of our lives." This is a false distinction, because the effort to think with and beyond a creative writer necessarily involves our making sense of our lives.

The principal and extraordinary achievement of *Criticism in the Wilderness* (it is a lonely eminence in this respect) is its ecumenical consideration of both the Anglo-American and the Continental traditions of criticism. Though Hartman tends to favor the Continental, he can discover the poetry, so to speak, in Anglo-American critical activity. Perhaps the empiricist strain in the Anglo-American tradition makes us suspicious of this kind of attention to criticism. Hartman's poetic interest represents a radical humanism. By forcing us to attend to the critic's psychology, temperament, and historical circumstances, Hartman resists the attempt to depersonalize criticism in the interests of science. He undermines the claim of the system builder by reminding us that all theory is canon-specific. *Criticism in the Wilderness* is an embarrassment of rich speculation that should stimulate and complicate our already complicated understanding of the state of criticism.

II Contemporary culture in conflict

8 *The New York Review:* a close look

The editorial credo of *The New York Review of Books,* which began publication in February 1963, was what one might expect of a highbrow journal.

. . . Neither time nor space [has] been spent on books which are trivial in their intentions or venal in their effects, except occasionally to reduce a temporarily inflated reputation or to call attention to a fraud. . . .

Almost immediately it achieved its modest though difficult ambition of becoming the only serious review of books in America. Against middlebrow art and taste, the *NYR* insisted on the necessity of making intellectually and aesthetically scrupulous judgments and of being invidious and dismissive when necessary – which was often, given the plenitude of bad and mediocre works. The fault of the *New York Times Book Review* (which in part provoked the existence of the *NYR*) was that it showed an undiscriminating hospitality to books good and bad.

The high, dismissive tone of the *NYR,* especially in its first two years, was an equivocal virtue. On the negative side, the reviews tended to be self-congratulating and condescending, and the acrimony in the correspondence columns often went beyond the bounds of normal intellectual aggressiveness. One sensed from the beginning an editorial impulse to exhibit the reviewer at the expense of revealing the book. The review was to be so impressive, it might even satisfy the appetite for the book itself. Or the writer might prefer to be reviewed by the *NYR* to the simple pleasure of being read. The writer and his book were always in danger of becoming a mere occasion or object for use. David Levine's destructive caricatures of writers with their large heads and little bodies – a traditional denigrating device of cartooning – are perfectly appropriate to this attitude. Moreover, there was an in-group atmosphere to the magazine, which encouraged "provincial" paranoia about the New

York literary establishment. On the positive side, the reviewers exercised that capacity for discrimination and judgment which is the best of highbrowism. And if their reviewing was often refractory, that was in part because reviewing became an exercise in thought, not a mindless report on the contents of a book. It was also in part a matter of style. The style of a book reveals its intelligence, its grasp of truth. The reviewer must cultivate style in his sensitivity to the style under review – and therefore inevitably call attention to himself.

The lead article in the first issue was a review by F. W. Dupee of James Baldwin's *The Fire Next Time*, which caught the strengths and weaknesses of Baldwin's politics through a perception of his style. "When Baldwin replaces criticism with prophesy, he manifestly weakens his grasp of his role, his style and his great theme itself." And Dupee goes on to demonstrate this: " 'White Americans do not believe in death, and this is why the darkness of my skin so intimidates them.' " (Baldwin.) "But suppose one or two white Americans are *not* intimidated, suppose someone coolly asks what it means to believe in death." (Dupee.) " 'The real reason that non-violence is considered to be a virtue in Negroes . . . is that white men do not want their lives, their self-image or their property threatened.' " (Baldwin.) "Of course they don't, especially their lives. Moreover this imputing of 'real reasons' for the behavior of entire populations is self-defeating, to put it mildly. . . ." (Dupee.) (Again Baldwin:) " 'In order to survive as a human, moving, moral weight in the world, America and all the Western nations will be forced to reexamine themselves and release themselves from many things that are now taken to be sacred, and to discard nearly all assumptions that have been used to justify their lives and their crimes so long.' " Dupee remarks: "Since whole cultures have never been known to 'discard nearly all their assumptions' and yet remain intact, this amounts to saying that any essential improvement in Negro-White relations, and thus in the quality of American life, is unlikely." By "coolly" asking what it means to believe in death, by catching Baldwin out in his exhortation to White America that it "discard nearly all [its] assumptions," Dupee is effectively deflating the pretensions of the apocalyptic political style.

Dupee's review is especially illuminating when one considers the achievement of the *NYR*, because it helps mark the distance the journal has come from its original attitudes. *The Fire Next Time* is a document of the emerging apocalyptic radicalism. Dupee responds in characteristic highbrow fashion. He is dispassionate, intelligently discriminating, sensitive to style, graceful, but without any strong political commitment.

It is the style of the unpolitical fifties, to which the *NYR* is heir. Its political rationale is that the truth is too complex and elusive to be contained by simple activist formulas. This commitment to "the complex truth" was honorable when sincere and necessary for resisting Stalinist distortions of political reality; but it was reprehensible when it became an evasion of unambiguous evils in our society, as it did in the denial by "revisionist" liberals in the fifties and early sixties that poverty was a substantial fact in this country. The civil rights movement in the late fifties and early sixties created a new activist atmosphere in the intellectual life of the country, and the sudden escalation of the war in Vietnam in 1965 became a main cause for the "radicalizing" of people of "moderate" persuasion. The attitude toward apocalyptic activism that is exemplified by Dupee's review becomes increasingly more difficult to maintain. The *NYR* simply changed with the times, reflecting the political evolution of a large portion of the intellectual and academic community.

I. F. Stone, the American journalist with a special gift for telling the untold story, is among the first to note "a steady degeneration in the conduct of the war." (April 22, '65.) The real focus of his article is on the government's unwillingness to tell the truth about the war, which Stone rightly sees as a challenge to the citizen's freedom of information, and consequently to his freedom of deciding and correcting policy through his elected representatives. In 1965 the truth is not entirely out. Harrison Salisbury's reports in the *New York Times* in the winter of '66 on the terrible effects of American bombing in Vietnam were old news to readers of the European press, who did not have to cope with the American government's challenge to freedom of information. It is to the great credit of the *NYR* that it gave Stone, Jean Lacouture, Bernard Fall, and others an early opportunity to give their version of the war to a wide and important audience in America. Moreover, the *NYR* showed a sure instinct for little-known books that revealed the sordid aspect of the American operation: for instance, *Air War: Viet Nam,* by Frank Harvey (reviewed by Robert Crichton, January 4, 1968), a book commissioned by the Air Force, which nevertheless documents the deadly use of napalm against Vietnamese civilians.

As the truth about Vietnam came out in the next three years, the attack on the system that permits and fosters the war became more radical and comprehensive. The *NYR* continued to publish Hannah Arendt, Hans Morgenthau, George Lichtheim, but it became increasingly responsive to the New Left, the "moral" stance in politics, the apocalyptic view. The journal featured the essays of Noam Chomsky on Vietnam and the culpability of the Liberal Establishment, Stokely Carmichael on Black Power, Jason Epstein on Community Control of the Schools, Andrew Kopkind on Radical Politics, Tom Hayden on the Newark riots. The disaffection from the conduct of the war, enforced by the feeling of domestic injustice, turned into an all-out assault on the Liberal Establishment, allegedly the responsible party.

The insurgence of the New Left in the pages of the *NYR* can be seen as an "act of conscience," an awakening of the liberal intellectual to a sense of his own moral and political culpabilities. Those who did not become conservative or militantly anti-Communist during the fifties became depoliticized, generalizing from their disenchantment with radical politics to politics generally. The turn from Stalinist radicalism was accompanied by the mixed emotions of bitterness toward the movement and self-congratulation about having preserved one's integrity or about having emerged from political immaturity. But the self-congratulation was not entirely warranted by the facts. There was the sorry spectacle of equivocation and fear in the face of McCarthyism, which could not be justified by anti-Communism. There were the temptations of position and prestige in or related to government, a possibility for the liberal intellectual since the days of the New Deal. And of course the liberal in and out of power in the recoil from the Stalinist movement could hardly be expected to be specially sensitive to the aggressions and self-interestedness of American foreign policy. The *practical* difference between the liberal and the avowed racist in their views of the Negro was seen as so small that the professed concern of liberal whites for the Negro's plight in America could be viewed as hypocrisy.

The New Left was hardly needed to score against out-and-out reactionaries. The liberals themselves had been doing that job. What was needed was an assault from the Left on the complacency of the American liberal conscience and the New Left, intimate with the failures of liberalism because in part at least it represented *the disaffection of liberalism from itself,* served the purpose. It is difficult to account for the curious "masochistic" hospitality of liberals in the past few years to the New Left in any other way.[1]

There has been a curious complicity between the "radical" and "the liberal," which suggests that one should not take the New Left attack on liberalism at its face value. Not only has the liberal become hospitable to the New Left attack, but the doctrinaire unwillingness of the new radicals to formulate, let alone implement, programs suggests an almost cheerful acceptance of their own powerlessness. The new radicals depend on those in power to make social changes, the need for which radicals can only dramatize. Liberal guilt and radical powerlessness have combined to make a strange political drama of the sixties. And given the diffuse unrevolutionary content of much "radical" action, liberals can afford the feeling of guilt.

The act of conscience is not the whole story, however; for it has occurred in a compromising atmosphere of fashionableness. The rightness of the New Left attack becomes less important than doing what is fashionably right. Some of the articles published in 1967 (e.g., those by Andrew Kopkind and Tom Hayden in August '67) are painful to read now. The absence of the critical faculty is so obvious that one can only surmise that the editors had relaxed their customary rigor because they wanted to be where the action was. Thus, Andrew Kopkind's mindless attack on Martin Luther King:

He likes the idea of a guaranteed annual income, more Negro elected officials, better schools, more jobs, and protection of rights. These are unexceptionable goals, but King has no real notion of how they are to be attained, or to what they may lead. Although he speaks of structural changes, he assumes structural preservation.

---

[1] One might also note in this connection a certain relaxation in political vigilance on the part of writers like Mary McCarthy who was a main figure in the period of disillusionment with Stalinist radicalism – as when she accepts uncritically the admission of the North Vietnamese that they were mistaken in killing 50,000 people in the collectivization program. "It is possible that [the purging of 50,000 people in the agrarian reform of 1955–56] could repeat itself in South Vietnam, if collectivization is attempted. Against this is the fact that the mistake was recognized and amends were made where still possible [The Rectification of Errors Campaign] and the point about an acknowledged mistake is not to repeat it" [January 18, 1968]. Her sharp sensitivity to the rhetoric of Stalinism should have made her suspect the term "error." How seriously are we to take a confession of error when it should have been a confession of crime? Opposition to the American role in Vietnam does not require our blinking such hard facts.

If King's goals are unexceptionable, why the absurd innuendo in "to what they may lead." Measured by Kopkind's standards, it is difficult to see what separates King from the new militants. Since when have wisdom about political tactics and a clear vision of the emergent political order been characteristic qualities of the political guerrillas Kopkind celebrates, they who have in fact distinguished themselves by their principled refusal to provide programs? The non sequitur about structural changes and structural preservation cunningly concludes the paragraph without a single shred of evidence. Kopkind then goes on to show his political clairvoyance when he declares that the new militancy has shattered the old order. But worse than the intellectual failure of Kopkind's "argument" is the animus that the article reveals. Kopkind concludes: "At least we know now that even if all Martin Luther King's programs were enacted, and all Jerome Cavanaugh's reforms were adopted, and the Great Society as it is described materialized before our very eyes, there would still be guerrillas."

But according to any genuine radical critique, the failure of a society is precisely its inability to live up to its ideals. If American society achieved the humaneness and decency dreamed of by Martin Luther King, poverty, racism, adventurism abroad would disappear. Who then would these remaining guerrillas be? Fascists resentful about the new justice and hungry for power? The feeling of *resentment* is painfully strong in Kopkind's piece.

As it is in Tom Hayden's "report" on Newark in the same issue. "A conscious guerrilla," Hayden tells us with all the authority of new revolutionary theory, "can pull police away from the path of people engaged in attacking stores." Can we trust a revolutionary who offers us the extraordinary formulation that "a riot represents people making history"? So does war or genocide. I don't mean to suggest that genocide and the urban riots are morally commensurable, but simply that Hayden is uttering dangerous nonsense, which we are supposed to take seriously because he has prestige as a "revolutionary." There are other instances of this low-level political writing in the *NYR*. Only a card-carrying Yippie could be expected to respond to the histrionic hysteria of Jerry Rubin, that is unless people feel that to be "with it" they *have to respond* (see *NYR*, Feb. 13, 1969). There is so much moral and aesthetic ugliness in American life at present, especially in the cities, that it is hard to see how the politics of unthinking resentful confrontation will make the necessary radical changes – though one can imagine how it could make changes for the worse.

These articles are of the moment, not about it. They are symptoms, not diagnoses. Given the open commitment of the *NYR* to *critical* writing and thinking (i.e., the deflation of a temporarily inflated reputation), the presence of these articles invites suspicion about the political seriousness of its editors. Clearly the standards of exposition usually demanded of contributors were relaxed in the cases of Kopkind and Hayden.

My complaint is not that the *NYR* changed. People, including editors, have the right to change their minds – indeed, have a moral obligation to change when events reveal a reality they have not perceived before. And the war in Vietnam is such an event. However, the content and tone of the disaffection do not follow automatically from the event. The hospitality to irrational forms of disaffection should be accounted for in the magazine. An atmosphere has been created in which the refusal to accept the escalation of political attitude and tone becomes embarrassing and awkward. Attitudes that several years ago had been considered reasonable by *NYR* writers now are peremptorily dismissed as indefensible. Dupee's statements about Baldwin have not been superseded by the new reality, but the effect of the political journalism in the *NYR* of the past two or three years has been a somewhat arbitrary recasting of the reviewer and the reviewed: it is as if Baldwin is now reviewing Dupee. One wonders what will happen when the New Left loses its cachet for the intellectuals: will the *NYR* turn to the next new thing?

The susceptibility of the *NYR* to political fashion reflects in part the depoliticizing of the intellectual in the fifties. There was good reason to respond to the sudden radicalization of the youth in the mid-sixties, but the quality of the response has too often been unresisting and uncritical, often lamely excused by an unwillingness to rock the boat. The fact is that style (the ideal of high-browism) has little to offer as a guide to political life. Moreover there is a deep connection between style and fashion. To have the right style, to be in the fashion means that one must be in tune with the *Zeitgeist. The New York Review's* need to be "with it" weakens its professed (highbrow) dedication to the making of discriminations and judgments.

Fortunately, the New Left has not been exclusively represented in the *NYR* by the likes of Kopkind, Hayden, and Rubin. The journal has published serious and important articles by Noam Chomsky, Christopher Lasch, and Paul Goodman among others – that is, by men of first-rate intelligence and character who were radical before the fashion. In his essays "The Responsibility of the Intellectuals" (February 23, 1967) and "The Menace of Liberal Scholarship" (January 2, 1969) Chomsky makes a serious and articulate attack on liberalism. (The essays constitute a sort of *summa* of one trend that has developed in the pages of the *NYR* since 1965.)

The argument goes like this. Liberal intellectuals in America have paid an enormous price in intellectual and moral conscience by becoming part of the political and economic Establishment. Through government contracts and even participation in the formulation of policy and the operation of government, the liberal intellectual has forgotten that his first responsibility is to truth. He has put whatever intelligence and technique he has in the service of an interventionist foreign policy. He has been concerned to make the execution of policy more efficient rather than to consider the morality and wisdom of the policy. The result has been, in Conor Cruise O'Brien's phrase, "counterrevolutionary subordination." The motives for the intellectuals' complicity with the Establishment range, according to the critics, from bad faith – i.e., the pursuit of status, prestige, and security (of which intellectuals have always been in relatively short supply) – to disillusionment with Stalinist Marxism in the forties and fifties, a disillusionment that for some led "logically" to the championing of American interests. It has also been suggested that elitism is a bias of the intelligentsia, and that the opportunity given to intellectuals to make and execute policy merely encourages the normal self-righteousness and arrogance of intellectuals, who assume that they know better than the people of an underdeveloped country, for instance, what is good for them. The liberals often named in the charge are men like Daniel Bell, Arthur Schlesinger, J. K. Galbraith, Irving Kristol, Nathan Glazer, and Daniel Moynihan, some of whom were associated with the New York intellectual world out of which the *New York Review* emerged.

As a description of what has occurred, this argument made by Chomsky and others has much to recommend it. It is strong evidence against Mannheim's view, for instance, that intellectuals by virtue of their hard-earned knowledge and self-understanding have achieved a disinterestedness beyond ideology. But it strikes me as short on theoretical understanding and even seriously misleading in certain respects.

What the New Left critic believes he is attacking is not a version of liberalism or liberalism at a certain moment in history, but the very idea of liberalism itself: its supposed incapacity to understand, in Chomsky's words, "moral truths about political life." The vices of the liberal intellectual – his elitism, his technocratic relation to political problems, his affinity for the establishment – are all seen as springing from the essential character of liberalism itself.

In an excursion in his essay on liberal scholarship, Chomsky does a survey of liberal historiography on the Spanish Civil War, and he uncovers "a failure of objectivity" in representing "revolutionary movements that are largely spontaneous and only loosely organized, while rooted in deeply felt needs and ideals of dispossessed masses." Chomsky remarks that "it is a convention of scholarship that the use of such terms as those of the preceding phrase demonstrates naïveté and muddle-headed sentimentality," a convention "supported by ideological conviction rather than history or investigation of social life." The essay is entitled "Objectivity and Liberal Scholarship,"[2] and the failure of objectivity, it turns out, includes Communist intellectuals. If "Bolshevism and Western liberalism have been united in their opposition to popular revolution (in its anarchist manifestation)," it seems to me misleading to assign simply the blame to "contemporary liberal ideology," unless one wishes to extrapolate bolshevism from liberalism. The view of Eric Hobsbawm, for instance, that the anarchist movement in Spain during the Civil War was a "disaster" for the Loyalist cause, may be motivated by a false estimate of the pragmatics of conducting an efficient military campaign against Franco or by an elitist mistrust of the spontaneous action of the masses, but it is hard to see that this is a peculiar phenomenon of liberalism. One would sooner expect such a view from an *anti-liberal* bolshevism, with its open commitment to revolutionary elitism.

The willingness of intellectuals to join the Establishment proceeds (as critics have often remarked) from motives deeper than ideology, such as the desire for status, prestige, security, and in some cases the more admirable desire (deluded as it may be) to "make a difference." But this kind of "sellout" is by no means unique to Western liberalism. The history of the intelligentsia in the Soviet

---

2   An excerpted version of the essay appeared in the *NYR* in the January 2, 1969, issue with the title "The Menace of Liberal Scholarship." The passage on the Spanish Civil War is in the unabridged version printed in Chomsky's *American Power and the New Mandarins* (New York: Pantheon, 1969).

Union is hardly a history of radical disaffection and responsibility to the truth. There have been notable exceptions of course, but that is precisely the point: responsibility to the truth is finally a matter of intellectual capacity and moral perspicacity and courage, whatever the going ideology might be. It is the work of a "moral elite" to use Chomsky's surprising phrase. It is true that a given ideology may provide the rationale and terms of the "sellout": in the Soviet Union, the scholasticizing of Marxism gave an inquisitorial cast to political actions and discussion. In holding an opinion, one could be risking one's life. The appeal to authority became the fatal style of intellectual life under Stalin.

Liberalism becomes an abstraction in the New Left attack, a convenient handle for attacking the adversary. (To say the liberal is the real enemy has, for intellectuals, the shock and fascination of paradox.) As it gets to be used ritualistically, the term "liberalism" introduces an opacity into political discussion and debate, which avoids complication. One has only to reverse the situation to see what is wrong. Imagine dealing with radical activity and scholarship by continuously identifying radicalism with bolshevik perversions of truth. It is not liberalism per se that has been discredited but certain programs and attitudes. For it is implicit though not admitted in the current argument that in its ideal commitment to maximizing the moral and rational elements in political life, in its belief in democratic procedure, liberalism is or should be a feature of *every* humane political philosophy.[3] Radicalism and liberalism are not necessarily antagonistic. It is the strong feeling that liberals have betrayed their own ideals that has made liberal philosophy itself seem indefensible. All this verges on platitude, but it is a mark of the extremity of the disaffection from liberalism that this no longer seems evidently true.

In light of the scientist piety about objectivity, the view of Noam Chomsky, Christopher Lasch, Eugene Genovese, and others that irresponsibility to truth may be the result of moral failure or insensitivity is valuable. For instance, it takes courage to see and express

---

[3] I am attributing these qualities to liberalism as an idea. The historical reality of liberalism is another matter, for like any other political type a liberal in practice may betray his ideals. The temptation to betray the ideals may be an unwitting feature of the ideology, but this must be demonstrated. If terms like "liberal" and "radical" have any meaning they unavoidably contain an element of abstraction, of definition: they stand for certain things. Indeed, the terms become opaquely "abstract" when their ideal content as well as their historical reality at a given moment is ignored.

an unfashionable truth, and courage is a moral emotion. But in this view there is an illicit confusion between the idea of moral commitment (telling it like it is, regardless of the consequences) and left-wing ideological partisanship. Such a confusion easily becomes an excuse for an unself-critical indulgence in ideological passion. In "The Responsibility of the Intellectual" Chomsky cites with contempt Heidegger's pro-Hitler declaration in 1933 that "truth is the revelation of that which makes a people certain, clear and strong in its action and knowledge."

On the evidence of a good deal of recent militant Left ideologizing (e.g., the Cultural Revolution in China, black mythologizing), Heidegger's statement serves equally for Left and Right. When Lasch says that "scholarship has to give up its pretensions to scientific objectivity and root itself in moral commitment" (Nov. 11, 1965), he is using "moral commitment" in a vague and polemical way, for the test of the validity of this assertion is what one means by "moral commitment." In "The Education and the University We Need Now" (Oct. 29, 1969), Lasch and Genovese admit that "it would be disastrous if the attack on the irresponsibility of 'objective' scholarship . . . led only to the cynical conclusion that all scholarship is subjective and 'ideological' – the conclusion which some critics are only too eager to draw." But they fail to make clear why the conclusion cannot be derived from their own attack on "objective" scholarship – or why they obscure the issue by putting quotation marks around *objective* and *ideological*. Do they or don't they mean the words they use? On the face of it, the term *moral commitment* is less adequate as a guide to truth than the *objective* standards of a discipline.

If one means by moral commitment sensitivity to injustice, then one is beyond ideology. The moral insensitivity that Chomsky and others have dramatized is a feature of the complacency of privilege, whether the explicit political commitment is Left or Right. Sensitivity to injustice is generally a characteristic either of men who are the objects of injustice or of men who have the imagination, compassion, and courage to put themselves in the place of those who suffer injustice. The Left, when it comes to power, loses much of the sensitivity to injustice that gives it its moral strength out of power – which is why liberalism has kept insisting on democratic liberties in all societies. I recall a French leftist friend of mine saying in 1956 in the aftermath of the Russian invasion of Hungary, "Thank God for the Communist party – out of power." He meant that the French

Communist party was valuable as the only real party of the working class and therefore as the Left in French political life. But he would never trust the party *in* power.

The danger of "counterrevolutionary subordination" may be greater than that of revolutionary subordination in a society in which the Left has no power, but this doesn't lessen the need for unremitting self-honesty in the Left. For the habits it develops out of power will condition what it becomes if and when it ever achieves power. It is not enough for a movement consciously to disavow authoritarianism. Anarchism (one inspiration of the New Left) is doctrinally anti-authoritarian, but the problems of sustaining genuine spontaneity in political life and that of controlling authoritarian types who tend to take control in "spontaneous" situations have never been solved. It is difficult to envisage permanent success for a movement that tries to sustain itself simply by preserving its moral purity, its idealism and courage, that does not formulate an adequate theoretical account of political reality. "Moral purity" without honest realism tends to corrupt itself into self-righteousness and to be tempted to mindless violence.

The achievement of the *NYR* has been real, though seriously flawed. It has with some success performed the needed task of *haute vulgarization* for more than 90,000 readers. Articles on philosophy, art, economics are not simply responses to recent developments, but attempts to give in microcosmic form a picture of what is alive and relevant in a whole field. The level of exposition is above anything we might call the popular level (since the audience is sophisticated), but the impulse is to break out of professionalism, to speak about subjects in the common language of discourse. The literary and art criticism has not been overwhelmed by the latest "audacities" of the avant-garde. Reviewers like Rahv, Gombrich, and Haskell have responded with intelligence and authority to the current scene. The *NYR* is one of the few places where art criticism is at once unfashionable and unsquare.

The political criticism has been much more erratic, more responsive to the fashion. The *NYR* is too fashionable, too much "with it" to be characterized as I am sure it would like to see itself: the conscience of the intellectual community in political, intellectual, and aesthetic matters. As provocation, however, it has played an important role in our cultural life.

9   The new Apocalypse

> I have watched the soul, Ferdinand, give way bit by bit, lose its balance
> and dissolve in the vast welter of apocalyptic ambitions. It began in 1900.
> That's the date! From that time onwards the world in general and psychia-
> try in particular frantically raced to see who could be most perverse,
> salacious, original; more disgusting, more creative, as they say, than his
> little next-door neighbor. A first-class scramble. Each strove to see who
> could immolate himself the soonest to the monster of no heart and no
> restraint. . . . The monster will scrunch us all, Ferdinand, that's how it
> is, and rightly so. . . . What is this monster? A great brute tumbling
> along wherever it listeth. Its wars and its droolings flood in towards us
> already from all sides. We shall be swept away on this tide – yes, swept
> away. The conscious mind was a bore, apparently. . . . We shan't be
> bored any longer! We've begun to give Sodom a chance and from that
> moment on we've started having "impressions" and "intuition."
> –Louis-Ferdinand Céline, *Journey to the End of Night*

They advocate passion over the intellect, exalt the body over the
mind, prefer the perverse to the normal, the spontaneous to the
habitual, the risks of violence and disaster to the security of our
ordinary modes of existence. They can perhaps best be described as
apocalyptists, because they exist in a condition of expectation of
some event of a demonic or catastrophic kind that will transform
their lives. They are often politically radical though the old conception of political struggle (its Marxian version, for instance) is super-
annuated. (As Jean Malaquais puts it, "marijuana-soaked hip is the
long rejected bastard brother of the proletariat.") They might concede the importance of social reorganization, but the reorganization
would presumably follow the revolution in the body and the con-

This article was published in 1965. It describes in stark, unnuanced terms a new
mood that would play a dominant role in our cultural life. The new Apocalypse
forms part of the zeitgeist that I discuss in the piece that follows: "Eros, Politics
and Pornography."

sciousness of men. Religious idea and image loom large in this literature of expectation. ("I think there is one single burning pinpoint of the vision in Hip: it's that God is in danger of dying. In my very little knowledge of theology this never really has been expressed before." Mailer, of course, is naïvely echoing Nietzsche.) The apocalyptist appears in the familiar guises of the bohemian, the hipster, the beatnik and the militant homosexual. His artist-heroes are Nietzsche, Whitman, Rilke, Lawrence, Genêt, Henry Miller. (Norman Mailer has been the outstanding American publicist of the Apocalypse.) In a less familiar aspect, the apocalyptist has produced a body of "philosophical" work: the writings of Wilhelm Reich, Herbert Marcuse and Norman O. Brown.

In common with other "movements" there is a certain amount of internecine warfare. The purity of doctrine must be preserved from its seductive variants. Thus Norman O. Brown in *Life Against Death* dissociates himself from the "primitive" genital psychology of Wilhelm Reich (Reich would have undoubtedly repudiated Brown's "religious mysticism") and "the paradoxically conservative sexuality" of D. H. Lawrence, when he declares for the abolition of repression and the reconstruction of the Dionysian ego. Brown is an extreme left-wing Freudian, who believes that the New Jerusalem is embodied in his interpretation of psychoanalysis. As Brown understands psychoanalysis, the New Jerusalem is no metaphor, for in his heretical interpretation of Freudian thought, psychoanalysis rejoins religion – the mysticism of the body – and thus transcends its original atheism.

The apocalyptists are, of course, hostile to orthodox Freudianism. Psychoanalytic therapy, except in the most reactionary and ignorant view of it, is hardly radical. It is a therapy motivated by a desire to help the patient accommodate himself to "reality"; it presupposes a conservative view of reality as a given, alterable only within narrowly defined limits. And yet it is psychoanalysis that illuminates most vividly the source of apocalyptic thought and feeling. Freud had systematically argued that our civilization, as well as our individual lives, is a history of the sublimation of sexual energy. By sublimation, a term Freud took from the romantic poet Schiller, he characteristically meant a channeling of sexual activity into nonsexual activity. The part of Freud that was committed to civilization (and it is the major part) valued sublimation, and psychoanalytic therapy is an outcome of that commitment. But it is possible to argue from psychoanalytic premises that the "reality" of therapy is no more than a complex of illusions, a masking of libidinal energies. Norman O. Brown in *Life Against Death* and Herbert Marcuse before him in *Eros and Civilization* attempted this transvaluation of psychoanalytic values.

Marcuse's book is rooted in German political and social philosophy. A scholar of Hegelian and Marxian thought, he justifies his use of "psychological categories" by asserting that they have become "political categories." Whether Marcuse's book is genuinely concerned with the political is moot, but it is clear that *Eros and Civilization* is the response of a man who is deeply committed to the idea of political "salvation" (the metaphor is mine) and who is trying to supply the old political categories with the psychological content of Freudian thought. Brown, on the other hand, speaks of "the superannuation of the political categories which informed liberal thought and action" and the quasi-mystical atmosphere of his book suggests his greater kinship with current apocalyptic thought and feeling.

In the concluding chapter of his book, Brown addresses himself to the possibility of resurrecting the body and thereby finding a "way out" from the dilemma of a civilization whose progress is based on the attenuation – i.e., the repression – of human energies. Brown admits that he is engaged in utopian thinking; earlier in the book, he speaks of the "mad consequences" in which his argument issues. But he defends his "madness" as the only way "of affirming faith in the possibility of solving problems that seem at the moment insoluble."

Brown advocates the abolition of repression; that is, the recovery of "erotic exuberance" and narcissism that man had possessed in a mythical golden age. This erotic exuberance (Freud calls it "polymorphous perversity") entails the destruction of the mind-body dualism and a new, completely sensualized body in which Eros has moved outside of its "normal" genital zone and reconquered the whole body. Reconquered because polymorphous perversity is paradise regained, infant sexuality recovered on a higher plane. The goal of life, in Rilke's phrase, is to live out all the "unlived lives in the body." The resurrected body that Brown celebrates is the risen body of Augustine, the body electric of Whitman, "the greater life of the body" of Lawrence. Brown's characteristic instances are from the mystical tradition (Jacob Boehme) and visionary poetry (Rilke).

The consequences of the resurrection of the body are social, political and moral. In the New Jerusalem, repressive work is banished.

Work would be transformed into play and the aim of bodily activity would be instinct-gratification. The society of abundance that Marx envisaged in the formula "from each according to his ability, to each according to his need" is, of course, a precondition of this vision. This new psychology of consumption and pleasure would destroy our anal-oriented and self-destructive connection to money, permit the conquest of the fear of death ("only those who have unlived lives in their body are afraid of death") and subvert the regime of time (the past and future are real only to the impoverished body and the dissatisfied self).

Brown's antipathy to civilization, its past as well as present, is total. His "dialectical" view (in the Hegelian mode) makes it impossible for him to repudiate the history of civilization, but he sees it as ultimately negating itself. (He quotes approvingly Stephen Dedalus in *Ulysses:* "History is a nightmare from which I want to awake.") The history of civilization is a history of sublimation, in Brown's "dialectical" version of it, and is its own undoing. For Brown, sublimation is an unequivocal negation, "The dehumanization of man is his alienation from the body."

Brown does not confront the fact that even in his own terms there is an unbridged (perhaps unbridgeable) gap between our actual bodies and the resurrected one he envisages. If we abolish repression, then we may permit our disordered bodies to act in terrible ways, for there is no guarantee that the abolition of repression would mean a new body: it might mean nothing more than the old body acting without restraints. To achieve a body worthy of the freedom Brown conceives for it, something more is required than merely abolishing repression. About that something more, Brown has nothing to tell us.

Moreover, Brown (and other apocalyptists) tend to confuse repression with oppression or suppression. If repression is unconscious, as Freud maintained, then it cannot be "overthrown" by the will. The rational and conscientious psychoanalytic will can mitigate some of its more painful effects, but repression permeates the mind-body too thoroughly and too subtly to be regarded as an ephemeral tyrant. Brown cannot tell us how repression can be overthrown or how the body becomes deserving of a new freedom.

How to bridge the gap between our disordered bodies and the resurrected one is the unsolved (perhaps insoluble) problem of the apocalyptist. Narcotics, liquor, criminal self-abandonment, disease

(like tuberculosis), perversion: these are the traditional ways of release. Norman Mailer has called the new body psychopathic, and
Jean Genêt, the archhipster of Europe, and a greater artist than
Mailer, has made the most elaborate chart of the adventures of the
rebellious body.

But the kind of demonstration that Genêt makes, for instance,
emphasizes rather than solves the problem. For perversion, for all its
advantages of intensity and vitality, is a cul-de-sac. To say, as Mailer has said in the notorious essay "The White Negro," that the
psychopath "may be indeed the perverted or dangerous frontrunner
of a new kind of personality," is to beg the question. The evidence is
against the possibility. To pass beyond the psychopath, one must
make a detour: to go through it is to come smack against a wall.
Perversion, as Freud and Dostoevsky before him taught, is slavery,
not freedom. To be driven by a murderous impulse, or by the com-
pulsion to be beaten, may produce an ecstasy of pain and pleasure.
But it is not to be confused with the repossession of one's body that
one would expect in the resurrection.

Dostoevsky's *Notes from Underground* (written in 1861) is the *locus
classicus* for the connection between perversity and the dream of the
resurrected body. Throughout most of the story, the underground
man asserts his freedom from the "laws of nature." One law of
nature – as conceived by the utilitarians, the scientific psychologists
of the 19th century – is that the enlightened man pursues pleasure
and avoids pain. The underground man will suffer, and with full
consciousness, if only to prove his freedom from the tyranny of
psychological law. However, in his relations with his friends and
with a prostitute, he shows himself to be sado-masochistic. He
moves between gestures of self-abasement and self-humiliation, on
the one hand, and gestures of superiority and insult on the other. We
soon come to realize what we may have suspected throughout: that
the underground man's freedom is illusory, that he is the most driven
of men, that his actions proceed from terrible compulsions about
which he has some understanding, but about which he can do nothing. Our own realization is confirmed by the underground man himself who at the end acknowledges that he too knows his freedom to
be illusory, that in having invidiously distinguished himself from
others by asserting his uniqueness he has come full circle to the
knowledge that in his perversity he is no different from anyone else.
The paradox of the perverse rebel is that he is the most complete

victim of the order against which he is revolting, that his revolt is itself a mark of his enslavement and that even knowing this, he has no choice but to continue to revolt.

Jean Genêt knows this, but he doesn't permit it to darken his celebrations. *Our Lady of the Flowers* (a "novel" which is really a series of fantasies involving a cast of characters that Genêt has invented to satisfy his masturbatory appetites) and *A Thief's Journal* (a book devoted to the new trinity of Treason, Theft, and Homosexuality) are extraordinary efforts at an aesthetic transaluation of values. Genêt celebrates what I think is a general truth about the erotic apocalyptist: that he is an onanist, seeking in the love object not *another,* but himself. The apocalyptic hero is the sexually volatile hermaphrodite, the creature capable of becoming man or woman or both. Genêt also affirms the sado-masochistic character of his imagination. "If I continue, he will rise up, become erect, and penetrate me so deeply that I shall be marked with stigmata. I can't bear it any longer. I am turning him into a character, whom I shall be able to torment in my own way. . . ." The ultimate reach of this perversity and suffering is "saintliness," which Genêt defines at one point as loving what one hates. This is of course a rather playful perversion of the religious tradition. Genêt is like a Dostoevsky character who has preempted the moral authority of the novelist.

As moral speculation, apocalyptic "thought" is unconvincingly abstract and disturbingly inhuman. One can sympathize with Philip Rahv's complaint that those who should know better have been taken in by "the moral idiocy" of Genêt. Genêt, of course, is a more interesting counterpart to our own hip ethos, and the current interest in Genêt reflects, I would imagine, the fact that the hip ethos has fully penetrated intellectual culture. But it would be wrong to regard this phenomenon merely as a fad or as a symptom of cultural pathology. The apocalyptic vision is an important element in our cultural life, but its strength is in its poetry (and Genêt is, among other things, unquestionably a poet), not in its truth claims.

The poetry of Whitman, Lawrence and Rilke is an effort to extend the boundaries of the ego, not to be confused with the task of psychoanalysis, as Freud understood it, which is to insure the domination of the id by the ego. The visionary poets do not want domination at the expense of energy. They rather seek constantly to extend the ego beyond the area of safety, to create the adventure of the "spirit" in which even the destruction of the self is risked.

Self-dissatisfaction is the condition of the visionary poet's soul, and any resting within an area of safety is experienced as a kind of atrophy or death. The restlessness of the visionary poet is as much a curse as a blessing; half in love with easeful death, he yearns for a surcease of striving. (The negation of history, in Brown's view, is the end of striving and restlessness, which, one might add, would be the end of visionary poetry.) The visionary poet seeks the unattainable condition of divinity. It is no accident that he is apocalyptic, that his characteristic vocabulary is so often religious.

The current versions of the Apocalypse (its beat and hip manifestations) suffer from comparison with the really great instances. In "Song of Myself" Whitman declares:

> I am the teacher of athletes,
> He that by me spreads a wider breast than my own proves the
> width of my own
> He most honors my style who learns under it to destroy the
> teacher.

But Whitman's students (e.g., Ginsberg) are weak-chested. They have largely imitated the slackness, the stridency, the shrillness. They are not without gifts, but in the light of the largeness of their claims, they come off as unwitting parodists of the Apocalypse, confusing inspiration with slackness, automatism with spontaneity. Thus Allen Ginsberg in "Howl" imitates the Whitman catalogue, the least interesting and most vulnerable of poetic "devices." To be sure, the monotonous incantation is somewhat relieved by genuinely powerful and witty images: "angelheaded hipster burning for the heavenly connection," "ashcan rantings," "radiant cool eyes hallucinating Arkansas and Blakelight tragedy." But these images never coalesce into significant event. Whitman's best poems, "Out of the Cradle Endlessly Rocking," "When Lilacs Last in the Dooryard Bloomed," "Crossing Brooklyn Ferry" are poems of spiritual adventure and discovery: the journey into the "delicious" darkness of death in "Out of the Cradle" and "Lilacs," the epiphany in "Crossing Brooklyn Ferry" that the poet is suspended in "the eternal float" of community with other human beings. The egotism of Whitman and Lawrence is offensive and strident when they merely flaunt their vitality against the squalid world. In their best work, the "vitalism" is conditioned by their humanity. They know loss and impotence and guilt (see Lawrence's superb poem "Snake," for instance, or his novel *Women in Love*). The shout on the rooftops –

Ginsberg's characteristic utterance – is the rhetoric of vitalism, not necessarily an expression of vitality.

Of the writers of the Apocalypse, Norman Mailer has perhaps provoked the most attention. Mailer, it seems to me, has betrayed or mistaken the nature of his gifts. He is essentially a naturalistic writer in the tradition of Dreiser and Dos Passos. (Some of his best writing has, significantly, been reportage.) His justly admired short novel *The Man Who Studied Yoga* is strong on the observation of a semi-bourgeois, semi-bohemian life that Mailer knows so well; it is weak on dream and fantasy. (He need only be compared with Genêt, a genuine fantasist.) When Mailer tries to be a fantasist, he almost always becomes strident. His novel *An American Dream* is violent in plot and rhetoric, but it is curiously without visionary power, or without sufficient visionary power to redeem the book from its dross: arbitrary situations, inadequately realized characters, bad prose. It is very hard, if not impossible, to believe that Mailer's hero, Stephen Rojack, has sailed into "the harbors of the moon," that he is in communion with the demons of the universe and that the murder of his wife is authentic, so unreal are the emotional consequences of that murder. Crime without punishment, a Nietzschean transcendence of guilt and responsibility: above the genuine suffering and torment, Mailer is playing with abstractions barely disguised as fantasies. Mailer is a writer of considerable energy and talent, but an energy and talent that belong to the inspiration that produced *The Naked and the Dead:* the inspiration of realism.

In Mailer's recent career and in the public and imaginative career of some of the other apocalyptic writers, there is a strong element of buffoonery. It is hard to know when the buffoonery is intended or unconscious. But the comedy is often the most attractive side of beat and hip writing. It is almost as if the writer knows that he is not serious enough for his claims, or he is serious enough to know that the kind of gesture he makes is extravagant and ludicrous unless informed by genius and heroism – so he mocks his own gestures. There is a touching and amusing moment in *An American Dream* in which we get a glimpse of this kind of honesty – unfortunately only a glimpse, for Mailer prefers the frenetic and ultimately dull contortions of his "existentialist" fantasying.

"I can't get over the way you look," Deborah [Rojack's wife] exclaimed. "I mean you really look like some poor peddler from the Lower East Side."

"I'm descended from peddlers." [Rojack replies]
"Don't I know it, honey-one," said Deborah.
"All those poor materialistic grabby little people."
"Well, they never hurt anyone particularly." This a reference to her father.

Shortly afterwards, Rojack murders his wife. The peddler is forgotten or denied, and authenticity becomes gratuitous acts of violence. Immoralism has traditionally been linked to the aesthetic attitude (see, for instance, Genêt's invoking of the standard of elegance), and the value of that link was that art – with its emphasis on order, control and beauty, although a more flexible order than that of social morality – supplied a check to the excesses of the perverse imagination, a way of ordering it. The aesthetic justification may not be necessary for a genius of the order of Whitman and Lawrence (though we know what price they pay for such absolute trust in the power of their daemon), but it is necessary for minor talents. There is in fact an admission of this necessity in the hip ethos currently fashionable in some highbrow circles. Originating in a profound dissatisfaction with the forms of life available in contemporary America, hip has converted that dissatisfaction to a narrow belief in a particular style called swinging, which always verges on affectation: a style that is world-weary, cool and at bottom cynical.

The apocalyptic vision is necessarily lonely, aristocratic and tragic. It requires an authentic vision, fidelity in communicating it, a capacity to live in a permanent state of expectation, for no transformation would really satisfy. In its democratic *cultus,* as a "movement" of adolescents, dope-pushers, shrill solipsists and minor talents, we have a caricature of a valuable element in our cultural life.

10 Eros, politics, and pornography: a decade with *Evergreen Review*

Eight hundred double column pages of what is most alive and quirky in contemporary literature! With some notable exceptions virtually everybody who is anybody is represented in this monster anthology of the *Evergreen Review*. Here is a very partial list: Beckett, Robbe-Grillet, Williams, Pasternak, Neruda, Borges, Kott, Genet, Sontag. The anthology is a reminder of how *Evergreen* and its publishing house, Grove, were quick not only to sense which way the *zeitgeist* was blowing (one of the comic strips concerns a Phoebe Zeitgeist), but also to respond to genuine talent and good writing. The format, the print, the glossy texture resemble *Playboy*. One hefts the magazine, flips through the pages, feeling one is enjoying a pleasurable commodity. *Evergreen* learned sooner than anyone else the secret of combining the sophisticated and the vulgar, the intellectual and the sensational, avant-garde "integrity" and commercialism. The magazine is a classic instance of having one's cake and eating it. Not that it hasn't been "persecuted." Indeed, it seems to relish the moments when the authorities lose their "cool" and attempt censorship (for instance, the effort to censor Emil Caddo's nudes). The effect on sales of attempted censorship in our open society is well known. (The net sales of *Evergreen* for '68 were up nearly two million dollars from the same period in 1966.) And why shouldn't the editors enjoy the possibility of commercial success? In our pop world, of which McLuhan is prophet, compromise has become an irrelevant category. With the melting of high into low culture, artistic achievement into commercial success, *Evergreen* has helped lay down the new cultural trail.

If I were compelled to give a quick characterization of the editorial *persona* of *Evergreen*, it would go something like this. The hospitality to radical, avant-garde, pornographic attitudes has the easy graciousness of someone (Barney Rosset?) who found the guests amusing, didn't take the attitudes very seriously and was happy that everyone was talking about his parties. *Evergreen* is an American success story. The variety one finds in its pages (Burroughs, LeRoi Jones, Abdullah Schleiffer – unanthologized) has a common bond: "way out," extreme, but the threads of connection are very loose. Behind it all is commercialism, or perhaps more accurately, pornography. For isn't a "report" on the recent Arab-Israeli war by Abdullah Schleiffer, a renegade Jew, as titillating in its way as a nympho college girl's account of her nightly performance in Fort Lauderdale? This is not to deny that very gifted guests happen to come to *Evergreen*'s party, who in fact seem to justify it, and they come because of, rather than despite, the putative lack of conviction of the host. (We all know the repressive effect of a magazine with a strong editorial commitment to ideological positions in politics and art. The writer must learn to conform his intellectual and imaginative personality to the editorial requirements.)

All this suggests that *Evergreen* (despite its list of distinguished and interesting contributors) is hard to take seriously as a magazine. And yet the magazine is a cultural fact of first importance. In its content and format it has revealed and occasionally interpreted a sensibility that has become very powerful during the ten years of its publication.

The magazine exemplifies contemporary utopianism, the recent wedding of politics and eros. Contemporary utopianism has grafted the ecstasies of polymorphous perversity onto the old radical pursuit of reason and justice. The major philosophical instances are Herbert Marcuse and Norman O. Brown, who don't appear in the pages of *Evergreen*. (I will suggest later on why work by Marcuse and Brown would find awkward accommodations in *Evergreen*.)

The wedding of eros and politics is based on the Freudian premise that happiness is a matter of instinct gratification. Since civilization is based on repression, i.e., the renunciation of instinct gratification, human happiness (in Freud's view) is impossible. He cannot conceive a civilization that will permit the overcoming of repression. Whether it is possible to overcome repression is of course a problem for philosophical sociology. The relevant point here is that the sensibility of *Evergreen* not only assumes the possibility, it attempts to realize it. Photos of nudes walking the streets of Paris while the students have seized the Sorbonne suggest new political and erotic impatience for immediate instinct gratification: sex now and everywhere, political demands of the most extreme kind not compromised or delayed but immediately met in their full extent. It is not simply the ecstasy of pain or pleasure which the open erotic character of the magazine projects: it is *immediate* pain or pleasure, *immediate* justice. What all this means is that to the extent that we take *Evergreen* seriously as a magazine that has a personality and ideology it belongs to, indeed helped create, the contemporary utopianism of the polymorphous perverse.

An article by Julian Beck of the Living Theater in an issue of *Evergreen* manages to express the attitudes in their interrelatedness:

. . . this society cannot offer peace, love, joy, honor, and fulfillment to its citizens, but in their stead, offers varieties of hatred, competition, greed, a life of senseless pain, trivia, and early death. A society that can attain affluence and still let people starve to death makes the brain go tilt; a society that can indulge in the Vietnamese war is insupportable to those who are trying to recuperate their holy feelings. A society which bases its affluence on useless toil in which millions of lives are sacrificed to the production of goods made not for use but for money, in which the mind must die in order to protect itself from thinking, because thinking is too painful if you have to live out your life in senseless drudgery – such a society must be transformed.

Artaud's manifesto of feeling calls for assaults on the senses and the creation of cruel events in the theater, with the hope that such theatrical events will reach the spectator in the flesh, in the bowels, in the eyes, in the groin, there where he feels it. Then, once feeling something, other doors to the body of feeling will open, and, physically offended by the pain experience in the theater, the physical spectator will no longer be able to tolerate pain around him in the world outside the theater, and the revolution will burst into action.

The theater of the Revolution must mean new forms of acting in which the space trip that the actor takes is worthy of the attention of the spectator. The actor must discover forms of behavior and experience that unite the physical body with the mind if he is to serve the needs of the public. The mental theater in which the body is only the stage must mutate into a theater in which all the senses operate, receive experience profoundly, answer experience profoundly, and resolve experience according to the truth of profound feeling.

One of the interesting things about *Evergreen* is that it is a concrete instance of an idea, which is usually worried on an abstract level. Indeed *Evergreen* gives us not so much an idea as a sensibility or an attitude. For one thing, the magazine seems to encourage the note of hysteria, a note we hear in Beck's article. We live in a world in which it is regarded as a sign of compromised conscience or an absence of vitality to be dispassionate, to be intellectually and morally inhibited by a sense of complexity and problem. We know how moral cowardice often hides behind a ritual attachment to complexity and ambiguity, and it is this knowledge that strengthens this view of the world. But the effect of a *systematic* exercise of high moral impatience produces hysteria. An instance of this is a piece in the anthology by Nat Hentoff. In 1967 under the influence of the moral atrocity of Vietnam and the increasing awareness of injustice in our society, Hentoff laments our moral obtuseness and laziness in the following manner:

But of what am I guilty? Of what are you guilty? I can make it more specific. We read in *The New York Times* of people dying in the city hospitals because there are not enough nurses, not enough equipment. We read that of eighty thousand patients in New York State's mental hospitals, sixteen thousand receive no treatment at all. Not enough doctors. Not enough money.

Do we – those of us who convince ourselves that our concern for the powerless is more acute than that of the average hibernating bear – do we march on the hospitals, conduct vigils, place our harassing selves in front of functionaries and politicians? Don't be ridiculous. We can afford doctors who can get us into the good private hospitals.

But consider the political effect in the city of New York if five thousand of us were to mass at Bellevue as citizens concerned with other citizens. Absurd, you say, it'll never happen. Auto-anesthesia is the nature of the human beast when he himself is not threatened, all the more so when he is compressed into cities.

It is hard to quarrel with the facts. And indeed, Hentoff's rhetorical questions have been answered by "confrontation politics." But one misses the distinctive characteristic of this passage, if one doesn't listen to the voice that is uttering it. It is the voice of exasperated indignation, of a desire for immediate action not necessarily based on reflection. Do anything, anything (it utters in the most exasperated manner), anything that will wake up our slumbering moral consciousness. Its tone (moving toward moral self-righteousness) suggests that any question about the manner of formulating the issues is a kind of cop-out, an instance of bad faith. Moreover, it is the kind of exasperation that is very hard to sustain in one's minute to minute existence without disfiguring one's character. One can more easily express it in an article.

We know how unpleasant moral self-righteousness can be, but unpleasantness is hardly a crime and not even a vice. It may be a virtue when pleasantness is a mask for complacency. To be unpleasant to people who refuse to be disturbed in their thoughts and actions when intolerable injustices exist in their society is admirable. if not lovable. Those who attack the moral self-righteousness of radicalism on the ground of its unpleasantness do not deserve to be taken seriously. The *moral* peril of moral self-righteousness is injustice. So intense is the rage. the indignation. that the indignant person loses his perception and control of the issues. The morally self-righteous man is more interested in satisfying his feelings than in the question of justice. and the effect is the opposite of the original intention of the indignation – the passion for justice. When the blacks at Brandeis feel that they must assert their manhood by characterizing Morris Abram as a Georgia Cracker (see their ''Black Manifesto #2''). they are concerned to satisfy their passion for indignation rather than to tell it like it is. When LeRoi Jones in *Evergreen* lets loose against the ''joos.'' he is manifesting the pathology of the resentful man. confusing his intolerance with the objective fact of intolerable situations.

What *Evergreen* makes one see is the erotic element in this moral self-righteousness. In rejecting the Great White Society. Julian Beck affirms the youth and the blacks who are ''free to reject this society that cannot offer peace. love. joy. honor and fulfillment of its citizens.'' And on stage asserting his doctrine of love. he assaults his audience with a passion of hate. justified by the a priori assumption that his audience is the detestable Great White Society. Begin by assuming the moral authority of one's instincts and passions. the vile corruption of everything external and opposed to it and the pursuit of justice and fulfillment slides into the cruelty of moral self-righteousness. Neither reason nor self-irony (based on humility about oneself) is possible.

It is not necessary to turn this view of the *Evergreen* sensibility into a fierce polemic against it. the usual temptation. For something so strong and so attractive to many of our best people as this sensibility cannot be moralized away. It is ultimately a symptom of political. economic and cultural conditions that so irritate and exacerbate the sense of justice that the process described above becomes irreversible. Something in the quality of our life (which the war in Vietnam merely triggered) has lowered the threshold of endurance to a point where to discriminate among occasions for protest becomes an irrelevancy.

Those who have been puzzled by the apparently gratuitous character of much revolutionary feeling in America (after all. the young people who are rebelling come from affluent homes. etc.) have failed to realize that it is precisely the affluence and the increased expectation and the expanding sense of possibility that accompany the affluence which have generated and intensified "revolutionary" feeling. Create a sense of infinite material and even spiritual possibility (as technology and the imagery of American mythology have done) and then suddenly abort that sense of possibility by forcing young men into the army to fight a cruel and stupid war, and the intense desire for immediate radical change naturally follows. Contrast the sense of possibility fostered by American mythology with the hitherto *unexperienced* sense of universal suffering provided by the communications media and the threshold of endurance becomes increasingly lower. A man can suffer poverty and malnutrition quietly, even without bitterness, but if you constantly tantalize him with images of an opposite way of life, you attack and enrage his self-respect and it becomes a point of honor to fight in any way possible (and perhaps even impossible) for his dignity.

Most of the criticism of the "irrational" side of black revolutionary activity fails to account for this. There is no need to argue with LeRoi Jones' anti-Semitism, for that would dignify the substance of what he is saying by admitting the possibility of justice on his side. But justice or truth is not the motive or the reality. Jones is engaged in making a symbolic gesture of self-defining hatred. Hatred of whites and of Jews (the eternal middlemen) nourishes the feeling of militancy, which for many blacks is existence itself. Justice is the luxury of the privileged.

There may be moments in the history of a people when the empirical perspective, i.e., telling it like it is, must surrender to the need to *create* and sustain an identity for oneself. For instance, the reality of black life in the urban ghettos is probably like what the Moynihan report describes. The resentment of black militants to the report is in part at least a reaction against the reality. What we want, what we need, the black militant seems to be saying, is not a rehearsal of the awful circumstances of our life, but a mythology made out of the elements of our existence, which will enable us to change those circumstances.

Black studies, black art: this is all necessary mythology, and myth, we have learned, is not necessarily pejorative, for all of us are sustained in our lives by myths. To be sure, the black militant doesn't put the case this way, because he would experience the distinction between *finding* and *creating* one's identity as subversive of his enterprise. But to those who are bewildered objects of his resentment, it is necessary to make the distinction as a basis for sympathetic understanding. I think that without knowing all this *Evergreen Review* (white and liberal) provided Jones with a forum for a reason like this. What cannot be justified, however, is the particularly noxious (indeed, ultimately self-defeating) character of the anti-Semitic myth.

The hang-up for the liberal comes in the sympathy he feels for the gesture of survival in the Negro, a sympathy to which the Negro replies: "Just get off my back." The liberal reacts either with indignation or with hurt bewilderment and incredulity. If he persists in his "sympathy" it is out of hopefulness which says we can solve the problem together if only we all generate an atmosphere of good will. The militant has every right to be cynical about this hopefulness for the evidence of history is with him. For the white liberal (even if he refuses to acknowledge it) the situation is tragic. And the reason for the tragedy is not that there is a disagreement about objectives, but that the white simply cannot enter the skin of the black militant and understand the sense of urgency in his demand for justice. From the white point of view, it is viscerally, if not intellectually, experienced as impatience. I think it entirely a mistake to see the tragic gulf as a matter of disagreement about specific issues like centralization and decentralization, integration and separation. When the blacks argue for decentralization and separation, they are not arguing for ultimate principles: they are historically conditioned goals which can be and will be abandoned when the historical circumstances change. What is at issue is the tragically inevitable gulf between those who suffer a particular kind of humiliation and those who do not – which "sympathetic understanding" alone cannot begin to overcome.

Having said all this in trying to understand, if not extenuate, black anti-Semitism, one must exercise equal justice and sympathy in understanding the Jewish response to black anti-Semitism. It would be moral callousness to expect Jews not to respond keenly to anti-Semitic utterances of any kind. The point is that racism and anti-Semitism release powerful memories and emotions and one cannot apply different standards to the understanding of the two phenomena. If one tries to understand the emotional dimension of racism in the victims of racism, one must also sympathetically understand the emotional dimension of anti-Semitism in its victims. To say that the Jews have made it in American society and consequently the issue of anti-Semitism is fabricated, whereas the blacks are suf-

fering every minute of their lives, impresses me as utterly meretricious. A black militant like Jones or an official of CORE who says
that Hitler failed to complete the job is not speaking out of the
anguish of ghetto suffering. He too has made it, and he must bear
responsibility for his utterances. It is part of the definition and reality
of a leader that he is sufficiently liberated from the circumstances of
his oppression that he has the power to lead.

What is tragic from the point of view of the Negro (particularly the
poor Negro) is, as I have already remarked, the self-defeating character of his anti-Semitism. The Jewish entrepreneur in the black
community, for all his vices, is not the real villain (certainly not in
his Jewishness). He may be part of the White Establishment or, as
has been traditionally the case, the intermediary between the Negro
and the White Establishment. To see the Jew as the enemy is to
divert energy from the proper object. The fact is that anti-Semitism is
a convenient tool of black capitalists who might want to justify their
own economic depredations of poor blacks. I know of an editor of a
leading Negro newspaper who was threatened with the loss of their
business by his advertisers if he repeated an editorial "best wishes"
to his "Jewish brethren on the Passover holidays." The Marxian
analysis of exploitation and oppression appears to be not entirely
dated, after all.

Both blacks and Jews are capable of fabricating the issues of
racism and anti-Semitism respectively for political reasons. I suspect, however, that the deeper reason for the mutual escalation of
racist passions in New York has to do with the impatient apocalyptic
temper of our times, the kind of temper that we find in the *Evergreen*
sensibility. To take a "reasonable" or tragic view of the situation
means risking the charge of being morally and politically insensitive.

The sensibility has its aesthetic – to be sure, nothing like a systematic aesthetic. But in the fiction, poetry and essays *Evergreen* has
published during the past ten years there is a coherent outlook, and
one related to the political attitudes I have been discussing. I need
mention only three essays which help define the outlook. Susan
Sontag's essay "Against Interpretation" insists on the primacy of
the sensuous and argues for a return to the innocence of art prior to
interpretation or, if that is impossible, advocates "the overthrow of
any means of defending and justifying art which becomes particularly obtuse or onerous or insensitive to contemporary needs and
practice." ("Contemporary needs and practice" are left pretty

vague in the essay, perhaps because Miss Sontag wants to avoid *interpretation.*) Artaud's "No More Masterpieces" declares war on the very idea of a classic tradition in the arts, which necessarily has "lost all touch with the rude and epileptic rhythm of our time" and affirms a theater of cruelty in which "the spectator is the center and the spectacle surrounds him." (Among its progeny, of course, is the Living Theater.) Jan Kott's essay on *Lear* (which influenced the Brooks production) attempts a kind of translation of the play which will make it alive in contemporary terms and sees it as a Beckett version of "naked unaccommodated man." ("The theme of *King Lear* is the decay and fall of the world.")

The practical consequences of such an aesthetic are problematic. In a real artist, the call of reality may not only be valuable, it may be necessary. Indeed, one hardly needs an aesthetic for him, for he will instinctively search out the real rhythms of our life and incarnate them in appropriate forms. Grass, Beckett, Pinter, André Pieyre De Mandiargues: they exemplify not so much the aesthetic of the *Evergreen* sensibility as its hospitality. The more usual consequence of the aesthetic (and this comes clear only when one goes through the actual issues) is to give license to "artistic" frauds. There are too many gassy stories without substance or form, whose presence in *Evergreen* can be accounted for only by a taste for outrageous subject matter or the eccentrically scandalous attitude. *Épater le bourgeois,* while titillating him, so that he will ultimately be attracted rather than repelled seems too often the editorial guideline. Indeed, even in the anthology, which not only contains the best of the magazine, but which in absolute terms has much that is very good, the intellectual level of the work is strikingly low. An anti-intellectualist doctrine like Artaud's or Susan Sontag's need not diminish the intellectual density of a work: there are too many counter-examples for this to be the case. But the fact remains that there is surprisingly little of any intellectual substance which one can engage, agree with, quarrel with. This is not to deny the genuine intellectual charm of Suzuki's disquisition on Eastern consciousness or Octavio Paz's Mexican meditations on death. But all discussion about an *Evergreen* performance reduces itself to talk about sensibility, rarely if ever about intellectual substance. Small wonder then that a Marcuse or even a Norman O. Brown never appears in its pages: they belong to the repressive intellectual culture of *Partisan Review.*

There remains the question about the seriousness of the enterprise. How are we to take the sadistic eroticism of much of the fiction, for instance? It is not simply a matter of the raw damage that a sexually and aggressively "open society" might cause (the fears of puritanism vastly exaggerate the danger), but more importantly, a matter of the *quality of life* engendered by the liberation. Repression, for all the human devastation that it causes, has at least a resemblance to the virtue of discipline. The kind of rigor which makes even for passionate art may in some cases be as spontaneous and unrepressive as passion itself, but it has yet to be shown (and *Evergreen Review* offers little evidence) that spontaneity, the purely "liberated" gesture, is the ground of all virtues.

There is a kind of humor, mostly in the photos and the comic strips, which read like embarrassed recantations of the extreme positions taken. In the absurd strip about Phoebe Zeitgeist, one of Phoebe's would-be sadistic ravishers responds to her whimsical (that's the tone) question: "Why? What have I ever done to you?" with the answer: "Poor Child! Be not so naive as to believe that cruelty and violence must necessarily be motivated! The malicious act, set apart from the commonplace, lackluster treadmill of goal-oriented drives, attains a certain purity of its own being." This is a sophomoric parody of, say, the moral psychology of *The Story of O,* a section of which is in the anthology. The difference between the two is the matter of style: not style as transformed perception, but simply as surface grace. *Evergreen,* I suspect, is ultimately a liberal cop-out, the self-parodying gestures are "sophisticated" winks to the audience, as if to indicate that the extreme radical stuff in the magazine is little more than a kind of erotic play with possibility.

The people making and reading *Evergreen* are not making the revolution.

11 The deradicalized intellectuals

The movement of the political pendulum doesn't characterize the general population, whose conservative instincts have been fairly reliable, but rather the volatile "intelligentsia," which seems to thrive on changes of opinion and mood. Thus, since we have begun to mark our "progress" by decades, it was inevitable that after the radical sixties a conservative reaction would begin to emerge in the seventies.[1] One of the visible signs of this reaction is the current editorial policy of *Commentary*. As Nathan Glazer remarks in a recent article on his deradicalization, *Commentary* in the early fifties had given some impetus to the formation of a new radical conscience in America by, for instance, bringing the work of Paul Goodman into prominence. Now apparently viewing the work of this conscience during the past several years, *Commentary* has decided it has had enough and is openly espousing the "conservative" cause. Thus Norman Podhoretz remarks editorially, apropos of Glazer's article:

> In 1970 some of us who came a decade earlier to radicalism via the route of ideas rather than the route of personal grievance are convinced that it has become more important to insist once again on the freedom of large areas of human experience from the power of politics, whether benevolent or malign, than to acquiesce in the surly tyranny of the activist temper in its presently dominant form. It is in this sense that we consider ourselves deradicalized, and not out of any sudden lapse into indifference over the remediable ills which afflict the world and to whose removal the spirit of radical activism has come to stand, for all practical purposes, in a stubborn and perverse and most intractable opposition.

---

[1] I believe this article accurately reflects the ideological character of what has come to be called neoconservatism. What I did not foresee was its immense political success: The fact is that despite Podhoretz's cautionary remarks about the limits of the political will, he and his magazine seem to have politicized all issues – cultural, artistic, sexual, and so forth.

The work of the radical conscience during the sixties is vulnerable to criticism, even radical criticism, but Podhoretz's polemical posture (and those of recent contributors to *Commentary*) suggests an insensitivity (despite the disclaimer that there has been no sudden lapse into indifference) to the fundamental fact that we are suffering a moral and political crisis of considerable magnitude and that this crisis has not been brought about merely by radical willfulness. "Personal grievance" hardly covers the profound feeling against the war in Vietnam or the fight for social justice at home, unless by *personal* Podhoretz means that people have felt personally menaced by American policies; for instance, the threat of the draft, as well as the feeling of the moral indignity of the war itself. If Podhoretz's earlier radicalism was merely intellectual (he of course intends to suggest its superiority, because presumably it was disinterested and reflective), it could not have been a very substantial or *experienced* radicalism. Podhoretz suggests that whatever their limitations, he would much prefer to return to the sophistications of the fifties after the wild sixties.

At the same time, Podhoretz obviously feels uneasy about the word "conservative." In an article on him in *The Wall Street Journal*, he is reported to disclaim any connection between his line and the politics of Richard Nixon. "The truth is he's 'a democratic socialist or a social democrat.' " The use of the word "conservative," he says, is part of a strategy against the fashionable radicalism of his fellow intellectuals. He grants that he had another option which was to reserve the virtuous term "radical" for himself and to denounce "pseudo radicals." But that he didn't choose this course is significant, not only for Podhoretz but for many intellectuals and other people who have wanted to react against radical excesses but were worried about what they were reacting in behalf of.

Podhoretz is not simply responding to the excesses: he seems to be responding to the radical idea itself. He is *not* in the position in which Alexander Herzen found himself in the 19th century when he too recoiled from radical excesses.

Everyone now plays with his cards on the table, and the game itself has become greatly simplified, it is impossible to make mistakes: in every corner of Europe there is the same struggle, the same two camps. You feel quite clearly which you are against, but do you feel your tie with the other camp as clearly as your hatred and disgust for that of the enemy?

The result of this new conservatism (there is nothing intrinsically dishonorable in the conservative idea) is I think to divert attention from the real evils to which radical consciousness has addressed itself.

The hysterical side of the radical argument has been clear enough. For instance, a Luddite dismantling of technology is not only impossible, it is undesirable. I heard a proponent of the counter culture argue to American students in Paris the joys of the primitive life on the very day that hundreds of thousands of Pakistanis were facing the natural elements unencumbered by repressive Western technology. But does the romantic illusion about the joys of a world without technology justify the opposite illusion that the solutions to our problems are contained within the natural progress of technology? Despite the tone of "realism" of Glazer's essay, his response to the radical critique of our cancerous economy is astonishingly complacent:

The radicals answer that much of the remaining 90 per cent [of the Gross National Product, which according to Glazer is nonmilitary] is also life-denying, going to such unnecessary or harmful products as cars, roads, and television sets. But the vast majority of the population sees in these things the essence of the good life. Human wants can be met in many ways, but they cannot be met by dismantling the machinery, physical and institutional, of modern society. Only a drastic reduction in standards of living – and radicals are the first to insist that standards are already too low for large numbers of our people – or a drastic reduction in the total number of people is compatible with the degree of freedom from organization, control, discipline, and responsibility for the support of others that seems to be the special demand of contemporary radicals.

Glazer simply asserts the by now traditional American desire for the proliferation of commodities without showing any awareness of the costs in physical and moral health. Not a word about what the new conservatism intends to do about the auto industry or industrial pollution. Not a word about the *enlightened* conservatism of Paul Ehrlich, who sees in the traditional capitalist (and Marxist) psychology of abundance a threat to planetary survival, given the increasing discrepancy between the development of the means of subsistence and population growth. Glazer avoids entirely the question of the military-industrial complex with a sociological sleight of hand in the worst tradition of sociology: to say that the military budget is only 10 per cent of the GNP gives no indication of its enormous significance in the economic life of the nation. It is a permanent gain of the sixties that we now perceive the ambiguous moral force of technology and that whether it saves or destroys depends in part on moral and intellectual energies that are other than technological. Whether or not this was known earlier is irrelevant; radical consciousness in America made it a familiar fact.

One of the vices of the current radicalism is the indiscrimination of its attack and the resentful manner in which it is often launched. Examples abound. In a recent *Ramparts* article on the population explosion, Steve Weissman begins with this gratuitous sneer:

Paul Ehrlich is a nice man. He doesn't hate blacks, advocate genocide or defend the empire. He simply believes that the world has too many people and he's ready at the drop of a diaper pin to say so. He's written his message in *The Population Bomb*, lectured it in universities and churches, and twice used America's own form of birth control, the late-night Johnny Carson Show, to regale bleary-eyed moms and dads with tales of a standing-room-only world, a time of famines, plague and pestilence.

Ehrlich's study is a serious and sophisticated reconstruction of Malthus' argument on the menace of overpopulation. *Ramparts* in fact had published Ehrlich in an earlier issue. Weissman's manner is simply fashionable. So strong is the resentment toward the adversary position that one feels free to impugn motives or at least imply the moral insensitivity of the advocate of the position. The shortcoming of this manner is its failure to distinguish between a rank injustice, like the continuing war in Indochina, and a genuine problem like the population explosion. Another instance: the first issue of *Amistad,* a magazine devoted to black history and culture, promises that it will "tell it like it is." The editors assert that they "know that the truth of Western Civilization lies in precisely what has been omitted from its teaching." There is to be sure no teaching that does not omit or distort the truth. But we know that some truth has been taught. And we know that if truth has been omitted, it often requires strenuous work to discover and reveal it. Unless truth is simply the revelation of the undeniable sufferings of the oppressed – and even this has been taught. (I omit the more egregious instances from the underground press.)

But such failures hardly discredit the unremitting criticism of the American role in Vietnam or of the racist character of our society. And it is scarcely a contribution to the health of American political life simply to rehearse, as Podhoretz does without criticism, the myth propagated by members of both parties that the war in Indochina is winding down and that it is no longer an issue in American politics. Even if the war is winding down for *American soldiers on the field of battle,* it remains a grim reality for the Laotians and the Cambodians as well as the Vietnamese who continue and will continue to be bombed from the air.

As much as indiscriminate action, the inflated statement has been part of the "normal" political discourse of recent years. But it has not happened of itself; the inflated statement contains within itself the infection of American reality. The slaughter of innocents abroad; the continued talk about the disgrace of losing the war; the President [Nixon] flexing the muscles of the American giant, believing that he is performing a moral gesture; his nervous desire for understanding, as if villainy too deserved compassion; the chaos of urban life – it has been difficult to contemplate gross reality without feeling the impulse to jeer or rave or cry. That it is impossible to base a politics on jeering, raving or crying should be clear from the current mood of exhaustion on the campus. That it may be morally undesirable as a basis for politics is also evident from witnessing how the habit of outcry can foster unjust intolerance for differences of opinion and outlook.

But then it is not clear at all to anyone at this moment what constitutes an adequate politics. It is certainly a bad sign for the cause of reason in political life that it can so easily be coopted by a man like Spiro Agnew, who has no difficulty urging reason and patience. When Goneril urges Lear to be patient, the fact that patience is a virtue is irrelevant.

There is doubtless no single motive for the present crisis – though what with Vietnam and the urban predicament we have two formidable provocations. But since the crisis is as much subjective as objective, it is necessary to account for the evolution of our feeling that we are in crisis. What has happened is that we have lost confidence in our understanding of the political life. The fifties fostered confidence that with the "end of ideology" we had achieved not only wisdom but mastery of political, social and economic life. Despite all the foreboding about the inevitable doom of capitalism, America, in the dominant view, had miraculously discovered a way of avoiding doom and of leading the nations of the world to a glorious new future.

These feelings, enforced by increasing disenchantment of Left intellectuals with Soviet socialism, virtually extinguished radical sentiment in America. The sudden visibility of poverty in America (dramatized by unconverted figures of the Left, Michael Harrington and Dwight Macdonald), the increasing unwillingness of the blacks to be regarded simply as an unfortunate exception to the generally benevolent American dispensation, and Vietnam with its imperialist implications and its revelation of the incredible destructiveness of modern technological warfare began to undermine confidence that we had mastered political reality.

But except for the young and some exceptional adults, this loss of confidence did not provide the incentive for people to return to the Left positions that had been abandoned in the thirties and forties. The young could afford a commitment to the Left, because they had not suffered the experience or the sins of Stalinism. They could undertake a leftist politics in good faith, though this good faith was no assurance that they themselves would avoid, in Paul Goodman's words, "the power plays, factionalism, random abuse and tactical lies that aborted the movement in the thirties and the forties." Moreover, since their radicalism was deliberately ahistorical (because of the feeling that to forget the past was somehow to be free of it), it rarely achieved any theoretical interest. It consisted of actions (some of them admirable – like draft resistance and the refusal to pay taxes; many of them of undefined political purpose) and shallow rhetoric. The genuine insights into the technocratic nature of American political economy and its expansive nature became occasions for moral denunciation but it produced no *immanent* critique that would provide the knowledge for significantly changing American society.

Filled with moral feeling that things were seriously wrong, no longer confident in benevolent technology, unprepared to resume the traditional Marxist perspective, adults of liberal and radical disposition became vulnerable to every assault, justified and unjustified, upon their consciences. But since the moral anxiety increased without commensurate outlets in coherent and effective political action, the indignation of the radical young tended to become hysterical. Consciences were touched, in many cases deeply touched, but nothing seemed to happen. The understanding of political reality in America grew more confused.

The confusion is not about the fact of the horror of Vietnam or of racism or of poverty. It is about the sources and the remedy. If Vietnam is the result of the failure of the system, then only radical change will make "no more Vietnams" possible. And to make that change, confrontation politics alone is hardly adequate. We need to know what institutions must be changed, the manner in which they are to be changed, and the means by which the change is to be effected. Who will take power and how will radical reform protect itself against self-betrayal, which has almost become a law of historical development? (Existing Socialist systems are dubious models.)

Of course, no theory can substitute for the historical process itself, but theory is at least a necessary condition for the revolutionary or reformist action that will do more than simply shake up the system. However, such questions were rarely raised and confronted; instead there developed a habit of open-ended activism (most brilliantly argued for by Daniel Cohn-Bendit; the phenomenon was not confined to America) which was based largely on the assumption that history itself would raise the questions and provide the answers. One unfortunate consequence was the tendency toward indiscriminate attacks on all institutions. The critics forgot not only that institutions were absolutely necessary to social life, indeed to the *freedom* of social life, but that some institutions served as protections against the noxious working of other institutions (the university against the military-industrial complex, the courts against racism).

It should be said at once that the New Left in its principal groupings (SDS, Progressive Labor, etc.) has not been alone in theoretical inadequacy. Liberals who themselves felt the need for radical change (e.g., Galbraith) were often astute in their analysis of what was wrong, but had no real sense of what had to be done or what could be done. Electoral politics was felt to be no alternative to confrontation politics, because given the strong propensity in the system for Vietnam involvement and the enormous pressures to sustain it, it was not at all clear that even in the best of circumstances – a victory for Robert Kennedy or Eugene McCarthy, for instance – the system could decide deliberately to extricate itself from Vietnam on terms of acknowledged defeat.

The point to be made about this crisis is not that the political will has its limits, but that the political failures of the system have been a principal cause for the excessively large place that politics has come to occupy in our lives. It is true that there have been many instances of impossible demands and Faustian political fantasies. There *are* limits to what politics can accomplish. But to turn this truth into an occasion for avoiding the political failure of America to stop its criminal war in Vietnam by taking the long view of the killing, as

Podhoretz does now (in the long run we'll all be dead) is inexcusable. Certainly those who have demonstrated against the war have felt the resistance of the government to any significant change of position to be something like the force of nature, obstinate and insurmountable. The language of tragedy applies to our involvement in Vietnam only in its effect on the Vietnamese and the American dead and wounded. The appropriate language for our role in Indochina is moral and political and it concerns the corruption of our system and its agents.

Nothing in the radical performance of the sixties has discredited certain of its insights into American interventionism, technocracy and racism. The effect of the new conservatism – with its sweeping attack on all fronts – is to distort the perspective. (See Walter Goodman on the question of repression, Irving Kristol on the urban crisis, Tom Milstein on the Panthers, Midge Decter on Women's Liberation – with more to come.) Podhoretz has expressed confidence that he is going to win. If he does it will be a Pyrrhic victory – for all of us.

12 *The New York Review* loves an Englishman

In 1970 I wrote an article for *Dissent* on *The New York Review* in which I criticized its association with the New Left. I recall that Irving Howe, the editor of *Dissent*, suggested that I title the essay *"The New York Review* and Radical Chic." I demurred, because I thought it a possibly unfair characterization of the motives of the journal. Howe and I settled on the evasive and less vivid title: *"The New York Review:* A Close Look." It was difficult to know at the time just how much of the *NYR*'s politics was genuine conviction and how much a fashionable flirtation with radical attitudes.

Jerry Rubin, Tom Hayden, and Andrew Kopkind were hardly writers one had come to expect in the *NYR* given its high-brow concern for quality in thought and expression. "Given the open commitment of the *NYR* to *critical* writing and thinking," I wrote, "the presence of articles by Rubin, Kopkind, and Hayden invites suspicion about the political seriousness of its editors." And I wondered what would happen when the New Left lost its cachet for intellectuals. Would the *NYR* turn to the next new thing? Clearly, I shared Howe's suspicions about radical chic, but I also felt that the bond between the *NYR* and the New Left expressed a significant political reality of the time. The New Left in a strict generational sense was the offspring of the liberalism which the *NYR* had espoused until the mid-sixties and it represented the disaffection of liberalism from itself. Conscience-stricken particularly about the war in Viet Nam, the *NYR* tried to induce a sense of guilt in its readers. The *NYR*, after all, was "chic" (if that's the right word) before the advent of the New Left and by opening its pages to what was in the early sixties a marginal "movement," it bestowed some of its prestige on the New Left. The cynical view is that the *NYR* committed itself to the New Left because its editors sensed where the action was or would be.

The New Left has lost its cachet and the *NYR* has turned

to . . . what? Certainly not to the next new thing, neo-conservatism. In fact, it is one of the few nationally prominent journals that has not paid its respects to what John Kenneth Galbraith in the pages of the *NYR* calls the "conservative onslaught" (June 12, 1980). If anything, it has returned to its liberal origins. In the late sixties, the *NYR* was the forum for the radical view that liberalism was dead or dying. Now that liberalism has survived the New Left and the conservatives and neo-conservatives are once more invoking the corpse of liberalism, the *NYR* has found again its liberal voice. Galbraith, for instance, speaks of the simplistic solutions of Milton Friedman and his school and in true liberal fashion acknowledges the difficulty of finding solutions to our economic problems. The economic gurus of the *NYR* are Galbraith, Robert Heilbroner, and Lester Thurow, whose pragmatic liberalism would have provoked contempt from the New Left in the sixties. Thurow, for instance, proposes the ethos of Japanese industrialism with its remarkable combination of puritanism and feudal honor as a model for American economic recovery. American workers must learn again what it is to work hard, and American industrial managers must learn what they never knew, a kind of *noblesse oblige* toward their employees which will insure their jobs and create incentive for harder work.

In foreign policy, Stanley Hoffman, the admirer of Gaullist Raymond Aron, dispenses advice to Haig and company in a manner that should dispel any doubt about lingering radicalism in the pages of the *NYR*. One precondition for effective policy "is the need to minimize discontinuity. . . . When a new president . . . is of a different party from his predecessors, and there is a big shift in Congress, the temptation to repudiate the past and to put Creation in the present is overwhelming. But nothing is more destructive of confidence abroad, more dangerous and ultimately more confusing at home" (April 30, 1981). I am not disparaging the wisdom of this statement, I only want to stress the conservative character of this wisdom. To be sure, Hoffman's conservatism is directed toward possible reactionary changes in policy: the abandonment of Salt II, the unqualified support of a right-wing dictatorship in El Salvador, but Hoffman's comments about sudden liberal changes that Carter made when he was president, e.g., his "first proclamations about human rights" suggest that stability is the principal value for Hoffman. He speaks almost regretfully about "the management and steering of inevitable change." Hoffman is fully aware of the "formidable inequities" in nations such as Chile and Brazil and the Union of South Africa, but his critique is devoid of the moral passion that flooded the pages of the *NYR* in the sixties. The arrangements in those nations are, in the long run, "unworkable." George Kennan's plea for nuclear sanity is distinguished by its moral passion, but it is the passion of a realist, not of a radical ideologue (July 16, 1981).

If there is a lingering radicalism in the *NYR*, it is of the hard to define kind exemplified by its hospitality to a writer-criminal like Jack Abbott. Abbott's sponsor is Norman Mailer, one of *NYR*'s favorite contributors, who has a history of sympathy with what may be called anti-bourgeois criminal fantasy first expressed in an essay in the late fifties, "The White Negro." But one should not make too much of the Mailerism of the *NYR*, since it is also true that Gore Vidal, another *NYR* favorite, is a severe critic of Mailerism, accusing Mailer of responsibility for the actions of Charles Manson. Jack Abbott is a permanent possibility in the *NYR* sensibility, but hardly central to its present concerns.

When Jason Epstein was asked to explain the *NYR*'s politics, he replied, "There is no political line. We go from issue to issue" (Philip Nobile, *Intellectual Skywriting*, 1974, p. 279). The *NYR* is not an organ of a party or a movement, it is hospitable to a variety of writers, it does not have an ideology, but it has a liberal tendency. Which means that it is susceptible to periodic radicalization that may provoke within the liberal tendency itself a revisionist response. *Commentary*'s reaction to the *NYR* reenacts the reaction of revisionist liberals (a number of whom became conservatives) to fellow-traveling communism in the thirties and forties.

What the *NYR* lacks is an intellectual center that makes it possible to perceive the changes in its positions as the product of an internal logic. I don't mean that the intelligence required by a journal like the *NYR*, which must respond to historical change, can insulate itself from those changes. But anybody can go from issue to issue. The question is what one takes to the issue. It is not that those who write for the *NYR* do not write with knowledge and conviction. It is simply that they do not constitute the intellectual center of the journal. The center is the editor or editors who select the writers, and since the writers may change from decade to decade or from year to year, a question remains about the character of *NYR* politics, especially when the editors are reticent to the point of anonymity. The judgment I am making would not be made of *The Edinburgh Review* and *The Westminster Review* in the nineteenth century. It cannot be made of *Dissent* or *Commentary* or *Partisan Review*, for the editors of those journals are not reticent. Perhaps the ultimate limitation of the

NYR is that its occasions are with few exceptions books under review. The *NYR* is an extraordinary source of intelligent opinion and accomplished writing, but the absence of an editorial center makes the journal viewed over the course of its career an exceedingly rich document of changing intellectual and political attitudes rather than a critical journal with a set of clearly articulated convictions.

But I want to suspend for a moment the question about the politics of the *NYR* in order to say something about the New York character of the journal. The loss of its radical cachet enables us to see the journal more fully for what it is. We need no longer focus so exclusively on its political aspect as we were invited to do in the sixties. In speaking of her migrations from Berlin to Paris and then to New York, Hannah Arendt used to say that even the differences in language did not prevent her from experiencing the essential continuity of these cities. For her, they constituted a *sui generis* geography which made them for intellectuals at least closer to one another than to the countries of which they were a part. The Berliner is more of a Parisian or a New Yorker than a German. Hannah Arendt is expressing the myth of the world class city to which the *NYR* has made its contribution.

New York, of course, is not Paris. Paris is not only one of the great cities of the world, it is the only great city of France. However, resentful provincials may feel toward Paris, the city is the incarnation of the greatness of France. The intellectual, artistic and commercial energy of France has been concentrated in Paris at least since the days of Louis XIV. Paris is the unity in the provincial diversity of France. New York is something else. In the eyes of the rest of America New York is un-American. Its energy is alien and exotic and its giganticism suggests that it is a world unto itself. If not disloyal to its country, the city is not really a part of it and therefore to be mistrusted. New York in its Jewishness and its blackness, its reputation for nightmare, lunacy, and poverty has long fed the paranoia of the rest of America. It is also the place where intellectuals and artists can be free of patriotic cant if not actually hostile to America and what conventional wisdom says it stands for. In the eyes of the critics of the *NYR* the *NYR* does not simply pander to radicalism, it is "anti-American." Midge Decter makes the case in class terms:

It's more than just radical chic. The American upper-class WASP, the blueblood, has been radicalized for some time. He hates the country more than the Black Muslims. The literary community here has always been in love with the upper class, because they have a great common enemy – the bourgeoisie. So you get that and the kids and the blacks, and that's why they turned left-wing. (Nobile, p. 143)

Midge Decter is aluding to the *NYR*'s connection with the WASP smart set, mainly symbolized by George Plimpton and its publisher Whitney Ellsworth. There is an echo in this of Tocqueville's critique of the upper classes of France, which combined with the literary community in hatred of the *ancien regime* to make the revolution of 1789. What Decter misses is the New York character of the opposition, understandably, since she herself is a New Yorker who flaunts her patriotism.

With the demise of the New Left, the politics of the *NYR* has become the politics of the big city. A city planner like Felix Rohatyn dramatizes the anguish of the big cities, of the moribund Northeast and speculates about the possibility of reconstructing America (March 5, 1980). The interests of the big city and America are congruent. America itself, however, acquires life in the *NYR*, when it is under attack, for example, by an expatriate like Gore Vidal, who says that harsh truth-telling about America is impossible within America, though apparently it is possible in the pages of the *NYR*. Apropos of a discussion of the serious novel, Vidal animadverts on the United States in the following manner: "The sort of harsh truth-telling that one gets in Aristophanes, say, is not possible in a highly organized zoo like the United States where the best cuts are flung to those who never question the zoo's management" (Dec. 4, 1980, p. 10). Vidal, an American who used to live in Rome, has the privilege of being un- or anti-American.

Not all anti-Americanism is tolerated in the pages of the *NYR*. Vidal is capable of excess and sour grapes when he speaks venomously and loftily of America, but he knows his country, whereas a foreigner like Peter Conrad who has little to recommend him except animus needs to be deflated, not in the interest of America, but in the interest of true observation. Elizabeth Hardwick's review of Conrad's *Imagining America* is precisely the sort of sophisticated corrective one might expect of the *NYR* (April 3, 1980). America is fair game, but you better know what you are talking about. One tolerates anti-Semitic jokes from a Jew, but if a *goy* tells the same joke, well. . . . Yet even in Hardwick's review one detects a note of chagrin about the performance of this particular Englishman. The *NYR* loves an Englishman. Here is a perfect example of a style to which the *NYR* is hospitable: Clive James (an Englishman in the guise of an Australian) writes on Evelyn Waugh: "Behaving as if recent history wasn't actually happening was one of Waugh's abiding characteristics. It is the main reason why his books always seem fresh. Since he never fell for any transient political belief, he never dates" (Dec. 4, 1980, p. 3).

In loving an Englishman, one of course loves a Tory (whether one's politics are left or right, liberal or conservative). The Tory looks down upon America the way in which he looks down upon the plebeianism in his own country. An issue of the *NYR* features a massive excerpt of a satiric poem by Clive James, dedicated to Prince Charles: "Charles Charming's Challenge on the Pathway to the Throne." The point of view is that of Prince Charles in this unfunny condescending portrait of Rayon Woollens (i.e., Raymond Williams):

> His name was Rayon Woollens, come to teach
> Some form of politics. Earnest of speech,
> In mode of dress he was no whit less grim.
> The Trendy Left could lay no claim to *him* –
> His Leftness harked back to an older school
> As stubborn as a mule and grey as gruel,
> A stagnant pool of glutinous viscosity
> Where failed polemics foundered in pomposity.
> "You represent a Ruling Class attempt,"
> Droned *Woollens,*
>   "to behave as if exempt
> From Social Thrusts by which Manipulation
> Becomes habitual to the population –
> And yet you form in fact part of the Flow
> By which a given television show
> Resembles any other . . ."
>   On he canted
> Of how the helpless masses are implanted
> With standard patterns of response, and yet
> To *Charles* it seemed of all the men he'd met
> That this man's patterns of response were more
> Standard than anything he'd heard before,
> As well as tedious beyond belief . . .   (July 16, 1981)

F. R. Looseleaf (i.e., Leavis) comes in for similar treatment. This is the wit of a man, if one may apply Clive James's characterization of Evelyn Waugh to James himself, who "behaves as if recent history wasn't happening." It is perhaps the mark of a split personality that the *NYR* on the one hand cherishes the condescensions of the Tory style and on the other hand behaves as if recent history *is* happening. In any event, when the *NYR* is radical, its radicalism is often of the Tory kind.

The analogy between anti-Americanism and anti-Semitism is not entirely gratuitous, because the anglophilia of the *NYR* is not simply a mark of its distance from – should I say – middle America, it is also a mark of its distance from its Jewish cousins, *Commentary,* even *Partisan Review.* Norman Podhoretz in his recent memoir, *Breaking Ranks,* occupies himself a good deal with the political differences between Jason Epstein and himself, that is, between *NYR* and *Commentary.* Podhoretz's earlier book *Making It* makes clear that the difference between Epstein and Podhoretz was also a social difference. Epstein was upper-middle-class, had gone to private school before going to Columbia, Podhoretz was the precocious slum waif from Brownsville. In *Partisan Review* and *Dissent* (the other significant New York quarterlies), the trace of an earlier immigrant experience with strong political resonances persists. The *NYR* in its tone and style suggests the crystallization of a meeting between Lionel Trilling and Isaiah Berlin. The Jewishness is barely remembered in the names.

It is not fortuitous that the emergence of the *NYR* as a dominant intellectual journal corresponds with the breakthrough of the American Jewish novel into national importance in the early sixties. New York intellectuals, artist and publicist, Jew and gentile, were being listened to, even courted by political figures of national importance for the first time. In *Breaking Ranks* Podhoretz describes a lunch meeting with Eugene McCarthy in 1968 arranged by a mutual acquaintance apparently at the request of McCarthy to test the waters for his possible candidacy for president. Podhoretz also describes meetings with Kennedy and Johnson at the White House. Though it is never made clear precisely what influence Podhoretz or any of his friends had on Kennedy, Johnson, or McCarthy, the association is meant to indicate the new national importance of the New York intellectual. Podhoretz's friendship with Daniel Patrick Moynihan is, of course, well-known, and *Commentary* has become a forum for policy statements by significant political figures, among them Moynihan himself. We know that Jeane Kirkpatrick, the U.S. ambassador to the U.N., came to the attention of Ronald Reagan through an article she wrote for *Commentary.* And we also know that when Nixon moved to New York one of his first remarks to reporters asking him why he was settling in New York was that he hoped to make the acquaintance of the Podhoretzes and the Kristols. What is true for *Commentary* is true for the *NYR*, though the political persuasion is different. Should a liberal president be elected in the future, the president's talent scouts would undoubtedly scan the columns of the *NYR*. It is, of course, difficult to sort out how much of the encounter between New York intellect and national politics is a matter of genuine political importance and how much of it simply belongs to the gossip columns. The ambitious New York intellectual wants to think of himself as politically important in the narrow sense of politics. The politician probably likes the association with intellect.

If one simply concerns oneself with the internecine battles between New York magazines, one may miss what one can grasp more easily at a distance from the fray. Jack Richardson, a writer in the unique position of being a regular contributor to both periodicals, notes the sensibility common to both the *NYR* and *Commentary* (one might add *Partisan Review* and *Dissent*): ''I feel somewhat sad that this split occurred between two magazines which emerged from the same sensibility. America doesn't have that many places where opinion is stated well. But I don't feel any deep ambiguity about it'' (Nobile, p. 223). Whether left or right, radical or conservative, the New York periodical maintains a superior distance from America. Even the recent flaunting middle-class patriotism of *Commentary* seems more negative than affirmative in its sweeping denunciations of upper-class WASPS, blacks and kids. A social history of New York periodicals will show this celebration of middle America to be an aberration. The New York intellectual sensibility, informed by European cultural, if not political, values is a subversive strain in the American tradition.

III Writing in America and elsewhere

13 *The New Country: Stories from the Yiddish About Life in America*

My reaction to these "stories from the Yiddish about life in America" is complicated by a fact of my adolescence. I had read some of these stories and others like them in a Yiddish *schule,* and they became part of the militancy with which I – and others who shared my experience – confronted the world as a Jew and a "progressive." (Several of the writers anthologized here, in fact, taught in these *schules.*) When the stories weren't merely exercises in reading they were lessons in right action and right feeling, and as one might expect, the lessons were clear and unambiguous. We shared the exploited sweat-shop worker's indignation and his hope for a better world. If we had never experienced the terrors of immigrant loneliness and poverty, we came to know them intimately, partly through our reading of the stories and, of course, partly through our parents. I suspect that these stories satisfied the adult reader in much the same way. They consoled him in his suffering, encouraged his indignation, relieved him somewhat of his bewilderment in the New Country either by a nostalgic evocation of the Old Country or an apocalyptic vision of an earthly paradise.

The characteristic voice of the Yiddish writer in America – and we hear it in this collection – was that of a sympathetic friend or brother who had suffered like his readers. He too had lived in a tenement or worked in a sweat shop. His stories perhaps lacked the sophistication of a richer culture, but his audience was openly grateful that he had not evolved to that complexity of artistic utterance which might make him introspective and difficult and even alienate him from them. Henry Goodman, the editor and translator of these stories, reflects this feeling in his introduction: "Realistic as some of these writers become, the tight-lipped coldness, the clinical aloofness admired in some American and other non-Yiddish writing, are utterly out of keeping with the feeling, approach, attitude, and practice of the Yiddish writer."

I have used the past tense in characterizing the bond between the Yiddish writer and his audience because that bond is in fact a thing of the past. A reader who comes to these stories cold may indeed wonder whether many of them are stories at all. They seem more like the beginnings of stories, sketches, anecdotes, excuses for social criticism. He might respond to the naive charm of Abraham Reisin's "Rockefeller and Rothschild," in which a newly arrived immigrant and his Americanized cousin debate in a crescendo of anger the respective merits of the two millionaires. He will, of course, find pleasure in the selections from Sholom Aleichem's *Motel Pessie in America*. (Sholom Aleichem is the one indubitable genius in this collection, though he is not represented here at his best.) The reader might be somewhat astonished by the incongruous presence of a writer of such authentic power and skill as Chaimowitz, who has read Goethe and Mallarmé and combines folk wit with an exquisite responsiveness to nuances of feeling. For the most part, however, the stories are primitively conceived and executed. If they still engage the reader's interest, it is because the very primitiveness of conception and execution reflect not so much a lack of talent – there is evidence of talent even in some of the least successful stories – as a significantly characteristic inability of these writers to come to imaginative terms with the new experience.

Like the people they write about, they have not been able to disengage themselves from the feelings of bewilderment, self-pity, hysteria in order to present those feelings with the necessary detachment and freedom of art. The expense of spirit of Jewish provinciality, for instance, is recognized only by an artist like Sholom Aleichem, who is capable of seeing – through the wonderfully cruel eyes of the boy, Motel Pessie – the greenhorn for the grotesque that he is.

But the firm irony of Sholom Aleichem is not typical. One can hear as one reads the book an irritatingly persistent lament: "the faint sound of a Russian song, like smothered weeping," the insatiable regret of childless parents, the inconsolable Jew, victimized by the landlord, the boss, the oppressive heat of the city, or an ungrateful "assimilated" son. From time to time the lament is interrupted by a complaint or an outburst of indignation; the struggling poet of Chaver Paver's "Moishe the Poet" realizes, for instance, that it is not life that he should hate, but "the unjust practices in life." "There's laughter, too" – the title of Part IV of the anthology – but even in the "laughter" one can hear the wail. The range of feeling and attitude in this collection is limited by an enormous self-love, the other side of Jewish self-hatred.

Rarely is there a surprising or unpredictable turn in these stories, and "the point of view" is typically uncomplicated by a sense of the complex or ambiguous nature of experience. Thus in the stories that concern parents and children, the villain is usually the Americanized son who has become an allrightnik, while the wonderful affections and values of the older bearded generation are eulogized. Reisin's "The Americanized European" is unusual in its sympathy for the younger generation, trying to live the life of the New Country. The ferocious conflict between parents and children that has become a commonplace of American Jewish culture has its origins in part in the frightful Old Country myopia of the older generation, so lovingly rendered in these stories. What these stories lack can be found, say, in Alfred Kazin's *A Walker in the City:*

Our parents, whatever affection might offhandedly be expressed between them, always had the look of being committed to something deeper than the *mere* love. . . . They had met – whether in Russia or in the steerage or, like my parents, in an East Side boarding house – whatever they still thought of each other, *love* was not a word they used easily. Marriage was an institution people entered into – for all I could ever tell – only from immigrant loneliness, a need to be with one's own kind that mechanically resulted in the *family*. The *family* was a whole greater than all the individuals who made it up, yet made sense only in their untiring solidarity. I was perfectly sure that in my parents' minds *libbe* was something exotic and not wholly legitimate, reserved for "educated" people like their children, who were the sole end of their existence. My father and mother worked in a rage to put us above their level; they had married to make *us* possible. We were the only conceivable end to all their striving; we were their America.

There is no lack of sympathy in this passage, but there is the hardness of true observation and the presence of a person who is not exclusively defined by the world he is describing, who has the knowledge of another world in terms of which he can understand this one. It is precisely that need for "untiring solidarity" of which Kazin speaks that deprived the Yiddish writers of the freedom of standing back and judging the quality of their lives. Zalmon Libin tells a story of a writer who is bullied by the Taracan *landsleit* into doing an article for their journal. He writes the article only to find himself at the mercy of other societies of Taracans at war with the first society, each demanding in turn an article for its journal. The story is scarcely more than the summary I've just given, and it ends weakly on a note of ironic self-pity: "Obviously, you cannot satisfy everyone in the world. The natives of Taracan, all Taracans without exception, are now enemies of mine." The writer's wistful complaint is, of course, Libin's. Like the writer in the story, he does not mean to give offense. This tender-mindedness, characteristic of so many of these writers, has caused him to muff a superb opportunity for satire on the fierce clannishness of the New York *landsmanshaften* and by implication of the Jews generally.

The tender-mindedness is one form that the defensiveness of the Yiddish writer takes. His secret – and sometimes, as these stories bear witness, not so secret – wish is to reproduce the squalid security of the old way of life in America. The fear of change, the desire to hold on to the old, especially in enemy country, are among the deepest of human fears and desires. And certainly the defensiveness of the Jewish immigrant, as these stories implicitly remind us, is the other side of that wonderful tenacity with which the Jews have held on to their identity. But the failure of these writers to realize the price that was paid for this defensiveness is finally their failure to emerge from parochialism onto the field that we call world literature.

14 *Three Novels*, by Daniel Fuchs

The Brooklyn of popular mythology is the absurd home of the Brooklyn Dodgers (now of Los Angeles), Coney Island and the famous bridge; the accent is funny, the people eccentric, the whole atmosphere as fabulous as Texas. Of course, anyone growing up in Brooklyn would find it hard to recognize himself or his borough in the myth. Brooklyn is a special place, but not for the mythological reasons given above. Not like Texas which is so American in its wide-open spaces, but, one imagines, like the East European *shtetl* on a macrocosmic scale: dense, airless, desperate. This was even truer thirty years ago before the influx from Puerto Rico, but the East European character of Brownsville or Williamsburg is essentially unmodified. Or, so it seems on every trip from "the city": one simply returns to one's past.

So that in reading these novels about Williamsburg (*Summer in Williamsburg*, *Homage to Blenholt* and *Low Company*, first published in '34, '36 and '37 respectively), one almost forgets that Daniel Fuchs is writing about an earlier time. The choking density of life in Williamsburg, the airlessness of street and apartment, the impossibility of privacy or anonymity in the tenement, the consequent irritability and tension of human relationships: Fuchs has given us the timeless "spirit of the place." In upper Brownsville people still seek the clearer *luft* of Eastern Parkway on a torrid summer night, as if they were ritualistically repeating the flight from the Old Country. Where else in America is the communal sense of oppression so great as in Brooklyn – and with good reason?

For Fuchs Williamsburg is the place where the great drama of the flight from Europe is reenacted, not in the older generation, but in the younger generation born and bred on this side of "the golden door." The immigrants themselves soon became fixed in their ways: some in the posture of tragic misplacement, selling newspapers at a stand during the day and at night smoking the eternal cigarette of

125

nostalgia and self-pity next to the window overlooking the desolate street; others took to the new opportunities with alacrity and evolved in varying degrees of corruption into the new breed of alrightniks. In the characters of Old Hayman and Papravel, the father and uncle of Philip Hayman (*Summer in Williamsburg*), Fuchs gives us vivid instances of both types. However, for Philip, the sensitive youth of the *erziehungsroman*, identity comes hard. Unlike his father or his uncle, he must choose a way of life, and the choice between his father's way and his uncle's way proves no choice at all. Papravel is a *gonif*, in cahoots with murderers, and the moral tenacity of Old Hayman is bound up with his resigned acquiescence in the squalor of Williamsburg. For the older generations, the world war and the Russian revolution were destiny; however great the terrors of displacement, there was nonetheless the exhilarating prospect of a new country, a new life. For Philip there is neither destiny nor self-knowledge; his *erziehung* is a perennial entrapment and frustration. He is finally a mere witness to the violence and death which inhere in all things. *Summer in Williamsburg* begins with the suicide of Meyer Sussman, the prosperous and kindly butcher, and ends with the suicide of his wife and children and the death by fire of Philip's romantically unhappy friend Cohen. In between there are numerous episodes of violence: a vicious cat-fight between two women in a Catskill *kochalein,* a beating of a slut, a murder by a member of the Papravel organization among other episodes. Fuchs is not merely documenting the era of Murder Incorporated. The combustible atmosphere is the moral condition of his people, the bitter expression of their terrible frustrations. The novel ends with Papravel's celebration of America: "America is a wonderful country . . . where in the world could a Jew make such a man of himself as right here in America." Fuchs' touch is as sure as Flaubert's; he has encountered the American Dream with the perfect irony.

The American Dream makes for wonderful tragi-comedy in *Homage to Blenholt*. Max Balkan, a *schlemiel* with Horatio Alger fantasies of wealth and power, is the hero of Fuchs' "classical tragedy." As the dreamer, the transcendent figure, he is the victim of the universal scorn of his neighborhood. At the funeral of the crooked politician Blenholt, whom he admired, Balkan "heroically" intervenes in a riot "to do something" only to have himself and his spectacles trampled upon. ("Crazy, crazy," Balkan's choric mother constantly complains.) And in the final punishment for his presumption, he learns through a *peripety* (there is a moment of joyful ignorance) that his idea for bottling onion juice had long ago been realized on the market. Like Tamburlaine (his literary idol), Balkan must suffer for his hubris. Again the sense of entrapment is very strong. In perhaps the most brilliant episode in the novel, a youngster in Balkan's tenement avenges himself on an older boy who has persecuted him by conning him into taking a trip in the tenement dumbwaiter and then locking the doors on every floor. The boy's terror reverberates through the rest of the novel. In another episode, the scholarly and bespectacled Munves, one of Balkan's friends, walks past a group of cab drivers and suddenly and gratuitously becomes the object of their aggression. In these two episodes we have the dominant themes of Fuchs' novels: the sense of entrapment and destructive violence.

For Fuchs' heroes then there is no escape and finally not even striving. Max Balkan "dies" into the responsibilities of manhood. The reflections of Max's father on the "death" of his son bring the novel to its "classical" tragic close:

Much had gone out of Max, aspiration, hope, life. His son would grow old and ageing, die, but actually Max was dead already for now he would live for bread alone . . . And regretting the way of the world, Mr. Balkan realized that he had witnessed the exact point at which his son had changed from youth to resigned age. . . . It seemed to him that this death of youth was among the greatest tragedies in experience and that all the tears in América were not enough to bewail it.
But all the same the evening sun that day went down on time.

What then is left to Fuchs' characters but the compulsions of death and violence. And in *Low Company* more than in his other novels Fuchs' fascinated attention to the disintegrative process has, so to speak, its fulfillment. The suffering moral consciousness of the earlier novels has all but disappeared. At the end Herbert Lurie, a proprietor of a hat store, who had been trying to make his escape from the oppressions of life in Neptune Beach, becomes witness to the terrible sufferings of a man whom he has despised and experiences one of the rare moments of conscience in the novel. "He had known the people at Ann's in their lowness and had been repelled by them, but now it seemed to him that he understood how their evil appeared in their impoverished dingy lives, and further, how miserable their own evil rendered them. It was not enough to call them low and pass on.'' The moment is genuine and moving but finally irrelevant, for Fuchs' powerful imagination of the waste of life has made the gesture of compassion a kind of sentimentalism.

The plot and tempo of *Low Country* are created by the compulsions of its characters, each apparently ''striving'' to free himself from some burden, while actually enacting the self-destructive law of his nature: the gambler vainly and desperately trying to make the killing at the race-track that will redeem his losses and save him from the murderous clutches of his creditor-brothers-in-law; the pimp imprudently asserting his human dignity and rights to a new cartel of gangsters who want to take over and run him out of town; the luncheonette owner with all the self-pity and miserly instincts of the *petit-bourgeois* going surely to his death in trying to save himself. Fuchs was artistically never surer of himself than he was in *Low Company*. The characters are vivid and unmistakable in motive and deed, each one held in the vise of his own making. The entertainment of the novels comes from the marvelous casuistry of his characters which keeps them from seeing that their lives are moribund. Enclosed each in his particular attitude and idiom, they pretend to be fully alive while the whole ''community'' of which they are a part is suffering an agonizing death. In the cacophonous atmosphere Fuchs' voice is heard: the voice of pathos, the voice of a man hearing himself think.

In a preface to this reissue of his novels, Fuchs speaks of *Summer in Williamsburg* as having been written in a ''state of sheer terror.'' The terror arose from a struggle with form, both aesthetic and moral. ''I was trying to find a . . . direction and plan to the life I had witnessed in Williamsburg.'' The novel reflects the struggle in Philip Hayman's bewilderment and its diffuse variety, albeit richness, of scene and event. Fuchs in the other novels found his *aesthetic* direction and plan, but the moral confusion and terror that he speaks of pervade all his work. ''Years later, driving through Williamsburg, I found myself shaking all over.'' Williamsburg was a trauma from which he never recovered. In the same preface Fuchs ingenuously justifies his farewell to the novel and departure to Hollywood as the understandable desire of writers ''to be paid a livelihood for the work they do.'' The ingenuousness would be charming if it were not followed by the disingenuous claim that Hollywood writers too ''are engaged on the same problems that perplex writers everywhere. We too grapple with the daily mystery.'' Whatever the personal reasons for Fuchs' "sellout" may have been, one is tempted to see a parallel between Fuchs' career and the recent history of the Jewish community (or a portion of it) in America.

The generation of Philip Hayman and Max Balkan left Williamsburg, some for the medical profession in better sections of the city, some for business and the suburbs, others for the academy and still others with creative talent for the Village or Hollywood. This by no means exhausts all the cases, but the general movement is clear. The escape *was* made into the airier (and emptier) atmosphere of American life. Papravel's belief in America was vindicated. Whatever one thinks of the quality of "assimilated" American Jewish life (one hears the condemnations of "the attenuation of Jewish identity"), it is clear, as the novels of Fuchs testify, that the escape had to be made. And yet the terror of which Fuchs speaks (it is also Kazin's terror in *A Walker in the City*) is mixed with a sense of magic that comes from the possession of the memory of a rich past, of a world. Fuchs lived on 366 South Second Street and even now when he remembers the number it has a magic for him that makes him tremble. This, of course, is what we mean by the artist's sensitivity, but it is not every artist who is blessed with the right conditions for his sensitivity. For an artist, it seems to me, Fuchs' past was enviable; for all its squalor it had the brilliant efflorescence of a dying way of life.[1]

When Fuchs went to Hollywood, he disinherited himself from this world, much as did the doctors and the businessmen who moved into the better-heeled sections of town. Fortunately, Fuchs had already passed on his inheritance in three classic novels. It remains to be said in extenuation of the "sellout" that the impact of Williamsburg on Fuchs' imagination had the quality of trauma. What he lacked was an adequate sense of the future (a counter-image to his Williamsburg past) to overcome the confusion and despair that mark his work.

But, after all, Fuchs' psychic scars are the stigmata of his race . . .

---

[1] The moribund life in the American South too has its efflorescence and has produced a remarkable literature. Significantly, the most interesting contemporary American writers have been generally Jewish or Southern.

15 The demonic charm of Bashevis Singer

The reputation of Isaac Bashevis Singer is a recent phenomenon.[1] Until 1955 (the publication date of the translation of *Satan in Goray*, a novel written twenty years earlier) Singer was virtually unknown to the English reading public. His other novel, *The Family Moskat*, published in 1945 by Knopf brought him praise from the connoisseurs, but his reputation was still obscure. I doubt very much whether he was better known to Yiddish readers. The name Singer immediately evoked in the mind of the Yiddish reader his more famous brother, I. J. Singer, author of *Yoshe Kalb* and *The Brothers Ashkenazi*. Bashevis Singer's reputation rests not so much on *Satan in Goray*, an interesting though short-breathed work, but rather on the stories, which he has contributed to the *Jewish Daily Forward* since coming to the United States in 1935. A number of them were translated and finally collected in 1957 under the title *Gimpel the Fool and Other Stories*. Though he has been advertised as "the last of the great Yiddish masters," his reputation has been created not by the *Jewish Daily Forward*, but by the periodicals that have translated him, *Partisan Review, Commentary, Midstream*. The placing of Singer with the great Yiddish masters is unfortunate. That Singer is a genuinely gifted writer is beyond dispute, but his real affinities, it seems to me, are with writers outside the Yiddish tradition. Indeed, Singer is an alien figure in his own literature, in an impious relation to some of its most cherished assumptions. It is therefore an appropriate irony that Singer should achieve his reputation not in Yiddish, but in translation.

In spite of the folklore and the idiomatic flavor of Singer's stories, they seem to have little to do with the tales of other Yiddish writers. Yiddish literature, as I know it, has a strong ingredient of social

---

[1] This was one of the first extended discussions of Singer's work.

criticism. Its sentimentality serves a simple, though deeply felt, opposition between good and evil. The ambiguities of so much of Western literature are inevitably absent from a literature born of an acute sense of oppression. Yiddish literature moves between indignation and pathos; even its humor, which is rich and wonderful, is never free of either the indignant or the pathetic.

Nothing of this explains Bashevis Singer. To be sure, his people suffer from illness, pogroms, psychological difficulties, but Singer's imaginative response to the sufferings of his people is original. Nothing that I know in Yiddish literature anticipates him. The world as Singer sees it is demonic. The narrators of several of the stories are either imps or evil spirits and the kind of creature they are is wonderfully illustrated by the autobiography of the narrator of "From The Diary of One Not Born."

I, the author of these lines, was blessed by a good fortune that comes to only one in ten thousand: I was not born. My father, a yeshivah student, sinned as did Onan, and from his seed I was created – half spirit, half-demon, half air, half shade, horned like a buck and winged like a bat, with the mind of a scholar and the heart of a highwayman. I am and I am not. I whistle down chimneys and dance in the public bath; I overturn the pot of Sabbath food in a poor man's kitchen; I make a woman unclean when a husband returns from a trip. I like to play all kinds of pranks. . . .

The view that the world is demonic means psychologically that the human will is impotent, that there are forces not only in the external world, but in the human mind itself that have a life independent of the will. Unlike other writers who see the world as demonic, however, Singer is not a "psychological" writer. He gives us an actual fairyland. There are real unmetaphorical demons and imps who are often more alive than the people they victimize. This difference is of no casual significance, for the actual fairyland is a function of Singer's refusal to be "psychological": his refusal, that is, to become sympathetically involved with the "inner feelings" of his characters.

Though Singer's work doesn't belong to the same order of achievement as the work of Dostoevsky, it is instructive to compare them in respect to "the point of view" from which a story is told. In Dostoevsky, the action is narrated from the point of view of the victim, the sufferer. When in *Crime and Punishment* Svidrigailov, Raskolnikov's demon, presents himself to Raskolnikov our sympathies and apprehensions are immediately with Raskolnikov. The same is true in *The Brothers Karamazov* of the confrontation between Ivan and the diabolic gentleman who drives Ivan to insanity. Our sympathy is always with the victim. The ultimate effect of a Dostoevskian work, despite a genuine comic strain, is tragic. One might expect the same effect from Singer. His people too are victims of unspeakable suffering, but the effect of his stories is the opposite. Where Dostoevsky's world is terrible and tragic, Singer's world is perversely charming and comic. This strange situation arises from the fact that the action is seen from the point of view of the demon, not the victim. We are made to share with the demon the pleasure of the cruelty he inflicts upon his victims. How is it possible not to be charmed by the demon who narrates "From The Diary of One Not Born"? Every time our sympathy goes out to the victim the demon intervenes in his charming way and we see the suffering comically. In "The Mirror" Zirel's sufferings are forgotten in the pleasures of the devils:

This fun has been going on for a thousand years, but the black gang does not weary of it. Each devil does his bit; each imp makes his pun. They pull and tear and bite and pinch. For all that, the masculine devils aren't so bad; it's the females who really enjoy themselves, commanding: Skim boiling broth with bare hands! Plait braids without using the fingers! Wash the laundry without water! Catch fish in hot sand! Stay at home and walk the streets! Take a bath without getting wet! Make butter from stones! Break the cask without spilling the wine! And all the while the virtuous women in Paradise gossip; and the pious men sit on golden chairs, stuffing themselves with the meat of Leviathan, as they boast of their good deeds.

What is the point of Singer's comedy? Clearly Singer is a serious artist. His stories are not capricious acts of sadism. For reasons of his own, Singer deliberately turns things around, bewildering us out of our customary moral responses. In almost every one of his stories there is a deliberate confounding of conventional moral distinctions. The story that gives the title to the collection, "Gimpel the Fool" concerns a type that appears elsewhere in Yiddish literature. Gimpel, like Bontche Shweig, in Peretz's classic story, is the perennial victim, the silent sufferer, whose innocence is a constant temptation to the mischief makers and the pranksters. Unlike Bontche, however, whose suffering in a sense dehumanizes him, Gimpel attracts the sympathy of "good people." But the secret of Gimpel's charmed life is in the passivity, which makes him so accepting of the actions of the world. Gimpel has his own doctrine, a doctrine that has contradictory propositions. Near the end of the story he says:

I heard a great deal, many lies and falsehoods, but the longer I lived the more I understood that there were really no lies. Whatever doesn't really happen is dreamed at night. It happens to one if it doesn't happen to another, tomorrow if not today, or a century hence if not next year.

And shortly afterwards, he speaks of the world as "an entirely imaginary world, but it is once removed from the true world." [2] Is the imaginary real or the real imaginary? Gimpel seems to be making both assertions. The result is that we begin to wonder what reality is or how real reality is.

It is not simply that reality turns into illusion or illusion into reality. Nothing is that certain in Singer's view – reality, seen as illusion, becomes reality again. One cannot tell where the real begins and the illusory ends. In "Fire," a man plans to burn down his brother's house. When he arrives at the house, he finds it already burning. Impulsively he rushes into the house to save his brother and his brother's family. Not being able to explain the reason for his presence on the scene, he is accused of arson. Another writer might have turned this into an opportunity for complaining against the injustice of the world or "the irony of fate." Singer, however, remains true to form.

Until now I have told this story to no one. Who would have believed it? I even kept it a secret that I was from Janow. I always said that I was from Shebreshin. But now that I'm on my deathbed, why should I lie? What I've told is the truth, the whole truth. There's only one thing I don't understand and won't understand it until I'm in my grace: why did a fire have to break out in my brother's house on just that night? Some time ago it occurred to me that it was my anger that started that fire. What do you think?
"Anger won't make a house burn."
"I know. . . . Still there that expression, 'Burning anger!' "
"Oh, that's just a way of talking."
Well, when I saw that fire I forgot everything and rushed to save them. Without me they would have all been ashes. Now that I'm about to die, I want the truth known.

2 The world, as we know it, is a world of illusion, and though Singer makes ritualistic reference to the other world which lies beyond the world of illusion, he shows no active belief in it. He is not a religious writer. Rather he uses the metaphor of religious experience to enforce our sense of what the actual world is like. His preference for the characters who are orthodox and traditionalist belongs to his quietism, which I define later in the essay.

No judgment is made, no complaint registered. We are left in a sort of uncertainty between the two statements: "Anger won't make a house burn" and "Still there's that expression, 'burning anger!'"

Singer performs his subversive acts in so charming a way that we are hardly aware of what is going on. We are certain only that we have been charmed. And indeed, the charm is essential to Singer's purposes, for he is performing for us a kind of abracadabra by the magic of his art. But the question remains why? What is the purpose of his black magic?

Though Singer finds the world as other writers have found it: a miserable place, full of suffering, terror and impotence, he refuses to assume a moral attitude toward it. Singer has none of the moralist's impulse to reform the world. Mitya's and Ivan's question, "Why must the innocent suffer?" is rarely asked in Singer's stories; when it is asked as in "Joy" it is not intended to elicit the sympathetic moral response that Dostoevsky elicits from his readers. There is a sense of the injustice of the world running through Singer's stories, but it never converts the fundamental attitude which is one of complete acceptance of the world as it is.

Singer knows that the impulse to reform the world often leads to worse suffering. *Satan in Goray,* for instance, is concerned with the messianic expectation that has sustained the Jewish people through the ages. The novel is based on an actual historical episode. In the seventeenth century, the notorious Sabbatai Zevi, the false messiah arose, after the disastrous Chmelnicki pogrom, to promise the Polish Jews the kingdom of heaven only to bring them more misery. The apocalyptic dream of the dissolution of the old world is seen by Singer as a dangerous falsehood. The story "The Gentleman from Cracow" has the same moral. And Singer's long novel *The Family Moskat* ends in a way that signalizes Singer's characteristic response to the apocalyptic hope for a better world. The novel concludes with the Jewish experience of the Nazis in Warsaw:

Hertz Yanover burst into tears. He took out a yellow handkerchief and blew his nose. He stood before them confused, ashamed. "I've got no more strength," he said apologetically. He hesitated for a moment and then said, in Polish: "The Messiah will come soon."

Asa Heshel looked at him in astonishment. "What do you mean?"

"Death is the Messiah. That's the real truth."

The apocalyptic dream for Singer is invariably the dream of the charlatan visionary – the man who wills not to see and accept the truth.

Of course, truth and reality are questionable categories in Singer's world. Singer's suspicion about the messianic hope seems to have behind it Pontius Pilate's question to Jesus: "What is truth?" The truth that Singer holds onto amidst his confoundings and bafflements is that the truth cannot be known. The lie is in the claim to know it. And this is what the moral will claims – that it can discriminate between true and false, good and evil. The supreme delusion in Singer's world is that one can actually know life's mysteries. Those who suffer from this delusion are doomed to misery. Rabbi Benish's judgment of his community in *Satan in Goray* is Singer's own judgment: "They delved too deeply into things that were meant to be hidden, they drank too little from the clear waters of the holy teachings." The political implication of this is obvious. Singer is advocating quietism, a form of conservatism. He has no illusions about the political and moral nature of the world; there is in all his stories a sensitivity to its evil and corruption. But there is nothing that Singer distrusts more than the will and particularly the will in its best intentions. He prefers giving himself up to the world process to trying to make the world better. Those of us who have been brought up in the radical and liberal traditions find such a doctrine politically unpalatable. If we no longer believe in the automatic progress of the human race, we still believe in the power of the benevolent human will to make it better. Singer clearly does not share this view and, to do him justice, one must concede that the evidence of history is with him.

In *The Family Moskat* (a derivative blend of *War and Peace* and *Buddenbrooks*) the quietism is a sort of passive nihilism. The Nazi extermination of the Jews is regarded as the symbolic culmination of the death wish of the European Jewish community. The protagonist, Asa Heshel Bannet, has the chance to leave Warsaw but prefers to let things happen, i.e., to lose his life at the hands of the Nazis. His communist mistress, significantly a convert from Judaism, runs off, presumably to Russia, to fight the Nazis from there. For Singer's hero death indeed is the Messiah. The novel is "decadent" in its subject matter and its vision.

But the stories are unlike the novel. There fantasy dominates, an impish gleam dissipates the gloom. The stories are not "decadent." Despair often yields to joy. Rabbi Bainish in "Joy," who has suf-

fered like Job, curses God, giving his own version of the creation:
"In the beginning was the dung." But he dies murmuring, "one
should always be joyous." Men like Moshe Ber (in "The Old
Man") and Abba (in "The Little Shoemakers") have the wonderful
strength and appetites of the Biblical Patriarchs. The joyousness is
almost Hassidic, which is hardly surprising when one remembers
that many of his stories are about Hassidim. The joyousness, however, is uniquely defiant and diabolical. It never degenerates into
sentimentality.

Singer's elusive intention cannot be simply reduced to either politics or Hassidism. Singer experiences the world as an artist experiences the world – an object for wonder and contemplation. He
refuses to exercise his moral will, because, like Gimpel, he wants to
be in a passive relation to the world, permitting the life of the world
to flood in freely upon his imagination. For the artist, in one view of
him, is a fool, mindlessly acting out of inspiration, *breathing in* the
life of the world without understanding it. To compare once more
Gimpel with Bontche: the difference between them is in a way the
difference between Singer and what I would call the traditional Yiddish imagination. Bontche's passivity is his vice. When, after a life
of unrelieved suffering, all he asks for in heaven is a fresh roll and
butter, the angels hang their heads in shame. Through the shame of
the angels Peretz registers his disapproval. Bontche should have
asked for the riches of Paradise, which are rightfully his. Peretz's
story can be interpreted as a thinly veiled allegory on the absence of
political and social awareness in the lower classes of Polish Jewry.
Peretz's attitude is immediately moral – as one might expect from a
Yiddish writer. Singer refuses the moral attitude. He chooses rather
the passivity of the artist.

The passivity of the artist is, of course, deceptive. "The Mirror"
is intended as an image of the reflections of art: the art of the story
which is being told. But the demon who tells the story inhabits the
mirror which consequently does more than reflect. He converses
with the women who stand before him. Attracted to their beauty, he
flatters, cajoles and finally seduces them. Like the purposes of the
artist, the demon's purposes are mysterious even to himself. He
knows only that he possesses a power (beyond his will) to affect
whatever he gazes upon and that all he can do is to remain faithful to
that power. The ultimate questions he cannot answer.

Is there a God? Is He all merciful? Will Zirel ever find salvation? Or is
creation a snake primeval crawling with evil? How can I tell? I'm still only a

minor devil. Imps seldom get promoted. Meanwhile generations come and go, Zirel follows Zirel, in a myriad of reflections – a myriad of mirrors.

If "The Mirror" is an allegory of art (the imps we are told are fine punsters), of Singer's own art, then he has merely enforced his sense of life as an enigma, which even the artist cannot solve.

One result of Singer's doctrine is that it robs the world of its terrors. Even Gimpel, whose life has been extremely troubled, seems remote from his suffering as he tells his story. It is almost as if his demon were telling the story. Singer's comedy is finally the lyric celebration of what is: of truth and illusion, good and evil. It is the refusal to gainsay anything – the insistence that life is a mystery, that the claim to understand, to know life is an act of desecration. The demons are the bundles of energy that perform actions in the world, usually suffering actions. Singer is enchanted by the energy and nothing, not even the pain, will diminish his impulse to celebrate that energy. In his unique awareness of the absurdity of suffering, Singer has made comedy of a rare order.

Obviously then our response to Singer cannot be the simple affectionate response that we make to other Yiddish masters. In affirming the traditional and the conservative, he has performed the radical act of subverting our pieties. He unmasks the devil in his virtuous guises not so much to expose him as to appropriate him. And the final paradox of his stories is that his *moral* point is made by the unmasked devil.

16 The thirties revisited: Meyer Liben's *Justice Hunger and Nine Stories*

It happens in the best of fictions, the way it is written: "After three months," or "In the year that elapsed." I find such phrases very unpleasant; usually they mean to me that the author is avoiding the hard reality (he is not alone), the difficulty of everyday life, so he creates these vacuums of time, and then moves to some exciting moment, to something more *interesting*. It is what makes difficult the description of a working day or of a day-to-day married life. We see the peaks of existence, but all dramas, revelations, epiphanies – call them what you will – require a matrix of experience, of behavior, the necessitous and not always inspiring acts and dreams of the working day, the working marriage. No essence without *materia*, if I quote the philosophers correctly. . . .

–from "Justice Hunger"

Since Henry James one of the clichés of literary criticism is that the story-teller (whatever the size of the fiction) should *show*, not *tell*. Dramatize, dramatize, the Master insisted, and it has become a piety if not a fact of the fictional performance that the writer is devoted to the rendering of the action and feel of experience. When he begins to talk *about* his characters and their experience, he has somehow failed to do his job.

Meyer Liben always talks *about* his characters and tells *about* their experience: there is a minimum of showing, but something in his manner or voice inhibits the almost automatic impulse to pass judgment. The passage quoted above hardly seems promising: "*matrix* of experience, of behavior, the *necessitous* and not always inspiring acts and dreams of the working day, the working marriage": one hears the sociologist's cant in these words. The manner, if not always the matter, is the heavy-minded speech of the New York Jewish intellectual of the thirties. I assume that Liben knows how portentous his (or his heroes') style can be. In "A Note on Chivalry," the unnamed hero of the story throws a book at the head of a sociologist in conversation with a girl whom the hero admires, because he

138

wanted "to save her from the sociologists." Sociologists are "killers of [the] language," smotherers of "the new-born truth and beauty (for truth and beauty are always new-born)," doing their work "by an apparatus, an effluvium, gobbledegook, words that have lost all relation to the object, to language itself." Curiously, the language of accusation is somewhat infected by the idiom of the "killers." Liben knows this. He takes the risk of presenting his hero without irony – that is, of incurring the charge of heavy-mindedness himself, because (I assume) that for all its squalor of speech and experience Liben wants to be *inside* that mind, discovering its values as well as its failures. The stories are invariably told in the first person, and in one story which begins in the third person ("The Business of Poetry"), Liben can't sustain the "fiction" and the narrator admits "I am the Ned of whom I have been talking about."

The heaviness of the voice, the ponderosities of vocabulary, the pedantic wit ("and so he held us back, making us feel like the wedding guests in the poem [though the Mariner stopped one of three]") at first embarrasses us with the suspicion that perhaps this isn't fiction at all, but a kind of confession. Moreover, the peculiar intimacy with the heroes (really an identification with the mind of the past, the mind of the New York Jewish intellectual of the thirties) creates the impression of work already dated. Arguments about the respective merits of Stalin and Trotsky, the purges, the possibility of Socialism in one country are presented without the modification of contemporary sensibility as if the contemporary perspective would destroy the integrity of the past.

We discussed the film, a powerful movie set in far-off Mongolia describing the rapacity and cruelty of Western imperialism and ending on a note of colonial struggle, the hero refusing to be used by his arch-enemies and leading his people against these enemies. The screen was filled with men speeding on horses, men with clenched fists, determined to undo, once and for all, these ancient wrongs and oppressions and to win a final freedom. "What freedom?" I asked (without denying the power of the film), and we got into a discussion of what was then called the "nationalities question."

The voice and accent are atavistic: the past is relived, not remembered, the "then" being superfluous.

Liben wants that past to renew its claims without interference from contemporary prejudices, so that we can discover the struggling humanity behind the political clichés and philosophical ponderosities. It is a mark of Liben's integrity that he makes no effort to conceal the platitudes of his heroes, but under his influence we come to hear them not as intellectual obscenities, not simply as symptoms of squalor, but also of aspiration. The platitudes become incompetent, sometimes comic, efforts to be humane and tender and loving.

Toward the end of "Justice Hunger," the short novel that gives the book its title, the hero takes a walk in the city. The title of the chapter, characteristically, is an intellectual tag, this one a quotation from Thoreau: "To affect the quality of the day, that is the highest of arts."

> The city lived around me; I breathed its grime, smelled its odors compounded of monoxide, industrial fumes, and whatever nature had to contribute, tasted my tongue, touched here and there a wall, a railing, a window protecting merchandise against marauders, and saw the lovely mobility of our people, thinking of my friend who had gone south and felt that he was moving so *fast* down there. The faithful uses of objectivity, the strong sense of the reporter absorbing (*Queen of the Senses, renew me*) the life around.

The indignation is almost the canned product of the social criticism of the past two centuries: the hatred of the industrial revolution – "monoxide, industrial fumes," the *abstract* loathing of the property-minded bourgeois – "merchandise against marauders"; and yet we are made to hesitate by that unexpected phrase "the lovely mobility of our people" and the obscure reminder of the friend "who had gone south and felt that he was moving so *fast* down there." The hesitation prepares us for the extraordinary passage that follows:

> What was it that St. Augustine said about the world? That it was a place where the dying succeed the dead; why not where the living succeed the lifeless? But this was a shallow optimism, what we call, in the political sphere, a *vulgar* optimism. Look there! a strange sight. Two boys are teaching a blind boy how to catch a ball. He has the awkward stance of the blind – his feet are spread, his arms outstretched, anxiously, hopefully awaiting the arrival of the ball. One lad throws the ball, the other stands close against his body. He smiles the agonized smile of the blind. "Great! Great!" and the youth takes the ball from the blind boy and tosses it to his companion, who prepares again for the throw; again the blind boy adopts his curious awkward stance, awaits the ball with all that pathetic eagerness. Poor blind child, dear suffering boy, dumbly doomed. If you had to choose between blindness, deafness and dumbness (for who is without sense of taste or smell?), which would you choose?

The scene or rather the note struck by the scene is rarely heard in contemporary fiction: the note of compassion, of fraternal embrace.

We don't often hear this note, because the contemporary imagination is dedicated to the egoistic emotions and to the aesthetic of despair.

The virtues of the heart that Liben cherishes have a corresponding moral intelligence. Nothing simply happens in the stories: the mind anticipates events, worries them while they occur, dissects them afterwards. In "A Note on Chivalry," the hero is attracted to a girl at a party: "we merely looked at one another . . . a manner that bespoke the possibility, circumstances allowing, that we might get into an involvement more personal than the next, though not necessarily very personal." But circumstances don't allow it, because his sense of responsibility to his fiancée chills his imagination of the possibility of being "*carried away . . .* down some turbulent river, into some unknown sea" with this young woman. "I've only known her twenty minutes, I thought, and here I was engaged to my childhood sweetheart (I meant by that thought that I knew my childhood sweetheart ever so much longer). I was pleased with this truly responsible thought." He would as soon be unfaithful to his childhood sweetheart as betray his comrades.

It is not simple instinct that keeps him faithful but a continuous and anxious reflection about possibilities. Recollecting a discussion about the Soviet Union, the hero of "Justice Hunger" remarks truthfully, if somewhat ponderously: "It was a typical discussion of the times, not in itself convincing but influential nevertheless, because people changed their views, slowly, under the impress of hundreds of such discussions, for most of us were willing to learn, prepared to change our views, to listen, to compare, to allow the play of the critical reason, to break up the emotional investment." Liben's heroes are conscientious men, filled with a painful sense of responsibility, tediously worrying themselves sick about doing right – which in part accounts for the peculiarly inhibited narrative style of the stories. By the standards of our own time they are insufferably square. They do not drink, they make love behind the scenes (only tender glances and warm embraces are visible), their one obsession is the moral life: doing right by the group, by their families, friends and sweethearts and by themselves. It is customary to dismiss the intellectual gestures of the radicals of the thirties as merely ideological. And certainly there is much "intellectual" talk in Liben's stories that is ritualistic rather than genuinely reflective. But by contrast with the cult of irrationality in a good deal of the new radicalism, how thoughtful and humane the oldtime radicals seem to be.

Whatever claims are made for them, however, they are fallen creatures – to use the metaphor of another tradition – uncertain in their affections, confused in their minds. They touch us, entertain us, even provoke our admiration on occasion, but they are unheroic men incongruously dedicated to the revolutionary imagination – that is, to an imagination beyond their capacities. Liben has rendered their world – or a portion of it – with imagination and tenderness, and without sentimentality.

17 Bernard Malamud's
A New Life

In a recent issue of *Commentary,* Philip Roth delivers a long complaint against "the American reality" from the point of view of the
writer. "The American writer in the middle of the 20th century has
his hands full in trying to understand, and then describe, and then
make *credible* much of the American reality." Roth is understandably appalled by the extravagance of a culture that has produced
Charles Van Doren, Roy Cohn, David Shine, Sherman Adams, Bernard Goldfine and Dwight David Eisenhower. He speaks ironically
of the American reality as "a kind of embarrassment to one's own
meager imagination," and what he means, I suppose, is that the
writer cannot expect from his world a center or poise that will make
it possible for him to see his world whole. The point Roth is making
has been made in a somewhat different form by Mary McCarthy in
an article in which she examines the failure of the modern novelist to
contain a whole society in his imagination.[1] The achievement of a
Balzac or a Tolstoy no longer seems possible. The self-enclosed
discreteness of modern experiences has broken the chain of being
which enabled the nineteenth century novelist to see the whole world
(or nation) in the individual destiny. So that no contemporary writer
seems able to produce, for instance, the resonance of the Tolstoyan
sentence: "The previous history of Ivan Ilych was the simplest, the
most ordinary and therefore the most terrible."

Bernard Malamud is an interesting case in point, for his novels
and stories are especially moving in the modest and natural way in
which they apparently open out from the local and temporal fact into
the larger spaces of myth and history. Yet despite the reverberations
and resonances of Malamud's fiction, one is still puzzled by what
they signify. Has Malamud been able to find in the baseball player

---

[1] Mary McCarthy, "The Fact in Fiction," *Partisan Review,* XVII (Summer, 1960),
pp. 438–458.

143

(*The Natural*) or the Jewish grocer (*The Assistant*) or the assorted characters that inhabit his short stories (see *The Magic Barrel and other stories*) successful instances of the American (let alone the human) destiny in its latest stage? Are the resonances of his fiction signs that Malamud has done what none of his contemporaries has been able to do: to sustain authentically in the immediate fact the imaginative power for those larger spaces of myth and history? Or are those resonances simply the product of extraordinary gifts of rhetoric and fantasy? *A New Life,* perhaps more than his earlier work, provokes these questions.

The hero of Malamud's new novel is Seymour Levin, who arrives in the mythical western town of Marathon, Cascadia, with suitcase and valise, an immigrant from an alcoholic life in New York City. With his wonderful ear for the Yiddish idiom, Malamud recalls the Yiddish immigrant tale. "Bearded, fatigued, lonely, Levin set down a valise and suitcase and looked around in a strange land for welcome." Levin is greeted at the station by Gerald Gilley, Director of Freshman Composition at Cascadia College where Levin will teach as an instructor in English, and Gilley's wife. Cascadia College, a science and technology school (much to Levin's dismay) is an obvious opportunity for the kind of satire on the academy that has become fashionable in recent years.

The main academic drama is a rivalry for departmental chairmanship between C. D. Fabrikant, a somewhat dryasdust scholar with integrity, and Gilley, the amiable mediocrity, whose concern with the pleasure of the State Legislature far exceeds his concern with literature. The retiring chairman, Professor Fairchild, whose textbook *Elements of Grammar* is in its thirteenth edition, is one of those oppressive presences in American academic life, friendly to mediocrity and hostile to intellect, and yet redeemed by the complex ironic sympathy in which Malamud envelops him. His passion for grammar genuine, Professor Fairchild utters his dying words in Levin's arms, "the mysteries of the infinitive." Levin, one of the few friends of intellect at Cascadia, discovers what is by now merely a painful truism, that the life of the academy has little to do with either intellect or moral courage. The Fairchilds, the Gilleys, the Bullocks (George Bullock, a handsome athletic type has special sympathy for athletes, and together with the coaches steers his boys through gut-courses): they constitute the provincial academy.

Malamud is knowledgeable about American college life. He has caught perfectly the traditional speech of the departmental chairman (or the College President) at the beginning of the term, welcoming a new faculty member whom he hopes will "enrich us from his experience in the East," or a returning faculty member who has completed his dissertation on *Piers Plowman*. ("The Ph.D. is our *conditio sine qua non*, and everyone who has not acquired the degree should be working for it, no matter how rigorous the course.") Malamud knows that a new instructor is likely to have an affair with one of his students and that the chances are good that he will have an affair with one of the faculty wives. He knows too that courage and genuineness are as rare in the academy as elsewhere in the world.

The ultimate effect of Malamud's scenes of academic life, however, is neither satire nor sociology. The provincial academy, set in nature, the latest version of America's "manifest destiny," becomes the arena for a kind of Tolstoyan exploration of LIFE and the pursuit of happiness. It is certainly no accident that the hero's name is Levin, for like his namesake in *Anna Karenina,* he demands nothing less than the meaning of life and the full measure of human happiness. Clumsy in the social world (in his adventures and responses he resembles the Yiddish *schlemiel*), Malamud's Levin, like Tolstoy's, is a worshipper of nature.

The sight of the expectant earth raised a hunger in Levin's throat. He yearned for the return of spring, a terrifying habit he strongly resisted: the season was not yet officially autumn. He was now dead set against the destruction of unlived time. As he walked, he enjoyed surprises of landscape: the variety of green, yellow, brown and black fields, compositions with distant trees, the poetry of perspective.

Like that of the elegy, the rhythm of *A New Life* is determined by the seasonal changes. And in "the open forest," Levin finds his fulfillment with Pauline Gilley, the wife of the Director of Freshman Composition. Malamud has done a rare thing in modern literature: he has written a pastoral romance. His hero and heroine live in an earlier time of romantic hope, free of the corrosive modern cynicism about love. Neither the pain nor the absurdity can dim the glow of their expectation of renewal. In order to protect his romantic imagination from the eye of satire, Malamud has rejected the realistic mode. The fantastic complication of plot and event, the charmingly whimsical lyricism of style sustain the atmosphere of romance. Counterpointed to Fairchild's sterile musings on "the mysteries of the infinitive" are the conjugations of Levin and Pauline.

> He hung his trousers over the branch of a fir. When he knelt she received him with outstretched arms, gently smoothed his beard, then embraced with passion as she fixed her rhythm to his.
> He was throughout conscious of the marvel of it – in the open forest, nothing less, what triumph!

The little academic drama is complicated by Levin's affair with Pauline and by a strange, poignant memory which all the characters share of an irrepressibly rebellious Leo Duffy, Levin's predecessor, who was fired and subsequently committed suicide. Duffy is the specter from the East. Radical and explosive, he exemplifies the virtues of an earlier time: intellect, courage, erotic fulfillment. (And like Frank Alpine, the "assistant" of the earlier novel, Duffy is the kind of *goy* that serves Malamud's demonstration that all men are Jews.) Even after his death, his memory threatens the philistine repose of Cascadia's English faculty. The test of a character is his attitude toward Duffy, and most of the people in the novel fail the test. Fabrikant, who supported Duffy for a while, proves a last minute failure. Pauline, it turns out, was Duffy's soul-mate and she relives her love for Duffy in her affair with Levin. Levin, as expected, reenacts Duffy's career, is fired, but leaves his Arcadia with Pauline to renew his *Vita Nuova*.

What significance are we to find in the little academic drama? If Duffy is the ghost to Levin's Hamlet, then it is clear that the bitter and tormented past that Levin is trying to forget must be bravely remembered and faced. Early in the novel, Levin tells Fabrikant that he has left New York, "seeking, you might say, my manifest destiny." Fabrikant replies:

> This corner of the country was come upon by explorers searching for the mythical Northwest Passage, and it was opened by traders and trappers in their canoes trying to find the Great River of the West, the second Mississippi they had heard of. Then the settlers came, fighting the Indians, clearing the land, and building their homes out of their guts and bone. . . . "There were giants in those days." Their descendants are playing a defensive game. Their great fear is that tomorrow will be different from today. I've never seen so many pygmies in my life.

The novel opens out from time to time to this kind of vision of the American past. The past is at once irony and possibility, for if the present appears filled with "so many pygmies" in the ironic light of the past, there is nevertheless the reminder of the possibility of renewal to anyone with the capacity and courage to remember.

The Utopian impulse in *A New Life* is very strong, and it accounts for the pastoral romance, the extravagances of whimsy and plot. And how else could Malamud have saved the immediate fact from triviality and inconsequence, if he had not abandoned the realistic mode? The squalor of contemporary fact does come through when at moments Malamud adopts the naturalistic manner (e.g., Levin's introduction to the Gilley household), and we can then perceive graphically the plight of the contemporary novelist. It is as if the novelist has to work *against* reality, to perform through fantasy, pastoral dream and mythic recreation of the past the acts of faith that make the celebration of life still possible. (Even in *The Assistant* in which the miserably gray life of the Jewish grocer is so *brilliantly* depicted, Malamud needs all the fantasy he can muster to elicit significance, and, indeed, one wonders whether for all his inventiveness, he has succeeded in realizing the full significance of his story. His stories sometimes fail to yield even when his fantasy works overtime as in "Lady of the Lake.") And it is for this reason that the novelist who chooses the mode of celebration and affirmation does not finally convince, for he expects us, despite the overwhelming presence of the actual, to believe in his fantasy. When Levin and Pauline drive off to their happiness, we read in disbelief. Having gazed at the immediate fact, Malamud, unlike the nineteenth century novelist, has found the absurd and the trivial, and has tried to redeem the fact through the *grace* of his art. For a moment we are enchanted by the gossamer loveliness of Malamud's dream, but when the actual world comes to us again, the dream becomes a kind of irony in our lives.

18 Ralph Ellison's
Shadow and Act

Collections of fugitive pieces suffer inevitably from certain disabilities: discontinuity, occasions that no longer interest, a journalistic thinness which only extensive revision can redeem, a revision that would alter the character of the enterprise. Only an interesting mind or presence justifies such a collection. Without the armor of scholarship (he must, after all, meet his deadlines), the writer has only his intelligence, his character and his wits to fall back on. He reveals himself perhaps more fully than on other occasions, and very few survive the test.

Ralph Ellison is among the few. He is a gifted man, but that is not the principal reason for whatever success these essays have. Actually, they are sometimes infelicitous, occasionally out of control: there is dross enough for the reviewer looking for trouble. The success of the essays consists in their revelation of an admirable man. Without the passion for self-dramatization that seems nowadays to be a necessary condition for ''making it'' on the literary scene, Ellison is purely devoted to the only task that justifies egotism, the task of understanding himself and his world in the hope that he will discover something of universal significance. Of another kind of egotism, Ellison has this to say: ''There is an American Negro tradition which teaches one to deflect racial provocation and to master and contain pain. It is a tradition which abhors as obscene any trading on one's anguish for gain or sympathy.''

The theme of self-exploration is immediately sounded in the book and persists to the end. Ellison tells us of his first ambition to be a musician, of his love of reading. Writing was at first a natural extension of his reading. After his meeting with Richard Wright, the possibility of a career as a writer became real, and Ellison began to make his extraordinary investment in the discipline of the novel. The references to *discipline* and *technique* are constant in the book, and one might object that the statements rarely go beyond an insistence on their importance. But this is a quibbling objection. What does emerge is a clear sense of the *morality* of such discipline. Whatever those procedures may be (and they can be inferred from Ellison's fiction), we are made to feel that in becoming an artist Ellison became a man, that his integrity as a human being, his capacity for experience was inextricably bound up in his art. There is a moving passage in an essay in which he defends himself against certain criticisms by Irving Howe that indicates vividly the continuity in Ellison's imagination between art and experience:

Do you still ask why Hemingway was more important to me than Wright? Not because he was white, or more "accepted." But because he appreciated the things of this earth which I love and which Wright was too driven or deprived or inexperienced to know: weather, guns, dogs, horses, love *and* hate and impossible circumstances which to the courageous and dedicated could be turned into benefits and victories. Because he wrote with such precision about the processes and techniques of daily living that I could keep myself and my brother alive during the 1937 Recession by following his descriptions of wing-shooting; because he knew the difference between politics and art and something of their true relationship for the writer. Because all that he wrote – and this is very important – was imbued with a spirit beyond the tragic with which I could feel at home, for it was very close to the feeling of blues, which are, perhaps, as close as Americans can come to expressing the spirit of tragedy.

The passage is important to the argument, because Howe has in effect made Ellison into a species of aesthete, a man more devoted to his art than to the life of the people. In a long and somewhat tortuous essay, Ellison tries to show that the dichotomy is false, that in serving his art, he also is serving his people. Moreover, he has no alternative but to be true to his *daemon*. This is not exactly Ellison's formulation of the issue, but it seems to me the main issue in reading these essays. It is certainly a *daemon* that keeps Ellison at it for so long in his rebuttal of Howe. There is a disproportion between Howe's criticism and Ellison's defense that invites Howe's contention that Ellison is out of control. The fact is that Ellison has been wounded, and in responding he reveals one of his deepest concerns. (Howe and his criticism at a certain point become irrelevant.) "I could escape the reduction imposed by unjust laws and customs, but not that imposed by ideas which defined me as no more than the *sum* of those laws and customs." He has been wounded by an idea that attempts to *define* him, to control him. Elsewhere, Ellison speaks of ideas (or stereotypes) as estranging one from one's reality. The essay on Howe, for all its polemical faults, is superb testimony to the power of ideas, particularly their power to hurt. Ellison wants his mystery, his human elusiveness respected. He is a Negro from Oklahoma, who now lives in the North, with experiences both characteristic of his people and peculiar to him, but there is also an irreducible human essence, an *invisibility* that each man possesses that is sacrosanct, the province of religion and art. And here Ellison's egotism touches on (more than touches, identifies) with something of universal significance.

Ellison's main quarrel with the American reality derives from its inability to recognize the humanity of the Negro. For Ellison humanity is a single community, and a denial of any part of it mutilates the entire community. One of Ellison's main tasks is to bear witness to the humanity of the Negro, to bring forward to the American consciousness its most taboo subject. In an essay on Twentieth Century Fiction, Ellison argues that the taboo has been a blight on American literature since Twain. It has enervated the artistic and moral character of our literature: "The artist is no freer than the society in which he lives, and in the United States the writers who stereotype or ignore the Negro and other minorities in the final analysis stereotype and distort their own humanity." (Only Faulkner is excepted from this general condemnation.) This is a debatable dictum and so is the non-sequitur that "the non-concern with ideas" in contemporary American literature stems from this failure to recognize the humanity of the Negro. But Ellison's point is more interesting than his polemical failures. For he is suggesting the true ambiguity of the Negro writer in America: he must give testimony to the special experience of the Negro, its richness and creativity as well as its poverty, illiteracy and violence, and he must at the same time cherish the irreducible essence that makes his fraternity with other men.

In essays on Mahalia Jackson, Charley Parker, Jimmy Rushing, Charley Christian and others, Ellison finds the lyric, tragic-comic confrontation with life that informs his own artistic vision. His intimacy with jazz and the blues is a musician's intimacy, and it gives authority to his argument against LeRoi Jones and others who would assimilate the music to the ideological purposes of the Freedom Movement. The process of distortion and reduction is not confined to one's enemies.

One's first thought is that Ellison is merely rehearsing the complaints of revisionist liberalism: that life is richer than any ideological formulation of it, more complex and more ambiguous than any militant view of it, ideology is a form of hubris, a violation of the sacred mysteries, etc. Ellison unquestionably has a good deal in common with revisionist liberalism, but it is misleading to reduce him to this position. The fact is that Ellison includes essays from a time when he felt the attractions of militancy. A piece on Negro working class sociology (written for *The New Masses*) and a critique of Gunnar Myrdal's *An American Dilemma* (which *concludes* the collection) suggest that Ellison is not simply participating in the rhythms of the *zeitgeist*. If these pieces are representative of his whole career. Ellison has been throughout committed to the liberation of America (Negro and white), not merely from the oppression of its laws, but also from false and dehumanizing ideas, from whatever quarter they may come. One may dissent from Ellison's particular views, but it is hard to deny the force and integrity of this commitment.

This commitment is of unmistakable *social* value, for if it states that the strident ideological stance is false to both art and life, it also implies that when the artist is true to his art (and when his art aspires to universality) prophecy and art become one. Ellison is not contradicting himself when, in an interview, he denies the distinction between "a purely literary work" and a work in the "tradition of social protest":

I recognize no dichotomy between art and protest. Dostoievsky's *Notes from the Underground* is, among other things, a protest against the limitations of nineteenth-century rationalism; *Don Quixote, Man's Fate, Oedipus Rex, The Trial* – all these embody protest, even against the limitation of human life itself. If social protest is antithetical to art, what then shall we make of Goya, Dickens and Twain? One hears a lot of complaints about the so-called "protest novel," especially when written by Negroes; but it seems to me that the critics could more accurately complain about their lack of craftsmanship and their provincialism.

One gathers from passages elsewhere in the collection a Kenneth Burkean idea of art as symbolic action, an acting upon the reader to create or convert his moral consciousness. The key term remains *discipline* or *technique,* for in that term Ellison finds the aesthetic counterpart to the dialectic between freedom and necessity, which is the history of both society and the individual. The process of mastering experience through form is partly a process of realizing one's limitations, personal and cultural. It is also the discovery (and the knowledge of preserving) the free mysterious element in life, the source of human freedom and transcendence. In the life of Wright, the songs of the blues and jazz people, Ellison finds evidence for the dialectic.

The essays provoke admiration more for their intention than their realization. One misses a fuller testimony to the richness and creativity of the experience that Ellison means to celebrate. The essays on the blues and jazz people are fine for that reason. On the singing of Jimmy Rushing:

> . . . across, the dark blocks lined with locust trees, through the night throbbing with the natural aural imagery of the blues, with high-balling trains, departing bells, lonesome guitar chords shimmering up from a shack in the alley – it was easy to imagine the voice as setting the pattern to which the instruments of the Blue Devils Orchestra and all the random sounds of night arose, affirming, as it were, some ideal native to the time and to the land.

On the art of Mahalia Jackson:

> It is an art which depends upon the employment of the full expressive resources of the human voice – from the rough growls employed by blues singers, the intermediate sounds, the half-cry, half-recitative, which are common to Eastern music; the shouts and hollers of American folk cries; the rough-edged tones and broad vibratos, the high, shrill and grating tones which rasp one's ears like the agonized flourishes of flamenco, to the gut tones, which remind us of where the jazz trombone found its human source.

And Ellison's own memories help supply some of the necessary texture. But elsewhere the abstractions are cumbersome or, to change the metaphor, insufficiently rooted in concrete detail. Sometimes a hyper-seriousness becomes a weight, a source of infelicities: "As I see it, it is through the process of making artistic forms – plays, poems, novels – out of one's experience that one becomes a writer, and it is through this process, this struggle, that the writer helps give meaning to the experience of the group."

The infelicities, however, are a fair price for the rewards of Ellison's self-explorations. It would be a mark of obtuseness in the reader not to perceive the moral grace that controls these essays.

19 William Styron's *The Confessions of Nat Turner*

We are within the consciousness of Nat Turner as the events of his life, the slave system of the ante-bellum south and the extraordinary rebellion that he led are narrated and described. But what does it mean to say that we are inside Nat Turner's consciousness? And who is Nat Turner anyway? William Styron has been praised for his capacity to get inside a black man's consciousness. But the black man is Styron's own creation. Styron himself tells us in a prefatory note that "there is little knowledge in regard to Nat," and that he has allowed himself "the utmost freedom of imagination in reconstructing events." It is highly doubtful that Styron's Nat has very much to do with the historical Nat Turner, who according to Styron, led the only effective revolt before the Civil War. Herbert Aptheker, who has written an historical account of the events, is appalled by the liberties Styron has taken. (He also claims that there were other effective revolts.) For him Styron's "freedom of imagination" amounts to a monstrous historical distortion. I do not want to enter into the tangled controversy about Styron's historical accuracy, nor into the related question of the novelist's obligation to historical fact in his "meditation on history," but the praise for Styron's empathy with the Negro consciousness, it seems to me, has been unconsidered. It has deflected critical discussion from the interesting problematic character of the book.

Toward the end of the novel, Nat and his followers in mid-rebellion approach the plantation of Richard Whitehead. Suddenly we are inside – no, Nat is inside, Whitehead's mind, imagining his white reaction to the black apocalypse descending upon him:

Twenty Negroes and more in a jagged line – all mounted, light glistening from ax and gun and sword – who burst from the distant woods in a cloud of dust which, obscuring us at the same time that it revealed our relentless purpose and design, must have appeared to him borne from the hellish bowels of the earth: the sight was surely a re-enactment of all the fears and

153

visions of black devils and heathen hordes that had ever imperiled his Methodist sanctity. Yet he too, like Travis, like all the others lulled by a history which had never known our kind before, was doubtless touched with disbelief at the same time that a portion of his mind grappled with the horror – and who knows but whether this was the reason that he stood rooted to the ground like a cotton plant, his bland divine's sun-pink face uptilted to the sky in vague bewilderment as we drew closer, perhaps hoping that this demonic apparition or vision or whatever, the result of undigested bad bacon or troubled sleep or August heat or all three, would go away. (410–411)

The issue here is not whether Nat had the sophistication for this kind of empathic entry into the white consciousness: it is rather whether a leader of a rebellion, particularly at the moment of its occurrence, would have the luxury for entering the thoughts and sentiments of his enemy. It is most unlikely that at the moment that Turner was performing his mission in full guiltless conviction that he was enacting the will of God, that he would see himself (through the mind of Richard Whitehead) in the imagery of black devils and heathen hordes. This passage revealed to me what I dimly suspected throughout: Nat Turner, in part at least, is a projection of Styron's own consciousness of the racial tragedy of our country. The passage is written out of the white man's apocalyptic fears.

Whether or not Styron has remained faithful to the historical facts, his novel is informed with the atmosphere and attitudes of the contemporary racial situation. One cannot, for instance, avoid the analogies between the slave revolt and contemporary black militancy. But the book simply will not sustain an allegorical reading: It does not have the unequivocal morality of allegory.

Nat Turner, as Styron conceives him, is in the tradition of the apocalyptic chiliasm that Norman Cohn describes in *The Pursuit of the Millennium*. The messianic figures whom Cohn describes appeared in the medieval periods of economic misery, possessed of a conviction that they were instruments of God's wrath. They destroyed in order to clear the path for the imminent entry of the graced into paradise. (Sabbatai Zevi is a Jewish analogue to the Christian Chiliasts.) These messianic characters (and Nat Turner is clearly one) were capable of monstrous acts. But Styron's treatment of Nat Turner, with its sympathy for the motives and aspirations of the slaves as well as its understanding of the objective historical circumstances of slavery, avoids the condemnation that characterizes Cohn's view of the medieval chiliasts. Three-quarters of the novel are given over to a depiction of the degradation of the slave system: the rebellion with all its monstrous acts is more judgment of the slave system than gratuitous horror. There are, to be sure, difficulties: the best of the white slave owners is cruelly murdered in Nat's passion for a uniform justice for all white men. The cruelest of the slave-owners escapes death, and a lovely girl, who established something like a human bond with Nat before the rebellion, is murdered by Nat himself out of mixed motives: the need to prove to his doubting followers that he can kill and a sado-erotic urge that miraculously leads to the recognition that he has loved the girl. The murder of Margaret Whitehead is Nat's only regret, and to the intelligent white man who takes Nat's confession he has no excuse for the enormities committed. Nat simply reiterates that he feels no guilt, but without defending himself. (*"Mr. Gray,"* Nat finds himself wanting, but curiously unable to say, *"what else could you expect from mostly young men deaf, dumb, blind, crippled, shackled and hamstrung."* Italicized by Styron because unsaid.) There is some temptation to see Styron's presentation as an indictment of Nat Turner's chiliasm and by implication the apocalyptic fantasies of Stokeley Carmichael, Rap Brown and the other black nationalists.

I do not think that Styron intends to make such an indictment, however. To be sure, the effect of the full revelation of motive and fantasy makes the kind of ideological endorsement Aptheker gives to the revolt impossible. No matter how gifted and spiritually inclined Nat Turner may have been, he was bound to have been motivated by feelings (among others) of resentment, of hatred, and perhaps of sado-erotic passion toward his white enemy. To be the disinterested agent of justice which Marxian apologetics often tries to make the revolutionary out to be would have violated the human truth of all reactions against injustice. In a system that breeds injustice, it is too much to expect that its victims be free of unjust motives. Nietzsche casts an excessively harsh light on the motives of the non-possessor, but he is illuminating when he declares that "The unjust disposition lurks also in the souls of non-possessors. They are not better than the possessors and have no moral prerogative; for at one time or another their ancestors have been possessors." Yet Nietzsche, interestingly enough, goes on to espouse the cause of social justice.

The effect of the enormities committed by Turner is mitigated by the imposing counterweight of the slave system, which is the main burden of the novel. Moreover, Nat Turner's consciousness has the elevation and poetry of the consciousness of the novelist himself: even at his most terrible he is seen in an exalted light. The atmosphere of violence which Nat inhabits in the last hundred pages has a transfiguring rather than degrading effect. (The monster is Nat's maniacal rival, Will.)

Indeed, until the last one hundred pages the novel is like a vast inert landscape, often brilliantly described, but immobilized, as it were, by the very institution of slavery. Suddenly the novel erupts into a kind of apocalyptic splendor, in which monstrosities and fulfillments seem inextricably connected. Two episodes in the part dealing with the rebellion itself illustrate the unpredictable "morality" of the novel. The first episode is Nat's attempted murder of his master (after failing, his insane rival Will succeeds), in which for the first time he looks into the latter's eyes, which are "acquainted with hard toil . . . and I felt that I knew him at last. . . . Whatever else he was, he was a man." In the death of his master, Nat Turner discovers his master's humanity. This is no judgment of the killing, for the killing has made the discovery possible. The other episode is the only death for which Nat Turner is directly responsible: that of the lovely Margaret Whitehead. There is an earlier episode of a trip that Nat and Margaret make in which Nat is sexually aroused by her loveliness and her kindness to him. But Nat represses the sexual impulse, the dutiful "action" of the slave. Now, confronted by her during the rebellion and wanting her with the intensity of the earlier episode, Nat unsheathes his sword and she awaits him, "bare arms still outthrust as if to welcome someone beloved and long-unseen." The killing of Margaret Whitehead is at the same time the emancipation of his male self from the mutilating oppressions and repressions of slavery.

I am almost suggesting that the "morality" of the novel is with Nat's chiliasm, a morality that would seem to receive sanction from the obsession with violence which characterizes so much American literature. With his master Faulkner, Styron shares the imaginative belief that violence liberates the self to new possibilities of experience. But the book issues not in "morality," but in tragic contemplation (or meditation, to use Styron's word). We observe the career of Nat Turner's passion with the emotions of pity, terror, admiration. We are beyond the realm of moral judgment.

For this reason, Styron's entry into Nat Turner's consciousness is factitious. For Nat Turner was a partisan, a man possessed of a vision of truth and justice, which *necessarily* denied the humanity of

Travis and Richard Whitehead. They were the white demons. How else could he want to destroy them? Could it be that Styron wanted it both ways: tragic consciousness and sympathy for black militancy which excludes tragic consciousness?

20 Donald Barthelme's
The Dead Father

The Dead Father is a mock-epic voyage of a half-dead, half-alive, part-mechanical being who, by means of a cable, is dragged by nineteen men through an indeterminate milieu called the country of the Wends. The goal is the mysterious Great Father Serpent, and the action consists mostly of odd, fragmentary transactions between the Dead Father and his children and between the children themselves. Events are presented rapidly and graphically, but since the logical thread of narrative has been snapped, they come at us apparently devoid of meaning or pregnant with undisclosed meaning. Not only is the rhetorical element absent (except perhaps as parody), but so is the explanatory function of narrative. One consequence is a release from moral responsibility: an event is in a free, irresponsible juxtaposition to what follows and what goes before, the effect of which may be grotesquely funny or horrific.

In epic fashion, there are stories within the story. At a campfire, the Dead Father asks Thomas to tell a story. "One day in a wild place far from the city four men in dark suits with shirts and ties and attaché cases containing Uzi submachine guns seized me, saying that I was wrong and had always been wrong and would always be wrong and they were not going to hurt me. Then they hurt me, first with can openers then with corkscrews. Then, splashing iodine on my several wounds, they sped with me on horseback through the gathering gloom." The Dead Father says "Oh! A dramatic narrative," underscoring the parody. There is the echo of Kafka in the abrupt, inexplicable sense of being wrong or at least of being accused. And the capricious terrorism which follows is an emblem of the narrative itself, which is filled with motiveless, violent suddennesses. The four men promise not to hurt the victim, but suddenly ply him with corkscrews. (Where did the corkscrews come from?) Donald Barthelme is the narrator of randomness, the parodist-naturalist of terrorism as quotidian event.

158

The story is told at some length, and the Dead Father is under-standably fatigued. But fatigue we know is part of the modern aesthetic experience. There is a moral in the story. Thomas is in search of the Great Father Serpent, who, he learns, will grant him a boon if he can solve the riddle: "What do you really feel?" To which the right answer is "murderinging." The Great Father Serpent grants him the promised boon, "the ability to carry out the foulness [of murdering his father], but then speaks Freudian, or is it Nietzschean, wisdom: "Granted then . . . but may I remind you that having the power is enough." Art is with us, so that we may not perish from the truth. Barthelme plays like an artist with violence.

The relation between the violence of Barthelme's fiction and the actual violence of daily life is not precisely that of verisimilitude, not because Barthelme is a fantasist, but because the line between true and false, the real and the fantastic has disappeared. Miss Mandible, a character in an early Barthelme story, knows what every reader should know – that everything he or "she has been told about life, about America is true." The following item from the *New York Times,* for instance, is pure Barthelme. "Mrs. Navaretti, who was kidnapped Nov. 26 on her way home from work at the International Technical Training Center here said she was kept in a tiny room 'without windows and so, so cold.' She said her captors chained her to a wall and cut off her hair, but gave her champagne and cake on Christmas Day." Our daily life is what Barthelme describes only in the sense that the images and messages of TV and of other media represent our life. They are the violent, stridently forced realizations of possibilities in our lives. Most of us have never been robbed or mugged and fear the possibility only because of the images projected by television and the newspapers. Barthelme differs from the media as conscious parody differs from unconscious parody. Blood in Barthelme is ketchup; skin is papier-mâché, though there may be the threat of something more in the *frisson* provoked by the punishment the Dead Father imagines for triflers:

On the eighth the trifler is slid naked down a thousand-foot razor blade to the music of Karlheinz Stockhausen. On the ninth day the trifler is sewn together by children. . . . On the eleventh day the trifler's stitches are removed by children wearing catcher's mitts on their right and left hands.

Barthelme's naturalism consists in his deadly ear for ordinary conversation, a characteristic possessed by many important modern novelists from Flaubert to the present. His fiction (Joyce anticipates him here) is nourished by the clichés of everyday life, just as psycho-analysis is nourished by its psychopathology. Cliché is a contagious disease of the mind of epidemic proportions: this is the satirist's view. Or it is part of the human condition, like Original Sin, and hence incurable. This, I think, is the view of Barthelme and Joyce.

As the incurable disease of the human condition, cliché or the very mechanism of ordinary speech becomes the object of sheer unac-countable fascination. In an early story (printed in his first collection *Come Back, Dr. Caligari*), the hero, who is a broadcaster, singles out a word like *nevertheless,* which he repeats endlessly. In its exposure "to the glare of public inspection the word frequently discloses new properties, unsuspected qualities." The *locus classi-cus* for this fascination is Flaubert who wrote:

Such a wide gap separates me from the rest of the world that I am often surprised at hearing the simplest and most natural sounding statements. The most ordinary word fills me at times with boundless admiration. Certain gestures, certain inflections of voice fill me with wonder, and certain types of ineptness almost make me dizzy.

One of the characters in *Snow White,* Barthelme's other novel, ad-mits that "he limits himself to listening to what people say, and thinking what pamby it is; what they say. My nourishment is refined from the circus of the mind in motion." On the other hand, there is the longing expressed by Snow White: "Oh I wish there were some words in the world that were not the words I always hear."

The photo of Barthelme on the jacket of *The Dead Father* may offer a clue to the character of his fiction. The face of Barthelme is an engineer's mask with large steel-rimmed spectacles. His tightly pursed lips suggest the precision of a slide rule. The brow is fur-rowed but unanxious. The look on the face or through the mask is very clever and wry. He is wearing a denim jacket; he may ride motorcycles. The very antitype of the alienated romantic artist. Bar-thelme's fiction is deliberately inorganic, arbitrary, synthetic, com-posed of the objects and events of high as well as pop and fashion culture. "No ideas, but in things." The fiction does not have so much a point of view as it does a temper or a temperament. There is a fierce chill in the writing, utterly un-Rabelaisian. The prose is bril-liantly perverse, without anxiety.

Flaubert, Joyce, Kafka are names that I have invoked to explain Barthelme, but he is by no means one of them. And it is not simply a

matter of talent or genius. Barthelme's fiction lacks the specific
gravity of major work, and he reveals his own knowledge of his
place in his playful relation to "the best that has been thought and
said" (cf. for instance, *Snow White*). Unlike contemporary French
experimental writing, which is invariably accompanied by ideological justification, American experimental writing does not pretend to
the status of ideology. Robbe-Grillet, for instance, is openly reflective about the epistemology of his fiction, and he has found his
perfect ideological critic in Roland Barthes. Barthelme's fiction is
filled with intellectual allusions, even the appearance of intellectual
argument which is animated by something like conviction (for instance, the moving passage on Kierkegaard's unfairness to Schlegel
in the story with that title), but it is impossible to fix him to an idea.
He seeks out "strange ideas," outrageous combinations, and jux-
tapositions. The effects are often brilliant, comic, sometimes moving. If there is an ideological bias, he may share the view of the
French antinovelists that the human world lacks depth or transcendence. There is, for instance, no genuine mystery in *The Dead
Father*, despite its surreal wildness. Perhaps, though this is only a
guess, Barthelme is a later-day aesthete for whom aesthetic "purity
is often consonant with madness," and "madness in the pure state
offers an alternative to the reign of right reason," the content of
which is rhetoric. But can we be sure, when in "The Explanation"
(the story in which this passage is to be found) he or rather the
anonymous character asserts that the content of rhetoric is purity?
Everything is turned to nonsense, and one is finally tempted to say
that Barthelme's imagination is a parodic simulation of our spirit-
alienated world.

21 Raymond Carver's *Cathedral*

The affectless narrative voice of a Raymond Carver story defends itself against surprise or shock or pain. The most banal situations propose inexplicable signs of menace that require, in response, a discipline of unemotional terseness. Nothing much happens at the dinner party in "Feathers," the first of the stories in Carver's latest collection, except for the weird appearance of a vulture-sized peacock, which stares at the guests and to which Jack, the narrator, responds at intervals with three "goddamns," as if the word were a talisman for preserving equanimity. The peacock, the plaster cast of misshapen teeth on top of the TV, the very ugly baby of the hosts give the story a quality of surreal menace that never quite materializes. Though nothing of consequence happens at the dinner, the friendship between the men (the wives have just been introduced to each other) is significantly altered. "We're still friends. That hasn't changed any. But I've gotten careful with what I say to him. And I know he feels that and wishes it could be different. I wish it could be too." Every detail conspires to estrange the friends from each other, whatever else they might wish.

The threat to Carver's characters lies within. They are vulnerable to their own weakness. Informed by his landlord that he must vacate a house he has rented, Wes of "The Chef's House" refuses to be consoled by his estranged wife. " 'Suppose,' [she asks him to imagine], 'nothing had ever happened.' " But Wes, a half-reformed alcoholic, can imagine no such power and freedom for himself. " 'I don't have that kind of supposing left in me. We were born who we are.' " Here the narrator is the wife who has imagined such freedom, a freedom that would make it possible for them to get back together, but who at the end acknowledges her husband's incapacity for it. "We'll clean it up tonight, I thought, and that will be the end of it."

Carver's characters are alcoholic, unemployed, occasionally violent to their spouses and children, victims of passion or circum-

162

stance. They are characters on the margins of middle-class life with the values and occupations of the middle class: sales people, teachers, business people, who nevertheless seem always on the brink of *lumpen* existence. They do not quite fall out of the middle class, but the threat of catastrophic failure seems always imminent. They live transient lives in rooms, apartments, and houses which either do not belong to them or to which they do not belong. Neither the utilities nor the furniture can ever be depended on – as if the external world had taken on the emotional uncertainty or inertia of the inner lives of the characters.

Carver writes of a time (the present) when everything seems to have gone wrong. In "Preservation," the breakdown of a refrigerator plunges the husband into despair because he remembers that his folks had one that lasted twenty-three years. Carver, with perhaps a bit too much contrivance, makes the fridge and the thawing packages of frozen food an objective correlative for the moral desolation of the time. Yet he also suggests that it may be an illusion that things have changed for the worse. The wife's parents, after all, were divorced, the father had disappeared from her life, and he had died in a car that leaked carbon monoxide.

Have things changed, or is change an illusion? Carver's answer to such a question is a double perspective, true to our experience of both past and present. The past seems better than the present until we recall the actual events of the past; but such recollection cannot alter our sense of *present* hopelessness or meaninglessness. Right now, whatever the past was and meant to the people who lived it, there is a general sense that things have not only gone wrong, but that they'll never be right again. America, the land of the future, suddenly seems at the end of its tether. Carver's fiction doesn't explicitly encompass conditions of structural unemployment, incorrigible violence in our cities, the closed frontier, and our sense of baffled manifest destiny, but he has superbly caught the mood generated by these conditions.

Even some of Carver's admirers have found the sad passivity of his characters a limitation of his art. In his review of *Cathedral*, Irving Howe mentions the judgment of a friend who finds the work "cold" and then goes on to construe the judgment as referring to "a note of disdain toward the people he creates," an impatience with "the resignation of his characters." Howe even hears in this note a wish that "they would rebel against the constrictions of their lives." I for one hear neither the note of disdain nor the note of impatience. The story "Chef's House" knows that Wes's inability to suppose is more authentic than the wife's desire not "to hear him talk like this." He is sorry, but he can't help it. " 'I can't talk like somebody I'm not. If I was somebody else, I wouldn't be me. But I'm who I am.' " His wife in effect acknowledges Wes's truth with an economical sympathy that is characteristic of the narrative voice in most of the stories. "Wes, it's all right, I said. I brought his hand to my cheek."

Wes could be speaking of the moral aspect of Carver's art as well as of his own character. In his first collection of stories, *In Our Time,* Hemingway presented characters, not unlike Carver's in their terseness, who refused to act up to feelings that they didn't have. The false note for Carver, as for Hemingway, is supposing yourself to be other than you are.

Like Hemingway's characters, Carver's characters possess a code (there is even the code of the alcoholic) which dictates their behavior. There is a right way and a wrong way to be despairing, or ineffectual, or lost. Carver actually gives us an aesthetic of failure. This is why I find Carver's prize-winning "A Small, Good Thing" flawed in its attempt to redeem the "evil" baker, who unknowingly intrudes upon the lives of the grief-stricken parents of a dead child, continually phoning them to remind them of the birthday cake they had ordered and forgotten to pick up. The baker, sullen and dimly conceived through most of the story, suddenly becomes a figure of compassion, who asks forgiveness for the kind of man he has become. "I was a different kind of human being," he says. Perhaps. But the concluding episode in which he tries to console the parents with coffee and freshly baked bread strikes me as a bit of willed Dickensian sentimentality.

There is, of course, the danger that the very limitations of these characters and the medium in which they live will produce monotonous art. The danger is reduced, however, by Carver's resourcefulness in creating a variety of events and effects. How different and yet alike are the two stories of ineffectual husbands, "The Chef's House" and "Preservation." Only on rare occasions does the weirdness of a Carver story fail to emerge "organically" from the situation and seem contrived, an unnecessary turn of the screw. In an early story, "Mr. Coffee and Mr. Fixit," the hero's mother is a sixty-five year old swinger, whom her son discovers kissing a man on the sofa of her house, an unusual but plausible scene of our time. But when the son remembers one of her former lovers, "an unemployed aerospace engineer," who walked with "a limp from a gunshot wound his first wife gave him,'' we seem to have entered the zone of jokiness. The integrity of ''The Student's Wife'' (a story in an earlier collection, *Will You Please Be Quiet Please?*) is also slightly compromised because it introduces the main character as an admirer of Rilke, whose poems he reads to his wife in bed. The rest of the story beautifully unfolds the insomnia and despair of the wife, who loses her husband every night to a heavy ''jaws clenched'' sleep. Rilke is an irrelevance. Carver's tact, his instinct for the right detail, is usually so sure that the rare failure jars.

One can see in the title story, ''Cathedral,'' which appropriately concludes the present volume, an effort on Carver's part to transcend his medium, or rather to find within the medium the gestures of fancy or imagination that will reduce its poverty. ''Cathedral'' is told like many Carver stories in a somewhat disconsolate voice, that of a husband bemused by his wife, who has invited home a blind man for whom she had worked as a reader and helper many years before. The disconsolateness disappears, however, in the extraordinary relationship that develops between the two men, in which the husband teaches the blind man to visualize a cathedral by having him hold his hand as he draws it. As in D. H. Lawrence's story, ''The Blind Man,'' blindness becomes a metaphor for imagination: the power of the mind to ascend to the spires. Carver's story risks pretentiousness, but wholly avoids it, for he preserves in the telling the simplicity and authenticity of language that characterize all his stories.

Carver's minimal art achieves maximal effects. Frank Kermode, I think, is right to speak as he did of Carver's capacity to evoke ''a whole moral condition'' in a seemingly slight sketch. One wonders where Carver will go from here. He is a lyric poet, who writes verse as well as stories. It is hard to imagine him working in the more extended form of the novel. In a revealing autobiographical essay (see *In Praise of What Persists,* edited by Stephen Berg), Carver describes his career as a short-story writer as a response to the baleful influence of his children, who did not allow him time for the longer effort of the novel. The circumstances of his life produced a ''discovery'' about the novel.

To write a novel, it seemed to me, a writer should be living in a world that makes sense, a world that the writer can believe in, draw a bead on, and then write about accurately. A world that will, for a time anyway, stay fixed in one place. Along with this there has to be a belief in the essential *correctness* of that world. A belief that the known world has reasons for existing, and is worth writing about – is not likely to go up in smoke in the process. This wasn't the case with the world I knew and was living in. My world was one that seemed to change gears and directions, along with its rules, every day. Time and again I reached the point where I couldn't see or plan any further ahead than the first of next month and gathering together enough money, by hook or by crook, to meet rent and provide the children's school clothes.

Although Carver's is not the only possible world, it is one in which many people live, and one he writes very accurately about. In the paradoxically lyric way of the minimalist writer, Carver has not only made sense of this world, he has given it value.

22 Saul Bellow's *Him with His Foot in His Mouth and Other Stories*

The title story of Saul Bellow's superb collection of stories is a portrait of the artist as an offensive man. Shawmut, a musicologist by profession, characterizes himself fairly as an utterer of "bad witticisms that well up from the depths of his nature," as good a definition of much of the inspiration of contemporary fiction as one would wish. "A surrealist in spite of himself," a random shooter from the mouth, Shawmut blames himself more than others. (" 'Oh, Dr. Shawmut, in that cap you look like an archeologist.' Before I can stop myself, I answer, 'And you look like something I just dug up.' ") The story, told in the form of a letter to the victim of the witticism, is an act of expiation. Shawmut is wise enough to know that the witticism is vile. But the temptation remains irresistible. Even his friendships seem to be defined by the temptation. His gimpy friend Edward Walish (shades of Valentine Gersbach, the villain in *Herzog*) reflects his own darker nature: "a wise guy in an up-to-date post-modern existentialist sly manner."

The wisecracking artist is endemic to contemporary fiction. In *God Knows,* Joseph Heller, for example, discovers that God is not an earnest social democrat, but (imagine the chutzpah!) the original comic Jewish novelist. The novel is a tissue of dumb wisecracks (King David on his marriage to Michal: "Michal, my bride, was not just the daughter of a king but a bona-fide Jewish American Princess. . . . I am the first in the Old Testament [*sic*] to be stuck with one" and on the comparative merits of the Moses story and his own story: "Moses has the Ten Commandments, it's true, but I've got much better lines."). Such inspired words should have been blocked and absorbed back in the system, as Shawmut suggests about his own bad witticisms.

The so-called avant-garde (bad witticisms, deliberately deviant imagination and all), paradoxically American mainstream, needs to be resisted. Thus Shawmut who writes with fraternal affection for

Allen Ginsberg (he has included the queer nation in the Whitmanian universal embrace) nevertheless doubts that "the path of truth must pass through all the zones of masturbation and buggery." Shawmut at least knows that "right speech" is based on self-control. Shawmut's story is a confession of sin, an attempt at purgation, so that he can hear words of ultimate seriousness.

The world's grandeur is fading. And this is our human setting, devoid of God, she says with great earnestness. But in this deserted beauty man himself still lives as a God-pervaded being. It will be up to him – to us – to bring back the light that has gone from these molded likenesses, if we are not prevented by the forces of darkness. Intellect, worshipped by all, brings us as far as natural science, and this science, although very great, is incomplete. Redemption from *mere* nature is the work of feeling and of the awakened eye of the Spirit. The body, she says, is subject to the forces of gravity. But the soul is ruled by levity, pure.

I listen to this and have no mischievous impulses.

It is hard for modern readers to refrain from smiling at words of ultimate seriousness, however eloquent – hard not to feel their futility. The saving grace in these words of seriousness is a holy "levity" to be distinguished from wisecracking. Still, it is not easy to get back the great nineteenth-century sentiment: the reverence for life. The language of art, as Bellow knows as well as anyone, may be aggressive and hard: how to keep it from mean-spiritedness?

Bellow's solution is to invent harsh, large-souled characters – like Wulpy, in "What Kind of Day Did You Have?." Harold Rosenberg-like in his giant physical size and intellectual sensibility, Wulpy is a prince of men, a world-class artist-intellectual who assumes "a kind of presidential immunity from all inconveniences." We see Wulpy's life through the eyes of Katerina, his lover (an admirable addition to Bellow's gallery of voluptuous, generous and suffering matronly women). Wulpy, with his gimpy leg and poor health, is as difficult and demanding a lover as he is an imperious intellect. Bellow shows Wulpy contending with the unpleasant realities of the lecture tour: air travel in inclement weather, missed connections, importuning characters who want to meet the great man, and loneliness in a hotel room. But the power of this story is in Bellow's aphoristic creation of Wulpy's character.

At the age of seventy, he had arranged his ideas in well-nigh final order: none of the weakness, none of the drift that made supposedly educated people contemptible. How can you call yourself a modern thinker if you lack the realism to identify a weak marriage quickly, if you don't know what hypocrisy is, if you haven't come to terms with lying – if, in certain connections, people can still say about you, "He's a sweetheart!"? Nobody would dream of calling Victor "a sweetheart!"

[Katerina] was with him in his lighthearted, quick-moving detachment from everything that people (almost all of them) were attached to. In a public-opinion country, he made his own opinions. Katerina was enrolled as his only pupil. She paid her tuition with joy.

Wulpy's adversary is the seductive filmmaker Wrangel, an intellectual entertainer and promoter of bad faith, who justifies his trivializing of ideas (he pretends to be a great admirer of Wulpy) by claiming that caricature clarifies abstract ideas. Another threat to Wulpy comes from Police Lieutenant Krieggstein, candidate for a Ph.D. in criminology and rival for Katerina's affections. Krieggstein is in the Bellovian line of reality instructors, who try to give people like Victor Wulpy "a better idea . . . of how savage it is out there." But, as Wulpy remarks, Krieggstein's own reality "belongs to the Golden Age of American Platitudes." He is beneath contempt for Wulpy: that is, beneath the ken of art, the only thing that counts. Wrangel puts it right: "Victor knows what the real questions are, and . . . that without art we can't judge what life is."

There is the risk of preciousness, but Bellow avoids it by reconceiving the bourgeois-bohemian conflict as a story of symbiosis, whatever the mutual suspicion. The "bourgeois" (the man of reality) in Bellow's fiction (whether he is a business *gonif* or a bona fide racketeer) is a kind of raw energy or material for the imagination. Bellow's artists or artist-types have nothing of the effete about them. Ijah, the artist-type in *Cousins,* mistrusts romantic inwardness, which has been the diminishing capital of so much art of the past two centuries, because he knows from his life in Chicago "that there were so many things going on in the *outer* world, the city itself was so rich in opportunities for *real* development, a center of such wealth, power, drama, rich even in crimes and vices, in diseases and intrinsic – not accidental – monstrosities, that it was foolish, querulous, to concentrate on oneself." But he refuses to concede this outer world to his racketeer cousin Tanky, for he too has experienced evil and "the dissolution of the old bonds of existence." If there is a resentment toward the outer world and those who incarnate it, it is because they want to deny it to the artist. In "Zetland: By a Character Witness,'' the father of Zetland, a success in business and an admirer of the arts, insists on a division of labor in which his genius son would be "all marrow no bone." If we cannot know life without art, an art that is cut off from the outer world is lifeless. Zetland's son fights to claim the world for himself.

But what does it mean in 1984 to judge life, from the vantage point of art or of anything else? Bellow's vision has become increasingly apocalyptic, as readers of his last novel *The Dean's December* have remarked with some displeasure. Ijah strikes the apocalyptic note: "And whether we are preparing a new birth of spirit or the agonies of final dissolution . . . depends on what you think, feel, and will about such manifestations or apparitions, on the kabbalistic skill you develop in the interpretation of these contemporary formulations." The aphoristic style is open-ended. Don't expect any final truth here.

Then what does the wisdom of art amount to? The implicit answer of these stories is the integrity of language: the truth, wit and eloquence with which it represents the world. The wisecrack and the cliché are degraded versions of the aphorism, the aspiration to express reality with "ultimate seriousness." We need only consider the trivializing power of the media through which we acquire so much of our political and moral "knowledge" of the world to appreciate the significance of Bellow's imaginative enterprise.

Bellow's work recalls Flaubert in his moral sensitivity to cliché. But unlike Flaubert, he does not confuse cliché with reality. (Writers like Donald Barthelme, who have the Flaubertian gift, have become complicit parodists of the cliché. Art is a matter of reduction: there is no higher and lower, no inner and outer. The pre-Columbian truth of the world is that it is flat.) For Bellow, art is not a bastion of purity to be preserved from the contaminations of the world. He has a healthy American or Chicagoan respect for the crude, even criminal vitalities in the world. Resistance comes, however, not only from criminal vitality, but from a higher self, which, as Shawmut remarks, "few people are equipped to observe." Bellow's quest for a higher spirituality, an ultimate seriousness, need not disquiet profane readers, for it has not extinguished his profane delight in the world. In these stories, spirituality is an element in a vision of complexity and balance that resists the reductions of experience to absurdity and despair.

23　The claustral world of Nadine Gordimer

Nadine Gordimer's novels with one exception are set in the Union of South Africa. The narratives describe the consequences – in the lives of whites and blacks – of apartheid, the dominant institution in the country. The characterization of Tom and Jessie Stilwell, the central couple of *Occasion For Loving* (her third novel), applies to the condition of most of the white liberals in the novels.

They believed in the integrity of personal relations against the distortions of laws and society. What stronger and more proudly personal bond was there than love? Yet even between lovers they had seen blackness count, the personal return inevitably to the social, the private to the political. There was no recess of being, no emotion so private that white privilege did not single you out there.

If "white privilege" is an aggressive intruder into the integrity of personal relations, then any effort to live out one's personal life free of politics is self-diminishing. The apolitical view, even the illusion of one, is possible only if one is free to constitute one's own personal realm: for instance to have and enjoy one's black or white friends, to intermarry. The answer to "white privilege" must be politics of another kind. To live apolitically even in the interest of the "integrity of personal relations" then is to accept implicitly the injustice of society.

The political life for the black and his white liberal friends in South Africa is inchoate. Characters allude to meetings, organizations, demonstrations, membership in the militantly anti-apartheid Communist Party. The threat of arrest is omni-present, arrests occur and we learn about torture, but the political interest of the novels lies in the sufferings of the white liberal conscience. Lacking access to a public stage, the political man exercises his politics in personal relationships – at times to absurd effect. Thus in *Occasion For Loving*, the liberal Jew Boaz Dias acts with extraordinary tolerance, even friendliness, towards the man who is having an affair with his wife because he is black. A character in the novel remarks: ''There's Boaz – he's so afraid of taking advantage of Gideon's skin that he ends up taking advantage of it anyway by refusing to treat him like any other man.'' Politics intrudes (sometimes irrelevantly) into the most intimate experience, because there is no other space available to it.

South Africa is not a totalitarian society. It is rather a democracy for whites, on this side of apartheid. In Gordimer's South African novels the absence of political opportunity makes it very difficult, if not impossible, to expand ''the circuit of self'' (a phrase from one of Gordimer's short stories) beyond the sphere of personal relationships. Unlike totalitarianism which induces the apathy that supports it, South African injustice provokes and thwarts the desire for justice. Politics is at once necessary and impossible.

The exception to Gordimer's South African novels is her fifth novel, *A Guest of Honour,* set in a country resembling Zambia, where a black revolution has triumphed. In order to write a fully realized political novel, Gordimer had to exit imaginatively from the claustral world of South Africa. If the liberal is haunted and hunted by political authority in South Africa, he can only contemplate that authority from a distance and perceive only the darkness of menace. He and Gordimer's readers are deprived of a vision and understanding of the workings of the South African political system. The scene of *A Guest of Honour* is the aftermath of the revolution which gives Gordimer's imagination an access to the political life in the public space. But the theme of apartheid (the South African theme) does not disappear; it continues to determine the new ''freedom'' that the revolution wins for black and white.

The novel provides us with an unillusioned view of black power in Africa, largely through the eyes of James Bray, the ex-colonial official who sympathized with the revolution, and has returned as a guest of the new African nation. The new Parliament is a sham, since ''African nations are in reality one party nations.'' In language that parallels Naipaul's condemnation of the mimic societies in the underdeveloped regions of the world, Bray characterizes the parliament of this new Central African country as a ''kiddies parliament which Africans think reproduces Westminster in their states.'' Adam Mweta, the first president, moves quickly to establish his power by instituting Preventive Detention, the principal object of which is to undermine the autonomous existence of the labor confederation and to abort the rival claim to power of his revolutionary mentor Shinza. Bray, the increasingly disillusioned friend of Mweta, makes the most profound criticism of the revolutionary process. ''But the effect was to make parties like PIP miss out on the vital stage of their function as political schools and ideological debating forums, a means of formulating the blind yearning to *have* into something that would hold good beyond the . . . grand anti-climax of paper free- dom. . . . And at the back of the minds of even the most intelligent and reasonable people there's a vague intoxication of loot associated with seeing the end of foreign rule.''

Bray's revolutionary idealism (shared by Gordimer) has disturbing implications. Mweta's policy of Preventive Detention is aligned with capitalism; the European company that Mweta invites into the coun- try to develop its economy wants docile workers. Gordimer con- ceives Shinza, the Marxist and mentor and now rival of Mweta, as a figure of virtue. But his Marxism is untested by the holding power, and there is nothing in the wisdom of the novel which assures us that Preventive Detention may not have been used by Shinza, if he had attained power. Gordimer chose Zambia as her model: What if she had chosen Ghana under Nkhrumah? Shinza's politics sound ominously like Trotsky's permanent revolution or Mao's cultural revolution. ''But we want instability, James, we want our instability in the poverty and backwardness of this country, we want the people at the top to be a bit poorer in a few years now so that . . . rock poverty . . . can be broken up out of its famous stability.''

The character of Mweta is a sort of blur in the novel. Gordimer rarely presents him in his own right, and he does not emerge co- herently from the perceptions that others have of him. He is a func- tion of the anxiety of others. For Bray, he is increasingly the ex- ploiter of friendship: Mweta wishes him to spy on Shinza, and in his mind Bray accuses Mweta of ''the oldest political trick in the world . . . incipient messianism.'' For Shinza, he is the traitor to the revolution. According to Roly Dando, Mweta's white minister of justice, Mweta plays for half-safety: ''to make great changes here you've got to take the most stupendous risks.'' Mweta simply lacks heroic capacity. His self-justification in the extended and brilliantly dramatized presentation of a party congress displaces responsibility for present difficulties to ''the colonial legacy.'' The response of the audience to Mweta's speech, however, registers the uneasiness that the reader feels with the self-justification. ''The general applause first swamped the different currents of reaction . . . part of the hullabaloo was simply polite – everyone's hands must be seen to move when the president had spoken. . . ." But none of the characterizations is convincing, partly because the novel presents the question of foreign capital in moral terms without adequate consideration of its economic implications. The political process is not a seminar in ethics.

Bray's ideological sentimentality (one suspects it is Gordimer's as well, because it is unchecked in the dramatization) compounds the confusion in the novel. Bray's quotation of Sartre: "socialism is the movement of man in the process of re-creating himself" could benefit from a deconstructive suspicion. The only movement? Is re-creation necessarily always a good thing? Is it true that socialism re-creates man? But the sentimentality pales next to the concluding callousness of Bray's little speech to a friend. "Whatever the paroxysms of experiment along the way – whether it is Robespierre or Stalin or Mao Tse-tung or Castro – it's the only way to go, in the sense that every other way is a way back. What do you want to see here? Another China? Another America? If we have to admit that the pattern is likely to be based on one or the other, which way should we choose?" To his liberal friend Neil Bayley's question – "You're saying socialism is the absolute?" – Bray responds with a resounding Yes! Only an ideological callousness or innocence would permit a characterization of what is already a fairly predictable process as an experiment. How many millions have to be killed for the "experiment" to be declared a failure? The answer is that the experiment can never fail, because it is not really an experiment: it has become an absolute.

This presentation of Bray is inconsistent with Bray's self-characterization in the following passage:

I was a sort of symbol of something that never happened in Africa: a voluntary relinquishment in friendship and light all around, of white intransigence that could only be met with black intransigence. . . . All Africans yearned for a situation where they wouldn't have to base the dynamic of their power on bitterness.

And it is inconsistent with Bray's sensitivity about inflicting suffering on others: "something may be worth suffering for as a matter of individual conviction, but nothing is worth bringing about the suffering of others." This is Bray's "own nature," which he finally decides to transgress and so become a participant rather than a mere liberal observer of the process of change. If Rebecca, his lover, offers a clue to our own affection for Bray, it is that, unlike her feckless husband, Bray "made life in accordance with some choice." But the choice, though brave (it ends in Bray's death) is abstract and futile – like the white politics in Gordimer's other fiction, and it is hard to resist the judgment of a minor character in the novel as perhaps truest to the quality of Bray's political life: "these nice white liberals getting mixed up in things they don't understand."

The judgment is that of Emmanuelle, a young woman who lived in Africa and has emigrated to England. She is an escapee, the opposite of Bray the participant. Emmanuelle fails to comprehend the deep need of the white liberal in Africa (a breed apart) not only to expiate his guilt, but more selfishly to participate in the public space, now denied him in South Africa. Only the undoing of white supremacy can disburden him of guilt and free him to live openly and expressively in society. The white liberal must lose power (which he never enjoyed) in order to gain it. And he may even have to accept the cruelties that attend the new society as the price for entry into the political process. This may help explain the apparent ideological obtuseness of the otherwise admirable and sensitive Bray. The title *A Guest of Honour* is, of course, not without irony. But it is a curious truth of Bray's situation that the new African nation has altered his sense of opportunity and possibility. Unlike the liberal South African white, confined to the margins of his society, fearful, ambivalent and frustrated, Bray can finally act in the fullness of conviction.

The novel even measures the distance Bray travels from hesitant observer to participant. When he arrives in Africa as a guest of his friend and protégé Mweta, he can do little more than observe with increasing concern the tendency toward a new version of the old oppression in Mweta's rule. But he hesitates to criticize his friend.

His mind switched to Mweta again, and his body shrank. He ought not, he was perhaps wrong to question Mweta about anything. He had made it clear from the beginning that he would not presume on any bond of authority arising out of their association because he saw from the beginning that there was always the danger – to his personal relationship with Mweta – that this bond might become confused with some lingering assumption of authority from the colonial past. I mustn't forget that I'm a white man.

The reader's first response is perhaps sympathy with Bray's scruple and an admiration for the delicacy of his political and personal intelligence. But Bray's reflections, it becomes clear on a little reflection of our own, are fraught with contradiction. In order to preserve his "personal relationship with Mweta," Bray feels that he "musn't forget that I'm a white man." Bray does not perceive the contradiction, because he regards the fact of his being a white man as liability. What he does not realize is that the necessity of remembering this fact already compromises "the personal relationship." Note the telltale shrinking of the body from the thought of Mweta at the beginning of the passage. The personal relationship is possible only if Bray is able to speak candidly and critically to Mweta as one human being to another. Bray ultimately overcomes his scruples and joins the struggle against Mweta.

The novels that follow *A Guest of Honour* return us to white dominated Africa. In *The Conservationist* and *Burger's Daughter*, the claustral condition of the white is imagined with even greater intensity than in the other novels. This intensity may correspond to an increasing sense of crisis in the social reality to which it corresponds. It may also be the effect of the imaginative experience of the political process in *A Guest of Honour*. The actions in both novels are internalized in the consciousness of the main character, virtually to the point of stream of consciousness. One is made to feel that significant action is not possible in the external world. And this condition is not confined to the white liberal. The central character of *The Conservationist* is an industrialist with a special pride of possession in the farm that he owns in the high veld. Though the farm ostensibly represents an escape from the pressures of urban and industrial life, it comes to be seen as an extension of European domination in Africa. Possession, however, is experienced not as power, but as vulnerability. Possession exercises a fascination for women, even a woman like his mistress Antonia, whose liberalism makes her relationship with Mehring one of love and hate. The relationship becomes a contest in which Mehring recognizes himself or his possessions as the object. "Smiling, pulling a face – Yes I know – I know. I want to change the world but keep bits of it the way I like it for myself. If I had your money. . . ." (All this is refracted in Mehring's consciousness.) For which Mehring has a just contempt: "That is why you will never change the world or have my money." Though he is able to dismiss his mistress' challenge, his resistance is finally a holding operation.

The real challenge to Mehring comes not from his white liberal compatriots, but from the blacks who work his farm. Jacobus, the black farmer to whom Mehring gives the responsibility for running

his farm, watches the workers dig the soil and in effect enact the
futility of the European presence in Africa.

It's necessary because there must be no skimping. The holes must be deep.
The earth must be properly trenched to a good depth. [Jacobus] cuts the thick
twine round the neck of the packing on each tree and carefully folds back the
plastic skin and the sacking beneath it. The clump of root and earth (this
earth has come all the way from Europe) has dried out a bit despite all
precautions. Some frail capillary roots look like wisps of fibre from an old
mattress. He tests them between finger and thumb; both limp and brittle. But
he will not allow himself to investigate the bigger root, visible though
embedded in the European earth; the trees must take their change.

The African soil rejects the European will to dominate it. Even the
blacks do not possess the soil. The novel implies a Faulknerian view
of the sacred inviolability of the land, which is given to men only in
trust. Mehring's death transforms the very idea of possession.

The one whom the farm received had no name. He had no family but their
women wept a little for him. There was no child of his present but their
children were there to live after him. They had put him away to rest, at last;
he had come back. He took possession of this earth, theirs; one of them.

Mehring loses to the blacks who work his farm, and to death.

What makes Gordimer's representation of white consciousness in
South Africa so compelling is that it does not reduce consciousness
to mere conscience. Not all the whites in her novels are guilty liberals, trying to do good as a form of expiation. But to the extent that
they are conscious of their situation as a privileged minority, living
as an enclave outside the howling distress of a black majority, they
experience a fortress mentality, which is itself a form of imprisonment.

The image of prison haunts the narrating consciousness of Rosemarie Burger (*Burger's Daughter*), who has grown up expecting the
imminent arrest of her communist parents. But the real power of the
image does not lie in the literalness of imprisonment, it lies in the
isolation of the heroine's mind (represented by a stream of consciousness), who finds herself excluded from the possibility of communion even with her black allies. In one of the most powerful
episodes in the novel, Rosemarie is ferociously challenged by Baasie,
a black to whom Lionel, Rosemarie's father, had given shelter. ''Why
do you think you should be different from all other whites who've
been shitting on us ever since they came. . . . I don't have to live in

your head.'' Baasie's view recalls the judgment of Bray in *A Guest of Honour*: ''These nice white liberals getting mixed up in things they don't understand.''

Claustrophobia is the pervasive moral and political disease of a society defined by apartheid. And its only cure would seem to be revolution. Gordimer has no illusions about the price that even the white liberal will pay in the coming revolution. In *July's People,* her most recent novel, the revolution is in process. The white liberals Bam and Maureen Smales are rescued from the terrors of urban war by their servant July who leads them and their children into a native village. The inversion of roles (July in a sense becomes their master), in a black setting utterly without the amenities of civilized urban life, allows the Smales to experience directly the deprivations and anxieties of the South African blacks. Maureen learns what it feels like to wash one's private parts without real privacy in unclean water.

Gordimer gives us in astonishing detail the physical character of life in the native village: the smells, the sounds, the tastes that the Smales simply cannot take for granted. Victimized as they are, the Smales do not relinquish easily, however, the habit of mastery. Thus when July tries incompetently to repair a vehicle, Maureen becomes ''unsteady with something that was not anger but a struggle: her inability to enter into a relation of subservience with him that she had never had with Bam. Leave it, she said of her lawn mower. – Leave it. He'll come and fix it. –'' And when the Smales anticipate an order from the chief to leave the village, the irony vis-à-vis apartheid is inescapable:

What business of the chief's to tell them where [to go]? He had not asked them to come here. A white arc of the hand; plenty place to go. And this was not *their* custom, but the civilized one; when a white farmer sold up, or died, the next owner would simply say to the black labourers living and working on the land, born there: go.

The novel concludes with the theft of the Smales' gun and with the ''high ringing'' of a helicopter flying over the village. The final image is of Maureen Smales on the run, like an animal who seeks neither ''a mate nor . . . [the] care of young, existing only for [her] lone survival.'' The novel seems to embrace with an unfaltering realism the coming powerlessness of white South Africa – as if such suffering were preferable to the claustrophobia of life in apartheid.

In writing about the political character of Nadine Gordimer's imagination, one risks an impoverishing account of her achievement. In her introduction to her *Selected Stories,* Gordimer speaks of her capacity "to let myself out and live in the body, with others as well as – alone – in the mind." And she goes on to compare herself to Camus. "To be young and in the sun; my experience of this was similar to that of Camus, . . ." This capacity appears throughout her fiction in passages of luminous evocation. It is particularly strong in her short stories, which are less determined by political preoccupation as, for example, in the following passage from the short story "The Catch," which suggests Lawrence more than it does Camus:

Water cleared it like a cloth wiping a film from a diamond; out shone the magnificent fish, stiff and handsome in its mail of scales, glittering a thousand opals of colour, set with two brilliant deep eyes all hard clear beauty and not marred by the capability of expression which might have made a reproach of the creature's death; a king from another world, big enough to shoulder a man out of the way, dead, captured, astonished.

Or a passage in which loneliness (or rather aloneness) becomes an experience of sensuous satisfaction.

She heard again inside herself the words alone, alone, just the way she had heard them fifty-nine years ago when she was twelve years old and crossing France by herself for the first time. As she had sat there, bolt upright in the corner of a carriage, her green velvet fur-trimmed cloak around her, her hamper beside her, and the locket with the picture of her grandfather hidden in her hand, she had felt a swelling terror of exhilaration, the dark, drowning swirl of cutting loose, had tasted the strength to be brewed out of self-pity and the calm to be lashed together out of panic that belonged to other times and other journeys approaching her from the distance of her future. *Alone. alone.* This that her real self had known years before it happened to her – before she had lived the journey that took her from a lover, or those others that took her from the alienated faces of madness and death – that same self remembered years after journeys had dropped behind into the past. Now she was alone, . . .

Isn't there a private life that has its intensities and rewards which one can live away from the political challenges of apartheid? Gordimer's short stories, more than her novels, give us periods in people's lives when politics are quiescent and she can explore the ordinary passages of life in which people work, make love and idle their time away. But those times are often deceptively quiescent. In the story,

"The Life of Imagination," Gordimer describes an adulterous affair between a doctor and the mother of a patient in which we are given a penetrating, though oblique, view of middle class marriage. At the end of the story, the doctor leaves the home of his lover before sunrise and forgets to close the door. The woman, lying in bed, sees "the gaping door" and "the wind bellying the long curtains" and suddenly there wells up inside her an anxiety that "they would come in unheard, with that wind, and approach through the house, black men with their knives in their hands." Political reality, "this stale fantasy," is always at the door of the domesticities that try to exclude it. Within the domestic round, political reality is like a concealed weapon that can fire at any time. Gordimer's gift is to make us feel the presence of the weapon even in its absence. Her fiction brings us to the wall that separates white and black, white and white and to the threshold at which momentous change is imminent.

24 V. S. Naipaul: virtuoso of the negative

I

Nothing is ever right with Naipaul's characters. Their incompetence is pervasive: in their speech, their vocations, their bodies, their possessions. In the early books they speak an English patois, a language of misconjugated verbs ("What happening there, Hat?") and misused pronouns ("But we have Americans on we side now."). When they speak English correctly, it is with visible strain and a loss of spontaneity. Lorkhoor, one of the amusing demagogues of *The Suffrage of Elvira,* speaks correctly English "in a deliberate way as though he had to weigh and check the grammar beforehand." He is regarded suspiciously by his compatriot Trinidadians as a tourist from Bombay. Indeed, the very correctness of his speech on occasion causes him to commit "a social blunder," when, for instance, he pronounces Mr. Cuffy's name Coffee as it should be rather than "Cawfey" as Mr. Cuffy in the spirit of the "incorrect" speech of his people prefers. The genius of *Miguel Street* (Naipaul's first collection of stories) loves to take auto engines apart but cannot quite put them back together again. Those who study hard to escape the squalor of life in Trinidad either fail their exams or their success is tainted by sloppiness and plagiarism. (Mr. Biswas' son's exam paper is a mess, making his success a puzzle. His father writes the exam essay, which he memorizes.) Mr. Biswas' muscles are like "hammocks" and the calves of his legs pathetically soft, as his wife Shama mercilessly reminds him. His houses are all makeshift affairs, vulnerable to destruction and appropriation. In the original design the solicitor's clerk (who sold Mr. Biswas his house) "seemed to have forgotten the need for a staircase to link both floors, and what he had provided had the appearance of an afterthought." In the six hundred pages of *A House for Mr. Biswas,* I can scarcely recall an episode in which something is properly made or done. The Negro

181

carpenter who begins to build a house in which Mr. Biswas is to live is discerning and competent but is given neither time nor money to complete the job.

The incompetence is modern rather than primitive. Naipaul's Caribbean characters are born into a world formed by modern things: movies, machines, contemporary English. The first story in *Miguel Street* is about a character who models himself on Bogart, another character resembles Rex Harrison. In *A House for Mr. Biswas,* a Trinidadian returning from an education in England sports a mustache which makes him look like Robert Taylor. And, as I have already noted, the genius of *Miguel Street* is an auto mechanic. In every case, Naipaul's characters are irascible, frustrated versions of modern man. They would be less at home in India than they are in the abortive modern world of Trinidad. Nostalgia for the old country, where it exists, is little more than a consolation for the insatisfactions of the present.

The early fiction has a charming exoticism, which may deceive the reader (though not for long) about the nature of Naipaul's vision. What we are given is not peculiar to the Caribbean. However precise the notations of Caribbean life may be, Naipaul manages to strike a universal note. (This becomes particularly apparent in his fourth and most ambitious novel, *A House for Mr. Biswas.*) Naipaul sees his characters in a particular time and place, but he also sees them by implication in a universal condition. "Ganesh," Naipaul remarks of *The Mystic Masseur* (his first novel), "is in a way the history of our time." Ganesh is that modern phenomenon: the sincere charlatan, the man who strenuously but inauthentically becomes "schoolmaster, author, masseur, healer, politician." The society Naipaul describes is thoroughly, though imperfectly, modern. Indeed, its very imperfection is a modern characteristic.

Naipaul's sentiment against the imitativeness of Trinidad society is thus somewhat misleading, for it is hardly unique in its susceptibility to American movies, songs, drinks and gadgets. Advanced countries like England, France and Germany are also susceptible. And indeed imitation (note cognate words: standardization, uniformity, the mass production of commodities) is a function of modernization. To be sure, mimicry does not exhaust the possibilities of advanced societies. There is a creative element as well. On the other hand, mimicry is the principal, if not the exclusive, capacity of underdeveloped societies, trying to become modern. What Trinidad, like America, does not have and the Europeans do have is the resisting legacy of a feudal culture. What Trinidad does not have that America possesses is centrality and power in the world economy. Naipaul does not misrepresent this situation, he simply applies to it an exaggeratedly moral contempt. Despite the exaggeration, it is fair to say that it is his clear-sightedness (on which he prides himself) that makes it possible for him to see through without dissolving the particularities of Carribean society to the universal condition.

What Surajpat Harbans says of his constituency in *The Suffrage of Elvira* could be said of life itself as Naipaul finds it: "Elvira, you is a bitch." In *A House for Mr. Biswas,* Naipaul writes with Dickensian indignation of the destitution that Mr. Biswas in his role as welfare investigator discovers everywhere.

Day after day he visited the mutilated, the defeated, the futile and the insane living in conditions not far removed from his own: in suffocating rotting wooden kennels, in sheds of boxboard, canvas and tin, in dark and sweating concrete caverns. Day after day he visited the eastern sections of the city where the narrow houses pressed their scabbed and blistered facades together and hid the horrors that lay behind them: the constricted, undrained backyards, coated with green slime, in the perpetual shadow of adjacent houses and the tall rubble-stone fences against which additional sheds had been built: years choked with flimsy cooking sheds, crowded fowl-coops of wire-netting, bleaching stones spread with sour washing: smell upon smell, but none overcoming the stench of cesspits and overloaded septic tanks: horror increased by the litters of children, most of them illegitimate, with navels projecting inches out of their bellies, as though they had been delivered with haste and disgust. Yet occasionally there was the neat room, its major piece of furniture, a table, a chair, polished to brilliance; giving no hint of the squalor it erupted into the yard. Day after day he came upon people so broken, so listless, it would have required the devotion of a lifetime to restore them. But he could only lift his trouser turn-ups, pick his way through mud and slime, investigate, write, move on.

Unlike Dickens, however, Naipaul neither indulges in moral peroration nor suggests a solution. And the reason is not, as one critic has put it to the disadvantage of Dickens, that Naipaul is simply "without any Dickensian sentimentality, apostrophizing and preaching." The fact is that unlike the great English novelists of the nineteenth century Naipaul cannot make sense of his society. Mr. Biswas, we are told, "investigated two hundred households; but after every classification, he could never, on adding, get two hundred, and then he had to go through all the questionnaires again. He was dealing with a society that had no rules and patterns, and classifications were a chaotic business."

This is ostensibly a judgment of Trinidad and not of advanced societies like England and France. But modern life has eroded the rules and patterns of all societies. Indeed, their apparent amorphousness is part of the definition of their advanced status, their modernity. Naipaul notes with regret that he was born and raised in a society in which no building is older than one hundred and fifty years. This is also true of most Americans, for whom the experience of rootlessness does not necessarily issue in powerlessness and despair. It is not true of Englishmen, though the presence of old buildings is not necessarily a source of national confidence and energy. (Thus the great city of London for Kripalsingh [the hero of *The Mimic Men*] is not a fulfillment, but an arena "in which we are trapped into fixed, flat postures." In the city, people have no sustaining identity. They are a series of separate encounters, "nothing more than perceivers. . . . The personality divided bewilderingly into compartments." In *The Mimic Men,* the entire world is the object of "a vision of disorder which it was beyond any one man to put right.")

What is disturbing, but essential to an understanding of Naipaul's work, is that all the alternatives are negative. He is scornful of the inefficiency and sloppiness of Trinidad society (its backwardness), yet he is also contemptuous of its Americanization, which leads to standardization, uniformity, all the well-known vices that issue from modernization. What are the alternatives: an organic society that never existed and could never be realized or simply the negative feeling that there are no alternatives? Occasionally Naipaul will value something that he disvalued in another context simply because it provides a contrast to something he dislikes even more. "As the Trinidadian becomes a more reliable and efficient citizen, he will cease to be what he is." And what is the valuable person that the Trinidadian suddenly appears to be?

If the Trinidadian has no standards of morality he is without the greater corruption of sanctimoniousness, and can never achieve the society-approved nastiness of the London landlord, say, who turns a dwelling-house into a boarding-house, charges exorbitant rents, and is concerned lest his tenants live in sin. Everything that makes the Trinidadian an unreliable, exploitable citizen makes him a quick, civilized person whose values are always human ones, whose standards are only those of wit and style.

A surprising celebration of the Trinidadian after the description in *The Middle Passage* (his account of travels through the Caribbean) of Trinidad as "unimportant, uncreative, cynical." Where are the human values? We are never given a demonstration of them. By placing Trinidadian immorality in the subordinate clause ("If the Trinidadian has no standards of morality etc."), Naipaul has displaced his own attention to what is normally an object of scorn or indignation. A virtuoso of the negative, Naipaul paradoxically achieves positive discriminations by ironically threading his way through negative alternatives, which he grades according to different standards at different times.

Despite the sentiment about the absence of rules, the social structure of Caribbean society has its strictures, taboos, rules. In a short story, "A Baker's Story," we learn that Trinidadian black people do not "forgive a man for being a black Grenadian," that Grenadians are given to prayer, that "Chinee people" work hard, that it is hard to get "Chinee people" to work for black people, that black people "get to believe that because they black they can't do nothing but work for other people," that the Chinese control the bread trade and Indians sell coconut.

And then I see that though Trinidad have every race and every color, every race have to do special things. But look, man. If you want to buy a snowball, who you buying it from? You wouldn't buy it from an Indian or a Chinee or a Potogee. You would buy it from a black man. . . . If a Indian in Trinidad decide to go into the carpentering business the man would starve.

The story, narrated by a black man who has become one of the richest men in the Port-of-Spain, is about the cunning with which he circumvents the occupational taboos of Trinidad society and becomes a successful baker. It is not that there are no rules, but that to the irreverent view of Naipaul's narrator the rules make no sense. "I ask Percy why he didn't like black people meddling with his food in public places. The question thrown him a little. He stop and think and say, 'It don't look nice.' " The narrative pauses for a moment to register its bemusement. One might note that these taboos can hardly be expected to withstand modern ways and that the exceptional success of the black baker is an omen of the triumph of modernity.

Naipaul's very precise and artful notations of social life in the underclasses of Trinidad society for all their comic and pathetic coherence do not issue in an understanding of the conditions of social life that one finds in the great nineteenth century novels. It may be, of course, that the understanding of the nineteenth century novelist was a false consciousness, an effort at optimistic social mastery. In modern fashion, he wants the truth, the concrete truth in all its limitations and unpleasantness. Naipaul presents us in *A House for Mr. Biswas* with the phenomenology of everyday life, which simply baffles the social understanding.

The sense of bafflement and emptiness is strangely combined with a powerful curiosity. When Naipaul enters a new place as a tourist (is there a more gifted traveller than he?), he misses nothing of the particularity of the scene, and yet the scene always proposes what is finally the truth of everything. It is not clarity alone that yields this truth, but a temperamental proclivity for emptiness. In a splendid piece from a journal of a trip through Egypt (which forms part of *In a Free State*), Naipaul gives us not only his capacity for observation, but the temperament that constrains it to a particular kind of observation. He describes a trip taken by him with a guide through the desert. There is a tense energy in the description as if it were moving toward some consequential revelation. But underlying the impression of consequence is a centrifugal quality, which threatens to dissipate the interest. The tourist's scorn for the squalor of the scene almost diverts us from the remarkable observations. "To me the boys, springing up expectantly out of rock and sand when men approached, were like a type of sand animal." The driver (his guide) shoos them away "with a languid gesture." "Grown up wearing trousers and shirt and good looking," the driver is bored and particularly with "the antiquities, the tourists and the tourist routine." And so is the narrator, who does not want to stay, who feels "exposed, futile" and "wants only to be back at my table." Naipaul has superbly caught the situation of the tourist almost anywhere. But what is particularly disturbing is his conclusion that the otherness which presumably draws the tourist is an illusion. Touring is "no different from actually living in the place." (The experience in Egypt recalls an episode in *The Mystic Masseur*, in which we are given "the poverty of Trinidad, nothing much to see." When Ganesh, the hero of the novel, takes some visitors on a "tour" of the island ["he used the word 'tour' "], they felt they had their money's worth.) Who can tell the boredom of the tourist from the boredom of the desert people?

In its power and coherence, Naipaul's own work is a sort of satiric antidote to the incompetence, emptiness and malice that turns up everywhere. It is, one should add, an antidote that does not reduce by one iota his vision of the negative. What makes for the coherence and power of Naipaul's work is an implicit ideal at once moral and aesthetic that amounts to an inverted or disappointed perfectionism. Naipaul sees the absurd, the grotesque, the deformed, the mechanical in all of life because of an acutely fastidious sense of the unachievable rightness of things. As a tourist, Naipaul finds in the "best" hotels the fixtures shoddily made, the help officious, the food not quite fresh. I would not for a moment doubt the accuracy of Naipaul's observations (no one observes as well as he does), but I am made uneasy by their more than occasional fanaticism and venom.

The narrator of the brilliant story "One Out of Many" in *In a Free State* sees Hindu dancers in Washington D.C. and discovers deformity:

. . . I felt for the dancers that sort of distaste we feel when we are faced with something that should be kin but turns out not to be, turns out to be degraded, like a deformed man, or like a leper, who from a distance looks whole.

The image of leper is powerful but excessive. Does Naipaul see deformity or does his seeing deform? It is interesting to note that the deformation the narrator sees is caused by the half-caste appearance of Hindu dancers appearing in Washington D.C. Naipaul's fastidious perfectionism extends to matters of race. The deforming aspect of Naipaul's vision (a paradox of his perfectionism) occurs almost gratuitously at the end of *The Mimic Men*, when the narrator-hero observes in a hotel a man eating, to whom he gives the name Garbage.

Garbage also sits behind a pillar. His hands are all I can see of him. They are long, middle-aged, educated hands: and their primary concern appears to be to convert a plate of meat and vegetables into a plate of acceptable garbage. While chaos comes swiftly and simultaneously to other plates; while meat is hacked and pushed around and vegetables mangled and scattered on a spreading, muddy field of gravy; while knives and forks, restlessly preparing fresh, mixed mouthfuls, probe the chaos they have created, and cut and spear and plaster; those two hands are unhurriedly, scientifically, maintaining order, defining garbage, separating what is to be eventually eaten from what is to be thrown away. What is to be thrown away is lifted high and carefully deposited on that section of the plate, a growing section, which is reserved for garbage. It is only when the division is complete – most of the other plates abandoned by this time and ready for surrender – that the eating begins. This is the work of a minute; the plate is ready for surrender with the others. The waitress passes. Stiffly, dismissingly, the out-stretched hands offer up their labour: a neat plate of garbage. I feel I have witnessed the first part of some early Christian ritual. For this is not all. After the plate of garbage comes the slaughter of the cheese. The big left hand arches high over the block of cheddar; thumb and middle finger find their hold and press lightly; the right hand brings down the curved, two-pronged knife. But at the last moment the hands pretend that the cheese is alive and getting away. The cheddar shifts about on the oily slaughterboard; there is a struggle; thumb and finger release their hold, but only to press down more firmly; instantly, then, the knife falls, in a strong clean stroke that continues until the cheese is truncated and still. And I almost expect to see blood.

The narrator observes this stranger as a garbage-making machine without any human interest. Since he does not make the effort to get to know him (and after all, what would knowing him mean?), the vision of Garbage is never threatened. My uneasiness may be exactly what Naipaul wants to provoke in his readers. All the trivial mechanisms, weaknesses and foibles that we take for granted in others and ourselves are, as it were, defamiliarized. We must not forget what a bitch life is.

II

What is the appeal of this virtuoso of the negative? Every scene in V. S. Naipaul's work is the occasion for mandarin scorn. It doesn't matter whether the scene is the half-developed or "mimic" societies of the Caribbean or the abysmal material squalor of India or the cruel places in Africa where revolutions are being made or, for that matter, the advanced societies of the West. Naipaul encounters one and all with a cold-eyed contempt. Even a place as innocent and unsqualid as the ivied Wesleyan University in Connecticut provokes contempt as the following passage of an interview with him in the fall, 1981, issue of *Salmagundi* shows:

Robert Boyers: Somehow it seems strange to meet you here in this setting, in the sedate environs of a Wesleyan sitting room.
V. S. Naipaul: I don't belong here, of course, although everyone has been very gracious. It's an intolerable place, really. Do you know that my students can't find a shop that sells the *New York Review of Books*? The college store apparently has never been asked by a member of the faculty to carry such a publication. . . .
Boyers: Still, the experience of teaching bright students must have its pleasures.
Naipaul: Are they bright students? I don't know. I think it's bad to be mixing all the time with inferior minds. It's very, very damaging to be with the young folk, the unformed mind. I think it damaging to one.

Boyers: Where do you look for better minds? Where is your peer group?
Naipaul: There are people. And you know, few things excite me more than
meeting a man I admire.
Boyers: Do you have a literary circle as such?
Naipaul: No, but most of the people I know tend to be people who would be
interested in my work, and have been for a long time. They are people
whose interest I think is worthwhile.

Readers may find the utter absence of ingratiation irresistible. Our
social lives are purchased at the cost of repressing the feelings that
Naipaul has the courage to express. It is not necessarily that these
feelings are just: they constitute, however, a freedom denied by the
democratic ethos of congeniality. Our democratic ears hear this mandarin freedom of speech as rudeness. And we respond, even thrill, to
it as to any forbidden pleasure. What a bastard, we mutter with
delight. To refuse to ingratiate (as a matter of instinct and principle)
is to have the power to say No, a rare power, in its articulate form, in
a democratic society. To say No, one must see clearly and have the
courage of one's clarity.

Naipaul values above all his clear-sightedness: it is a matter of
conscience, which he connects paradoxically with the holding of
certain prejudices. We, of course, all have prejudices; they belong to
our incorrigible subjectivity. But to flaunt one's prejudices as Naipaul does can be a rare virtue – or vice – in what I've called the ethos
of congeniality, which demands that we publicly tolerate one another, a condition that produces either hypocrisy (in which we affect
attitudes that we privately disavow) or self-deception (in which we
no longer recognize our true feelings). In either case, perception and
truth suffer. Naipaul does not self-reflectively tell us what his prejudices are. They are to be inferred from the observation of the scene.

There are unattractive prejudices – as for instance, when in an
Antigua boarding house, in *The Middle Passage* (the account of his
journey through the Caribbean), Naipaul responds to the information
that the company at dinner is about to sing "Happy Birthday" to a
Negro doctor who is entering the dining room by pushing his coffee
aside and running upstairs. The impression of snobbery, possibly
racism, is of course unpleasant. But more important than the particular
prejudices is the freedom to be prejudiced and the power to express it,
which is associated with the freedom and power of imagination itself,
as Naipaul himself recognizes in this admiring comment about Trol-
lope: "I wonder whether anyone anywhere will ever be able again to
write with his mid-Victorian certainty. . . . That unapologetic dis-

play of outrageous prejudices ('I hate Baptists like poison'), that fairness, that cruel humour without a tinge of self-satire, that deep sense of religion and good business. . . ." Certainly the mid-Victorian conviction is irretrievable, but "the unapologetic display of . . . prejudice" is as good a piece of self-description as Naipaul gives us. Prejudice, unlike religious or ideological piety, is ingrained in temperament or character. Prejudiced utterance is authentic expression. Naipaul's power as an observer of the ideological landscapes of the developing nations in works like *Guerrillas, A Bend in the River,* and *Among the Believers* owes a great deal to his prejudiced clear-sightedness.

Among the Believers is not his best work, nor for that matter his most successful travel book, but it is particularly interesting in the way it displays Naipaul's sensibility confronting events that are of the most immediate interest to us. I want to consider it then not simply as a report of Naipaul's Islamic journey, but as an expression of that sensibility.

Naipaul visits Iran, Pakistan, Malaysia, and Indonesia and everywhere finds a "fever of faith." The medical figure is not fortuitous. For the skeptical Naipaul faith is a disease. In the West skepticism is the force that corrodes faith. And the absence of faith often translates as a crisis of values, a failure of nerve. In *Among the Believers* Naipaul observes the scenes of his travels with an unremitting skepticism. In its encounter with resurgent faith in Islamic countries, skepticism emerges as a value. If the alternative is the "fever of faith," then we must prefer clear-seeing skepticism to faith, as we prefer health to disease.

Temperament and personal circumstances both contribute to the skeptical clarity that informs Naipaul's Islamic journey. As a man of Hindu origins, he would be expected to be both knowing and suspicious of Islamic claims. As a lapsed Hindu with a strong and acknowledged aversion for all religious fanaticism, he would find all that he needed in the Islamic revival to confirm his aversion. But Naipaul is not fundamentally hostile to Islam, as we can see in the following passage.

No religion is more worldly than Islam. In spite of its political incapacity, no religion keeps men's eyes more fixed on the way the world is run. And in the poetry of the doctor's son, in his fumbling response to the universal civilization, his concern with "basics," I thought I could see how Islamic fervour could become creative, revolutionary, and take men to a humanism beyond religious doctrine: a true renaissance, open to the new and enriched by it, as the Muslims in their early days of glory had been.

It is Islam's "political incapacity" combined with its inordinate political ambition that is dangerous. In Naipaul's account, Islamic fervor is an ignorant and destructive force: "Political Islam is rage, anarchy."

Naipaul has no counterfaith to offer as did the philosophes of the Enlightenment when they took on what they regarded as the barbarism of Christianity, though he values rationality, clarity, progress – all Enlightenment virtues. He does not, however, compose them into a philosophy. His responses are intellectual reflexes to bad faith and false consciousness. Thus in Hyderabad he examines history textbooks and finds them falsifying in their selective treatment of the past.

History as selective as this leads quickly to unreality. Before Mohammed there is blackness: slavery, exploitation. After Mohammed there is light: slavery and exploitation vanish. But did it? How can that be said or taught? What about all those slaves sent back from Sind to the caliph? What about the descendants of the African slaves who walk about Karachi? There is no adequate answer, so the faith begins to nullify or overlay the real.

There is a rapidity and abundance of observation in *Among the Believers* and Naipaul's other travel books that is at once disconcerting and revealing. In the passage above, one would expect a pause for speculation after the questions. "What about all those slaves sent back from Sind to the caliph? What about the descendants of the African slaves who walk about Karachi?" But Naipaul quickly moves on as if the authority of his discourse depends upon continuous uninterrupted observation of the particulars of the scene. Edward Said complains somewhere that Naipaul is all observation and no theory. We do not require of our witnesses who are imaginative writers that they be theorists, but in Naipaul the absence of a certain kind of speculation commensurate with his intelligence suggests an almost deliberate suppression – as if such speculation might interfere with the unadorned truth. Nothing must estrange us from a clear sight of the scene. Naipaul's anti-faith, anti-ideological skepticism is wedded to a kind of radical empiricism, a passion for observation. Observations do not gather into neat generalizations or conceptions. Given the frequent criticisms that he makes of people who do not seem to have thought beyond a certain point or deeply enough, Naipaul's speculative or analytical reticence (is it a journalistic limitation in him?) is at times disappointing.

But it is compensated for by another kind of attention: that of the novelistic eye or ear. One can hear something significant in the manner of someone's speech, in the tone of someone's voice. Tendencies, patterns, emerge, but what dominates is the particular observation. In Karachi, Naipaul visits a Mr. Mirza who "has been represented to [him] as one of the most distinguished men of Pakistan, one of the country's profoundest minds, and someone who would tell me all I wanted to know about the Islamization of institutions." An experienced reader of Naipaul knows what to expect in the sentences that follow: a quick deflation. The voice of the man immediately betrays his vacuity:

And there was no exchange of words: a low, even, unceasing uninterrupted babble poured out of Mr. Mirza. We are living in a satanic time; people were not interested in the truth; universities were not interested in the truth. We had a lot of information now, but too much information was as bad as too little information. No one could foretell the future; the "imponderables" were too many; the Tolstoyan view of history was correct. Was Mr. Mirza the only one interested in truth? Where was all this leading? It was leading back to the satanic nature of the age, to the need for Islamic belief.

Naipaul notes the response of the young men in his company who are "dazed with pleasure." The scene continues for another page, in which all that Naipaul can discover about the laws and institutions in Pakistan is that "they were not divine." Naipaul remarks: "Mr. Mirza had not thought beyond that point." The precise notations, the clarity of the scene that Naipaul presents is in ironic contrast to the vacuous profundities of the man he is describing. It is a characteristic irony in the book. And it is accomplished by Naipaul's extraordinary attentiveness to what counts in the scene: The monologic babble of the man signals the absence of any real knowledge, any real wisdom. Naipaul is incapable of being "dazed with pleasure," with being taken in.

Another scene: In Pakistan again, Naipaul meets a young teacher, who wishes to write a thesis on the political novels of E. M. Forster, Conrad, Graham Greene.

"Greene?"
"He wrote those three novels about Africa. *Heart of* something."

Immediately, we know the teacher is disqualified by his abysmal ignorance. *"The Heart of the Matter,"* Naipaul informs him. "I wouldn't call that political."
The young man's confidence is undisturbed.

"It is political. There is some dialogue there about natives being liars. But nobody said that it was because of colonialism that people called natives liars. People were made by colonialism. By history. But nobody says that."

Naipaul does not engage in this "argument" directly: he simply responds: "But if you think like that, then everybody is a political writer." To which the young man had no response, because, Naipaul surmises, he "hadn't thought deeply about his thesis." The young man then asks Naipaul about Kipling, whom he knows only by name. "Nobody has written as accurately about Indians. You can't fault Kipling there," Naipaul replies.

Though this passage does not contain any deep thought about the young man's "little idea," the basis for judging it is in the exchange I have just cited. First, there is the ignorance of the young man, who scarcely knows the first thing about his subject. What the young man has is an ideology that holds that colonialist ideology has invented the idea that the natives are liars. The possibility that there is native lying and that it may be a defense against colonialism is not even considered. Natives simply do not lie. Everything without the scruple of actual observation can be placed at the door of colonialism. Naipaul's remark about Kipling has a special force. Despite his imperialist ideology, Kipling wrote accurately about Indians. It is a misreading of Naipaul to see him as accepting or endorsing imperialist ideology. He is instead declaring its irrelevance to matters of art. It is not ideology that distorts or controls artistic perception: it is rather the ideologue who attributes ideology to all writing who prevents us from seeing the truth of the scene.

But for Naipaul the issue is not simply aesthetic. In this rough ideological indifference to truth, Naipaul sees the intellectual counterpart of Islamic revolutionary cruelty:

How could he read, how could he judge, how could he venture into the critical disciplines of another civilization, when so much of his own history had been distorted for him and declared closed to inquiry? And how strange, in the usurped Freemason's hall of Rawalpindi, to talk of the English political novel and the distortions of colonialism, when in that city in a few weeks, in the name of an Islam that was not to be questioned, the whipping vans were to go out, official photographs were to be issued of public floggings, and one of the country's best journalists was to be arrested and photographs were to show him in chains.

Naipaul is not denying the existence of colonialism, but he is denying the conventional Marxist understanding of it. The question for the young man is not whether natives lie, a matter for observation, but how the necessarily false view that natives lie came into existence. Reality for the ideologue is a deduction from ideology. And, ironically, it is ideology or scraps of ideology derived from the hated West, "ideas," in Naipaul's words, "twice removed . . . which the new Islamic missionaries had taken over and simplified in their many publications." (In a recent conference of Soviet dissident writers, the novelist Vladimir Voinovich remarked that the modern history of Marxism is the history of a fashion, which moves from the center to the periphery. As Marxism becomes discredited at its place of origin, it becomes fashionable away from its origin.)

A form of conceptualization, ideology itself is a feature of advanced societies. Ideology came into being in the Enlightenment, when thought itself became a political action. One could hardly deprive underdeveloped countries of opportunities that have long existed for advanced countries. It is also true that advanced countries have suffered the terrible consequences of ideological arrogance, the lessons of which are available to revolutionaries of underdeveloped countries. The willingness or capacity to learn them, however, may depend upon circumstances far more potent than the caveats of a writer like Naipaul. In any event, Naipaul is without illusion about his capacity to do more than represent what he sees.

Ideology may be too grand a term for what possesses the new breed of Islamic revolutionaries. It may be more accurately caught by the characterization of Bezdan, the first person Naipaul introduces us to in *Among the Believers*. Bezdan is "the kind of man who, without political doctrine, only with resentments, had made the Iranian revolution." It was Nietzsche who introduced resentment into our understanding of modern personality. Precociously sensitive to slights, tormented by feelings of exclusion, nourishing projects of revenge, inarticulate or half-articulate (unable, as Naipaul puts it, "to fit words to feelings," "feeling, uncontrolled by words"), the resentful man is the opposite of the aristocratic or mandarin personality, who possesses the earth and feels secure in his possession and his power of expression. It is under mandarin eyes that we perceive resentment, and it is through Naipaul's eyes that we perceive the resentfulness of the under- and half-developed personalities of the societies to which they correspond.

If Naipaul moralizes against anything, it is against resentment, which he regards as a passion that disfigures self and truth. He understands it as the necessary consequence of modernization. He writes of Indonesia: "Jakarta boomed. The city and the country needed wealth and skills. But these things created wounding divisions, and there was rage about the loss of the old order, the loss of the old knowledge of good and bad." Naipaul has little feeling for the old order and he regards the new one as a necessity. His realism tells him that the old order is not what it is now imagined by its elegists to be, and that in any case it can never be re-created.

How trustworthy is Naipaul as a witness? If the Shah was an oppressor (Naipaul does not deny the suffering of the Iranian people before the revolution, though he makes little of it in his book), how does one draw the line between the understandable hatred felt for the oppressor and the passion for revenge that then becomes the basis for a new tyranny? And even if one could draw the line, it would not, perhaps could not, be respected by those engaged in making the revolution. There is a "logic" to revolutionary passion that confuses truth and falsity, cruelty and justice, to a point where they are inextricably bound together. Moralizing against resentment may become a mandarin sentimentality, an exercise in futility. Naipaul speaks of the political incapacity of Islam. How would he distinguish it from the political capacity of Marxism, which can produce a comparable cruelty, perhaps a worse cruelty, because it is organized and not anarchic? I am trying to suggest the limitations of Naipaul's clear seeing, indeed the limitations of all clear seeing. His clear seeing depends upon an anesthetizing of compassion for the suffering of the oppressed, since sympathy with suffering can easily lead to the abyss of resentment. It depends upon an inhibition of those powers of conceptualization and understanding for which there may be no correspondence in what is present before one's eyes.

Naipaul's stress on clear-sightedness at the expense of ideology and related forms of conceptualization brings to mind George Orwell, who generalized his attitude into a hatred of intellectuals, men blinded by the ideas that possess them. Orwell's plebeian feeling for ordinary reality distinguishes him from Naipaul's mandarin sensibility, but the intersections in their work are remarkable – even in their uninhibited expression of prejudice and their common admiration of Kipling.

Naipaul is a tourist who cannot pretend to know the inner life of a country, no matter how clearly he sees and how well he reads. When Nadine Gordimer, for instance, represents the career of Marxist ideology in her novel *Burger's Daughter,* we can feel confident that she writes out of an intimate experience of that ideology within

South Africa over an extended period of time. We need not trust her judgments about Marxism or those of her characters to be persuaded that the representation is genuine. Naipaul's glimpses are those of a prejudiced Western observer. His perspective is "After the Revolution": the perspective that makes us keenly aware of revolutionary cruelty. His precocious sensitivity to resentment would probably make him an insensitive observer of, say, apartheid in South Africa, where the important fact is the exploitation and suffering of large masses of people by a privileged minority. It is hard to imagine what a book on South Africa by Naipaul would be like. All this is to suggest the limits of Naipaul's perspective, not to denigrate it; for it is always valuable for a writer from an underdeveloped country to refuse the ideological role that is usually conferred on literature about the colonies, whether on the side of the colonists or on the side of the natives. The best writing comes out of a resistance to the ideological role.

One does not expect to find a mandarin sensibility in a scion of a displaced Hindu family on an unimportant Caribbean island. From an outsider and a member of the nonpossessing class, one expects resentment or, on a higher level, a revolutionary sense of injustice. Naipaul, however, turns out to be one of our severest critics of social and political resentment and of every ideological articulation of it. It is tempting for those who share the revolutionary outlook of the Third-World insurgency to see Naipaul as someone who has internalized the values of the dominant culture.

But such a view is itself an ideological reduction of the man and his work. In Naipaul there is none of the insecurity and ingratiation one finds in people who borrow the manners and attitudes of another class. His confidence is absolute – or as absolute as is humanly possible. And the confidence shows itself in his writing: not only in the sureness of diction and tone, but in the comic mastery of the street dialect of Trinidad. I am referring to early books like *Miguel Street* and *The Suffrage of Elvira* in which Naipaul reveals with great charm the life of his native country. Those books could not have been written by someone who had made himself over in the image of a superior culture.

In experiencing Naipaul's manner as a puzzle and trying to explain it, one is of course resisting the possible view that a man may be a creature of his temperament rather than his circumstances. Since temperament cannot be explained, all one can do is describe it. We are so afflicted by the passion for explanation that we cannot help feeling dissatisfied by mere description or characterization. My own view is that temperament is an important part of the explanation of Naipaul's manner and attitude. Another word we use to describe the particular integrity and power of a person whom we cannot reduce to explanation is *genius*. But it is also true that temperament or genius does not exist in a vacuum: it unfolds itself in the circumstances of the person's life.

The principal fact or sentiment of Naipaul's life is his sense of displacement. As a Hindu, he was born in a place where he did not belong. But it is the particular strength of his temperament that he did not suffer from the sense of exclusion that might, for instance, make him resentful. Whatever wounds he may have suffered from the experience of displacement, exclusion, and poverty must have healed or been transcended. In *A House for Mr. Biswas,* a novel that has its source in the life of his father, Naipaul shows an unblinking and acute awareness of the material and spiritual squalor of Trinidad life. But his imagination remains secure from the infection of resentment. On the contrary, the experience of displacement simply confirms the artist's view of himself as separate and superior, which in the social sense is the mandarin sensibility. Naipaul does not want to join or achieve power within the society from which he is excluded. Rather he wishes to cultivate the powers that he possesses, which keep him apart. In one of the rare moments of self-revelation in *Among the Believers,* he describes a meeting with a young Pakistani intellectual who reflects Naipaul's own life. The Pakistani had tried to go to America or England to further his education, but was prevented from doing so by a lack of funds.

He didn't know how directly he was speaking to me. The idea of struggle and dedication and fulfillment, the idea of human quality, belongs only to certain societies. It didn't belong to the colonial Trinidad I had grown up in, where there were only eighty kinds of simple jobs, and the quality of cocoa and sugar was more important than the quality of people. Masood's panic now, his vision of his world as a blind alley (with his knowledge that there was activity and growth elsewhere), took me back to my own panic of thirty-five years before.

This does not mean that in going to England to be educated Naipaul wanted to become an Englishman and repudiate his Trinidadian background. Ethnic, national, or class affiliation is irrelevant to Naipaul's ambition. This is clear enough from the novels *Mimic Men* and *Mr. Stone and the Knight's Companion,* novels set in England, in which displacement or separateness is as strong as it is elsewhere in his work. Naipaul writes in *Mimic Men:* "We walked through the streets like disrespectful tourists." And elsewhere in the same novel he speaks of a "vision of a disorder which it was beyond any one man to put right." But for Naipaul England is a society in which "the quality of people" is important and where he can cultivate his intellectual and imaginative powers. It was a way out of "the blind alley" of arrested personal development. This is quite different from an experience of the sense of community or belonging in England. Naipaul remains separate and "disrespectful": a tourist wherever he is. Traveling for Naipaul one feels is the natural condition of his life, for it is always a way of living in a place without being part of it.

The societies in which the quality of people is held to be important are advanced technological societies. If technology does not humanize, it creates the conditions for a society in which the quality of people is valued. This may seem an odd view to those who have thought of technology as the enemy. Humanist critics have complained about the pernicious ascendancy of quantitative and mechanistic values in advanced technological society and have often constructed myths of a past that was more humane, more organic, truer to the claims and needs of the human spirit. Naipaul sees these nostalgic myths as travesties of historical truth and as the expression of psychological immaturity.

In Pakistan the fundamentalists believed that to follow the right rules was to bring about again the purity of the early Islamic way: the reorganization of the world would follow automatically on the rediscovery of the true faith. Shafi's grief and passion, in multi-racial Malaysia was more immediate; and I felt that for him the wish to re-establish the rules was also a wish to re-create the security of his childhood, the Malay village life he had lost.

But it is not simply that the return to the past is regression: it is not really a return, for there is only ignorance of the past. Sitor, an Indonesian poet, is an illuminating case in point.

Sitor's tribal past was further away; he had lost touch with it; and he had found that to write without an understanding of what he had come from was to do no more than record a sequence of events. That was why for some time he had put aside the actual writing and had concentrated instead on understanding his tribal background. He had gone back to his village in North Sumatra with a young Canadian anthropologist. She had helped to give him back some of his tribal past.

To gain access to the tribal past requires the achieved knowledge of advanced society.

Knowledge, power, possession: the plenitude that in the past characterized aristocratic civilization or the class that dominated and defined the civilization now characterizes modern society. Naipaul's wisdom about modern society is unconventional. Conventional humanist wisdom sees modern society as a democratic leveler, a degrading standardizer of things, an emptier of values. Modern society produces indistinguishable products, commodities. Both views have truth, but the more interesting, perhaps deeper, truth is Naipaul's. It explains how even the fiercest antimodernism retains a commitment to the achievements of modern civilization. In contrast, then, to fantasies of reversion, the actuality of advanced technological society offers the possibility of growth and maturity in which the virtues of mental clarity, intelligence, knowledge are cultivated.

Not that Naipaul is a complaisant advocate of any society, including technological society. That sense of separateness or displacement that I have described is the strongest element in his personality, the most persistent theme in his work. It has its origins, I believe, in a residual Hinduism. On his return from his first trip to India, which he described in his book *An Area of Darkness*, Naipaul discovers to his surprise that the society that he had seen and judged under Western eyes had entered his soul. He had seen India as a series of dung heaps, afflicted by filth and disease, only to find on his arrival in Rome from India "the deeper and richer Indian negation," which underlies his Westernized personality.

It was only now, as my experience of India defined itself more properly against my own homelessness, that I saw how close in the past year I had been to the total Indian negation, how much it had become the basis of thought and feeling. And already, with this awareness in a world where illusion could only be a concept and not something felt in the bones, it was slipping away from me. I felt it as something true which I could never adequately express and never seize again.

The mood is not a temporary one: it is the strain of stoicism that runs through all of Naipaul's work. In *A Free State*, the book that follows *An Area of Darkness*, the narrator declares: "All that my freedom has brought me is the knowledge that I have a face and have a body, that I must feed this face and clothe this body, for a certain number of years, then it will be over." This is the voice of Hindu consciousness, enforced in Naipaul's case by the experience of displacement. For what is the ultimate condition of displacement but the feeling that neither your face nor your body is finally your own?

In Naipaul, the "No" has its ultimate metaphysical source in a vision of the abysmal nothingness of life. The vision is not to be confused, however, with continental versions of the abyss, whose chief sponsorship has been existentialism. Naipaul's "nothingness" is an agnostic version of Hinduism, without the promise of reincarnation. Unlike existentialism, for which the abyss is an occasion for a creative leap, Naipaul's nothingness is an ultimate condition. And to the extent that it forms his sensibility, it provides a perspective on the futility of all created things. This feeling for metaphysical nothingness is, I suspect, a source of strength in Naipaul. It gives his vision equanimity. It permits him to gaze at the created forms of life without illusion – that is, with a knowledge of their final destiny.